LET'S CHAT

SHARDS OF JOY.

Hope you enjoy my stories.

Annie

Annie MacInnis

For my father and my husband - renegades with vast intellects, storytellers themselves

For my mother - you are everything I aspire to be

For my children - hearts of my heart, you were (and often still are) my inspiration to write

For my family, friends and readers who encouraged me to write this book

For my faithful old friend and walking partner, Teddy, best dog ever. Thank you for sixteen wonderful years of enthusiastic welcomes home, soul restoring walks, nursemaiding of the sick, cuddling and for listening to all our joys and sorrows. Until we meet again...

Thank you all for helping make this book a reality

Annie
Calgary 2013

TABLE OF CONTENTS

TABLE OF CONTENTS

TABLE OF CONTENTS

TABLE OF CONTENTS

A real hero

I open the closets and drawers and look upon the treasured accumulations of someone else's life. Clothes once loved, books read, cherished photographs of long gone loved ones, dishes, bits of memorabilia that were of great significance, or were they?

The single gorgeous gown, a pale lemon yellow vintage dress from the forties, all froth and glamour even after all these years. Where did she wear it and why save this one evening dress only? Nothing else in the closets suggested this extravagance was ever repeated.

I am in love with history. I love reading about it, learning about it, thinking about it and collecting stories about old things. I also love to cook and always note any history and details along with the recipe in my books. I recently came across a recipe I had not used in a long time and had forgotten about. In my handwritten recipe book I have this notation written across the top of the recipe "Murray's great-great-grandmother's Rolls."

This recipe is from my old and dear friend Murray. The recipe was passed down to him from his Uncle John Neil's mother who was William Hall's wife. The name William Hall will probably resonate with many Nova Scotians.

William Hall was born on April 28, 1827 in Nova Scotia. He was the son of two slaves rescued from a slave ship by the British Navy.

When he was a young man he joined the merchant navy. On leave in England, William joined the British Navy and served in the Crimean War.

In 1857 his ship, HMS Shannon, was sent to India at the beginning of the Sepoy Mutiny. Shortly after their arrival, four hundred sailors from his ship were sent to try to relieve the besieged British garrison of Lucknow. Many British women and children as well as officers and diplomats had by that time been under siege for four months in Lucknow.

The previous relief column sent to help had been decimated. The few survivors of that first relief column ended up taking refuge with the besieged they had come to rescue.

Hall and his fellow sailors were not trained or equipped to fight on land but they were the only British military forces available to help.

These gallant young men brought their ship's guns (eight inch guns and twenty four pound howitzers), their muskets and their swords. They dragged the eight inch guns and howitzers overland with them as they fought their way toward the beleaguered garrison.

They joined up with a small group of 93rd Highlanders encountered along the way to attack the 30,000 Sepoys besieging Lucknow.

Although the enemy was defeated and the siege broken by this second relief column, only two of the 400 sailors from the Shannon brigade survived the relief of Lucknow.

For his actions William Hall received the Victoria Cross *"for gallant conduct.at Lucknow on the 16th of November 1857."*

William Hall was the first man of colour in the British Empire to win the Victoria Cross. He was also the first Nova Scotian to win the Victoria Cross and one of the first Canadians to be accorded this honour.

Only 1,351 Victoria Crosses have ever been awarded. Of those 1,351, 94 have been awarded to Canadians.

Let's Chat

William Hall's Favourite Rolls
(the recipe from my friend Murray, William Hall's descendant)

Scald 2 cups milk, let cool until warm.

Sprinkle 4 teaspoons of yeast and a little of the sugar over the milk. Let stand 10 minutes. Stir gently.

Mix
1 cup oil
4 eggs
1 cup sugar
1 teaspoon salt

Stir together yeast mixture and egg mixture.

Gradually stir in 7 to 7 1/2 cups flour. When mixture gets too hard to stir knead in remaining flour. Knead until smooth and elastic.

Put dough in a large greased bowl. Cover with a clean tea towel. Place in a warm place to rise. When about double in size, punch down. Let rise again.
Punch down a second time. Divide dough in two. Cut each half into 12 pieces.
Roll pieces gently under your loosely cupped hand. Place in a 9" by 12" greased pan. Let rise again.

The recipe says bake in a medium hot oven until done. I do a 350 degree oven for about 20 minutes.

When I take the time to make William Hall's wife's rolls I think about a young man from rural Nova Scotia with the heart of a lion and a weakness for soft rolls.

Helen

Her name was Helen. She was one of those fierce, small, stringy older women. In a firmly buttoned and belted housedress, chastised hair, sensible shoes and thick stockings, she was the picture of tidy probity. She cleaned houses for a living.

She lived in a small house so clean my mother used to say you could comfortably eat off her floors. Soft spoken and meek in manner, she was a ferocious worker. Dirt dared not resist her. She cleaned our house Tuesday mornings. She had a particular order in which she did her assigned tasks throughout the house. This scheduled routine did not take account of those living in the house, with the exception of my father. He was the hallowed local doctor so if he had had a hard night his room was avoided while she cleaned quietly elsewhere.

That courtesy was not extended to feckless teenagers. Regardless of the night we might have had, she would slam the bedroom door open as she bustled in with the vacuum. Her lips would be firmed up as she recklessly vacuumed up stray small objects on our floors. She gave no quarter. You scrambled out of bed, grabbed your clothes and scuttled off under her disapproving eye or she would strip the bedclothes out from under you as she changed your bed. You were fully aware of the extent of her disapproval for your lax, spoiled lifestyle and you knew that all the details would be passed on at her other households for Helen had a funny quirk.

When Helen vacuumed, I am guessing she thought nothing she said could be overheard. (Although maybe I'm not thinking in Machiavellian enough terms, that is, maybe she fully intended to be overheard.)

Regardless, the whole time Helen vacuumed, from the moment she turned the vacuum on until the moment she shut it off, she raged and cursed about the people she cleaned for, her own family, and any people in town who had offended her or behaved inappropriately in recent memory.

She didn't just rant. She went into excruciating detail and used considerable profanity in the process. Few were spared the side of her tongue. If there was salacious gossip in town, Helen knew the details and judged the perpetrators accordingly.

Let's Chat

Maybe all that emotion accounted for her ability to clean so thoroughly. I know myself that there is nothing like feeling ratty at my husband or kids to send me off like a whirlwind through the house. A short while later I have a cleaner, tidier house and often can't remember, or no longer care, what I was irked about. Putting that irritation to use against a defenseless house is usually a lot more rewarding than getting into a row and I feel better when I'm finished. But, when I am feeling grizzly at a member of my household and cleaning and whipping up that internal dialogue about injustice, I usually catch myself remembering Helen and smiling. I'll never be as good at cleaning, or raving, at least while vacuuming, as Helen.

Panties

I am thoroughly disheartened. Oh, I'm putting a brave face on the day and I've had an extra coffee and put on one of my favorite work outfits that usually makes me feel great. I've made an effort with my hair and put on a little extra makeup so I look sparkly.

The plan is to look so normal on the outside that no one will take the time and trouble to look past the flash and see that I am not quite myself today. My life work balance has been seriously out of kilter for the past week. That delicate juggling act we all do to ensure we eat healthy, spend some happy time together with family members, get our work done, get some exercise and do enough housework so we aren't living in squalor has gone sideways.

We are persistently out of milk and bread. Baskets of clean laundry are piling up and wrinkling in the overfull baskets. The kitchen floor has some sticky spots. I actually threw a couple of food cans in the garbage instead of recycling. There is clutter everywhere. This happens to most of us occasionally. It's not pleasant and often leads to cross words between family members but that's not the actual problem today.

The situation is much, much worse and not something that can be kvetched about in polite company. No I haven't had a fight with my husband; my kids aren't pregnant or doing crack, nor is the house infested with fleas. It's much worse. Only I know the horrific, sordid truth.

I have been reduced to the dingy, grey, stretched out panties with the hole in the bum. Demoralizing beyond belief. Regardless of how much effort I have put into my outside today, I know the shaming truth. I am wearing panties that would make my mother drop any possible plans for the day and drive directly to the nearest SEARS rather than see me go out in public in this raggedy, shameful underwear. My mother would be aghast that I even possessed such pitiful back up panties. I know in my heart of hearts that she would not have gone to bed without hand washing a respectable pair.

So here I am out in the world just asking, just daring fate to send a speeding car my way, a patch of slippery ice, some medical emergency sufficient to put my into the hands of medical personnel so I will get my just desserts, my comeuppance for

Let's Chat

daring to venture into public blatantly ignoring that wise lesson to "always wear nice panties in case you're in an accident."

Annie MacInnis

When you wish upon a star...

It is wonderful when an unexpected gift comes your way! My mother was a church organist for more than twenty years, playing faithfully most Sundays year round.

I, on the other hand, was a callous, non-church going youth living 3,000 miles from my parents, when she became the organist. As the years went by, my visits home were more about me and my career and my life away and visiting with all my family than about me appreciating and celebrating my mother's accomplishments. So, for many years, my mother would slip off to church on a Sunday morning unbeknownst to me or get someone to play for her so she could visit with me.

Years passed, but I didn't realize they were slipping away. Then I became a parent and my visits home became consumed with fulfilling the needs of and soliciting admiration of my children. Like before, sometimes my Mom went and played but as a non-church goer with busy, young children, I didn't attempt church attendance.

Then one day my mother retired as church organist. She was honoured by the congregation for her many faithful years of service but, as usual, I missed the ceremony because I lived so far away.

I remained unaware of the extent of my loss until my daughter decided she wanted to begin attending church last fall. I committed to attend with her to keep her company. The services seemed hauntingly familiar yet in many ways so different from the church I remembered from my youth.

But, it was the organ playing that I kept coming back for. Each service I felt bereft as I thought of all the opportunities I had so thoughtlessly squandered. All those years, all those Sundays when I could have chosen to go to church, even though I was not a churchgoer, simply to hear my Mom play.

Of course, I heard her practice her pieces occasionally on our piano at home many times over the years but I never heard her perform. One never knows when inattention or carelessness will rob us of a moment in time that may never be able to be recaptured. How often do our thoughts turn to those words, "if only, I had known..."

Let's Chat

This summer, I was given a wonderful gift. My daughter had specifically asked to attend my mother's church with her. I had decided that I, too, would attend, since it had been so many years since I sat in church with my mother. The night before we went, my mother received a phone call asking her to fill in for the regular organist.

After all these years, when I had reconciled myself to never hearing my mother play in her church I was blessed to sit with my daughter at my side and hear her play. How fortunate I feel to have had that second chance, to know from now on, when I hear an organist play, instead of regret I'll be able to smile with sweet remembrance for that day when I heard my mom play.

Annie MacInnis

He is a Young Man now

Any minute he will be looking down on me literally as well as figuratively. He has the shadow of a moustache; darkening eyebrows, and a more strongly defined jaw. He argues like a lawyer (with everything I say it seems some days), and then is contrite like the little boy that has warmed my heart for 13 precious years.

As I see more and more glimpses of the young man he is becoming and less and less of my little boy, I see a future before me where I will share less and less of his life, less and less of his sorrows, his triumphs and his secrets.

The young man he is becoming is a delight to behold. He has such passion for knowledge, such conviction in his beliefs, such kindness is his heart and such dreams for his future. Yet, he still has the beautiful eyes that beguiled me from the moment he was first laid in my arms.

Letting go is easier with this second child. I still make mistakes but these days my mistakes seem more on the side of backing away too soon whereas with the first child I clung too long.

Funny how the lessons you learn in raising the first child so seldom stand you in good stead or even apply to the next child. Instead the role of the second child seems to be to teach you that all those aspects of the first child that you took credit for, as an "excellent parent" were really just serendipity and not to your credit at all, as evidenced by the behavior of the second child.

Looking back, I see clearly all the moments when I would have acted differently with hindsight on my side. All those times now come back to haunt me in the black self-doubting moments in the shank of the night when I lie sleepless.

Now that my children are teenagers, I am sure I will continue to make mistakes but I take comfort in the knowledge that whatever errors of judgment I make during these years will continue to be made through love and the best of intentions. I remind myself daily that my job is to strive to remain calm and loving in the face of all provocation and, above all, to be there if needed.

Every day now is just one more step away from me. As hard as it is, I let them move further and further from the safety of my loving guidance because that is what parents do for teenagers.

Let's Chat

We hang about in hopes they want to talk, make ourselves available for rescue, respite or food preparation, forgive all, remain grateful for any scraps of love and attention they carelessly offer, and always, always keep reminding them, "I'm here if you need me."

Annie MacInnis

Gypsies

Gypsies must live there, my grandmother would have said.

I wish I had a beautiful yard, a sanctuary where I could sit surrounded by a lush expanse of grass and beautiful flowers where gracious living and serenity took place.

I do not have that. What I do have is a yard that resembles a neglected war torn corner of some forsaken place made yet more pitiful looking by fall weather. There is a broken concrete pad littered with debris that has no home since we tore down the already falling down garage. There is a hedge that we tried to remove. The hedge prevailed and now rises phoenix-like from the surrounding dirt piles. There is an unfinished greenhouse floor project that isn't likely to be completed before the snow flies this year. The grass is pock marked with small bald spots where the dog has squatted.

Both my husband and I would like to have a beautiful yard but while we appreciate that the neighbours must be tired of heaving a great dissatisfied sigh whenever they cast their eyes our way, neither of us has the inclination nor the skill to create (or to maintain) such a yard. Nor have we the resources to hire someone who would and could make us look a tad more respectable.

I accept this state of affairs for the foreseeable future. I call myself a Darwinian gardener welcoming all plants that choose to grow in my yard. If a plant can survive lack of any care and attention, it is welcome in my yard.

However this attitude is not without peril. I was very proud of the beautiful (to my eye) tall purple flowers gracing my yard until a gardening friend spotted them and insisted I pull them all up immediately. Apparently these 'pretty flowers' are a pernicious weed that can grow anywhere even well trampled off leash dog areas and must be banned from all civilized yards.

Of course I didn't get around to pulling them up but when I finally got motivated one day to throw away many useless objects the change was short lived. Within hours my son and his buddies built a shrine with firewood on one of the dirt piles and the dog carefully redistributed all her precious bones and toys in suitable locations allowing easy access. The only upside is enough debris to have a nice fire in the fire pit. I guess my yard is a little

Let's Chat

like the Velveteen Rabbit, well used and well loved for all its worn appearance.

Happy Anniversary

February is a time when I reflect on marriage and love because Valentine's Day is my wedding anniversary.

We've been together 33 years and we are happy together most of the time. Our marriage has not always been smooth sailing. We have had some frightful squabbles. Words have been spoken that should never have been uttered. We have both, variously, been to blame. But there are more good times than bad times and we remain committed to each other 'for better or for worse'. Life's rough spots have tempered us but we always turn back to each other.

These days, however, I see our marriage reflected in our teenager's eyes. It's hard to explain long term relationships to teenagers. Hard not to feel our marriage is judged and 'found wanting' because our marriage is not a storybook or a movie romance.

Sometimes we are unjustifiably cross with each other or impatient or truly unkind and all this occurs with an audience. There is so much that the teenagers never see. The tender private conversations, the moments when we pause and truly see each other anew. They don't see the wealth of unsaid thoughts implicit in a touch of the hand in passing. They don't feel the sense of connection and shared history when we smile across the room at each other. They aren't privy to the shared history that makes us willing to set aside the awful moments and try again. When you've been a couple as long as we have, much is understood and much is forgiven because of all those other moments when we have been a comfort, a helpmeet, a hero, a true friend and a beloved mate.

My marriage is not my grandparent's marriage. They were unfailingly polite to each other. My Nanna prided herself that Mac had never been downstairs in the house without his waistcoat and jacket on.

My marriage is not my parent's marriage. They decided on their honeymoon not to fight and just have not.

Our marriage is far from perfect but we have grown up and changed and held onto each other without limiting each other and helped each other become better people in the process. Our marriage is a triumph over the adversity life has thrown our way

[20]

and a testament to our commitment to love each other 'come what may'.

It's not self-justification or sour grapes or settling to say that the unhappy and unpleasant moments of our marriage have contributed to the preciousness and poignancy and joy in all the many, many good moments.

When we were young and had a fight I would be distraught and mentally pack my bags all night, taking great pleasure in the thought of all the stuff I would claim.

Nowadays I try to embrace these moments in my life that I would prefer to forget because these moments remind me that we are both fragile human beings who make mistakes and are sometimes unkind and unwise and that I am blessed, most days, to find joy and comfort my marriage.

To the heart of my heart, my beloved and my friend, Happy Anniversary and Happy Valentine's Day.

What's For Supper?

They could say, "Hi, Mom, how was your day?" Or they could say, "Boy I had a busy day." Or "Wow I learned a lot today!" They do not. With the car door hardly opened, long before their bottoms touch the car seat, they always, unfailingly, ask those fateful, dire words, "What's for supper?"

Never mind I last saw them in this very parking lot before going to my office to work. I am tempted to retort, "Gosh, instead of going to work today I sat here for the past six hours just wondering that very thing. I have mentally reviewed what groceries we have in the house and have come up with fabulous supper options!" Or maybe I will sigh hugely and look about for the maitre'd and say, "Geeze, isn't your menu posted right there in front of you yet!" Or perhaps I could coo sweetly, "Gosh, I don't know but I'm really excited to ask the servants as soon as we get home." Or, "Hmmm. I'm not sure darlings. I've actually (self-depreciating smile here) not spent this time apart thinking about how best to tempt your palate this evening. Instead, I have spent this time making a living. Did you have something particular in mind for your supper?"

I don't say any of those things. Instead I smile bravely and patiently because I am a mother and sarcasm is neither a valued quality in a parent nor a wise parenting tool to set the tone for the rest of the day.

Before some helpful child offers "Actually I was thinking maybe we might have that…I think it was beef maybe but I'm not sure, recipe that you made once when I think maybe one of my friends was visiting and we loved it. Remember?"

Isn't it funny (in an awful kind of way) how cooking a lovely meal for your family can be such a pleasure and a source of pride when you have an idea and some supplies and such a source of despair when you don't?

I buck myself up. Since we are critically low on supplies, supper must be made from some combination of the following ingredients – frozen meat, frozen peas, orange juice concentrate, minimal salad stuff, (small) quantity of bread, (limp) broccoli, rice, cereal, canned soup, a little milk, yoghurt, and apples.

Let's Chat

I am reminded of my mother's various responses to the 'what's for supper' question. Sometimes the answer was one of my favorites, sometimes a new and exotic recipe like French Beef Stew with tarragon and fresh mushrooms, but sometimes the answer was, "Nothing new."

Annie's Mom's Recipe for Nothing New Chicken (otherwise known as Chicken Broccoli Casserole)

4 chicken breasts
2-3 cups broccoli
one can of cream of something soup
one cup sour cream or yoghurt
2/3 cup grated cheddar cheese
¾ cup of Just Right cereal
4 tbsp margarine

Preheat oven to 375.

Poach chicken in chicken broth or water and chicken bouillon cubes. Add broccoli for last few minutes.

Put chicken and broccoli in a 9"x12" pan.

Mix soup and sour cream and spoon over chicken.

Top with chopped green onions if that appeals to you.

Sprinkle with grated cheese, then cereal, then drizzle with melted margarine (or don't if you're watching your fat content).

Bake for 20 minutes.

Serve on rice.

With teenage help, in less than half an hour supper is in the oven waiting for the time bake to kick in. The time until supper spins out before us, rife with possibility for relaxation as the smells of a tantalizing repast soon begin to waft through the house.

* For a vegetarian version I use cauliflower instead of chicken and use vegetarian bouillon.

I have to pee

In my own defense I really had to go!

In a previous career I was a Senior Research Associate at the University of Calgary in the Strategic Studies Department. In that capacity, I was one of the escorts for a group of young mostly male university students on a field trip. We travelled by Chinook helicopter to CFB Wainwright to observe winter maneuvers.

Early our first morning we left with our guide. We would be spending all day outside so I dressed warmly. First stop after breakfast in the mess hall was an intelligence briefing. This was day three of these military exercises.

We spent the morning walking around with a young officer getting the briefing while observing the defensive positions and the preparations of one 'army' while learning of the attack plans of the other.

Those who stand to pee (everyone but me) availed themselves of ample opportunity to peel off from the group and discreetly do so throughout the morning. Increasingly desperate, I decided I was going to have to take advantage of nature's bountiful 'room to squat.'

I allowed the group to get considerably ahead of me before I veered toward a conveniently placed bush some distance away.

Once discreetly shielded from the group, I glanced carefully around me. Screened by the bush I saw nothing but fields, trees and snow. I paused only momentarily to grimace at my lack of forethought in wearing my old one piece parachuting overalls on top of one piece long underwear. I was going to have to strip from the ankles up. There was nothing for it but to quickly pull down the long underwear and pee. I hurriedly redressed without incident and caught up with the group.

About half an hour later our soldier guide led us perilously close to my handy bush. Stopping a little short of the bush he challenged the group to spot the several dozen troops in camouflaged trenches all around us!

Everywhere I looked on the ground I now saw smiling faces turned my way. They said nothing. Frankly appalled, I too, said nothing and certainly did not smile back.

I have no idea how I managed to walk to and from that bush without falling into one of those trenches or spotting the soldiers. I guess I was more focused on looking for people standing upright or walking my way. I shudder to think what those troops must have thought after three days of living in that snowy field fighting a simulated battle when a girl appeared out of nowhere, disrobed, peed (practically on them!) and then left.

For the rest of the trip, I could not walk anywhere on the base without sensing a ripple effect of discreet elbow nudges and subtle head nods in my direction. No one was ever so ungentlemanly as to allude out loud to the incident but I was the recipient of many huge overly friendly smiles from soldiers who obviously had seen a lot more of me than they ought.

Let's Chat

Unconscious Secretary

It definitely was not the best of times. It definitely was one of those *worst of times* weeks.

My husband had had a corneal transplant. Between post-operative pain and a surfeit of painkillers to address that, he was feeling a tad grim and grizzly. One kid had the puking-all-night-flu and was in need of being perpetually ministered to. I was tired, on crutches with a broken toe and feeling rather testy myself. The other kid (six) and the dog (almost three) were the only able bodied members of the family. The burden sat uneasily on their young shoulders. To make matters worse, the dirty laundry was close to critical mass (down the stairs in the basement) and the groceries were at an all time low.

Luckily Monday was Family Day so we laid low and ate what we could forage. Unfortunately Tuesday was a school day and my son was raring to go. I organized meals, ferried him to and from school with my broken toe pressing on the gas and brake, ministered to the sick and infirm and cringed at the thought of three more days of this.

Salvation came from an unlikely source.

The school secretary became ill and asked if I could substitute for the next three days. I took one look around the house and virtuously decided I should re-join the workforce this week.

I felt quite cheery at the thought of spending time elsewhere even though most of the house hassles would simply multiply in my absence. I'd have an actual coffee break today AND I'd get monetary remuneration in the fullness of time. What a deal!

Wednesday I sat placidly at the school office computer. I was proud of myself. The children and I had managed to get to the school half an hour early so I could start work on time and I hadn't lost my cool once.

Just then two small ECS boys entered the office. All I could see were the tops of their heads as they stood on the far side of the counter.

I gathered up my crutches, came around to their side of the counter and kindly asked, "Can I help you two?"

[27]

The boys were visibly nonplussed. I was not the regular secretary. After a brief whispered consultation they reached consensus and in small piping voices repeated as one, "Our teacher wants the regular camera. Can you please get it for us?"

I crutched into the utility room and looked fruitlessly for a few moments before returning to my small petitioners.

"I'm sorry boys," I said. "Since I'm not the regular secretary, I'm not sure where the camera might be. Can you go back to your teacher and ask her if she knows where it usually is? It's a little hard for me to do a big search since (and here I gestured to the crutches) I'm *on crutches*."

It's worth mentioning at this point that I'm from Nova Scotia. Despite living in Calgary since 1981, I have lost little of my strong Maritime accent. My unfamiliar accent may have been the cause for the resultant confusion. The boys stared at me, with stricken faces, the moment I mentioned I was *on crutches*. They didn't move. Finally I made a shooing motion with my hands and said, "Go." They immediately pelted down the hallway.

I shrugged my shoulders and returned to the computer.

Meanwhile, elsewhere in the school, the boys, burst into their classroom, skidded up to their teacher and breathlessly reported that, "The secretary can't look for the camera because SHE IS UNCONSCIOUS!"

"Unconscious?" asked the teacher.

"Unconscious," affirmed the boys.

The ECS teacher, aware the regular secretary had been unwell the previous afternoon quickly busied her children and whipped down to the office. She stopped at the sight of me sitting at the computer then remarked dryly, "Well, I understand you are unable to look for the camera because you are unconscious!"

We both burst out laughing.

The recurring mental picture of those earnest little boys rushing to report "an emergency" cheered me the rest of the week!

The Talk

Have you had "the talk" with any of your children yet?

Given that my daughter is nine, we have had several versions of "the talk" over the years. We started with very basic information when she was three and I was pregnant with her brother. A few general comments about a baby growing inside Mommy were sufficient this time.

However, once the new baby was home the topic arose once more. "No, I didn't *find* your baby brother and I can't give him back to the hospital because..." Her initial reaction to this gentle vague explanation was to blush and comment, "Euuww, gross" and return unconcernedly to what she was doing.

Over the years we have had more talks, gradually increasing the detail and range of our discussions and diagrams but until recently I had had only a few brief discussions about babies with my son. He usually expressed little interest in the topic. On each occasion the facts I offered were received with relative indifference and disinterest.

Recently though I overheard my son speculating about baby making to his sister. My son was wondering whether sperm would wear raincoats for their "dash" and whether sperm lived and worked in a factory when not swimming in races and whether any could fly or ride to go faster and whether the ones who didn't 'get' an egg were really disappointed...

Oops! I stood stock still, my mind reeling as I tried to assimilate the wealth of misinformation. My admittedly primitive little diagrams and occasional explanations had obviously gone seriously awry.

I resolved to go to the library that very day and choose age appropriate books for each child. As I decided this I felt good. I kidded myself that I would find a private moment to sit down separately with each child and tenderly discuss their questions and together we would look at their books.

I did manage to quickly clear out the children's sex education shelf at my library intending to vet the books at home and choose a couple of suitable ones. Unfortunately once I put them in the car, I forgot about them.

As luck would have it, the books were rediscovered several days later while we were stuck interminably in rush-hour traffic. It was Friday at 5 pm and we were on our way to the Park for a picnic supper (whose stupid idea was that!). The kids pounced on the books.

Next thing I know my daughter is giving my son "the talk" in the back seat using the completely un-vetted books.

I took several deep breaths. I counseled myself not to scar their psyches and any prospect of a healthy adult sexual life by shrieking at the children to "put that filth away!" until I could see if the books were appropriate.

I started to relax as I realized my daughter seemed to have picked out an age appropriate book to start with. These are sweet, colorful, charming books, I reminded myself; I'm sure I chose appropriately. I breathed a sigh of relief and realized what a gentle, sensitive job my daughter was doing.

Then she turned the page and uttered this phrase in a bright, upbeat voice. "Here are some of the ways that Mommies and Daddies fit together." While my mind boggled and I tried to crane my neck to see the book, the children dissolved into peals of laughter.

As I sat inching forward in traffic, I listened to my children as they discussed these 'ways'. They laughed and laughed. I thought of my well-laid plans for Kodak moments and glared bitterly at neighboring drivers.

Finally the traffic began moving and we eventually arrived at the Park. It was a Kodak evening after all – sunny, crisp autumn weather, happy children and dog, good friends, and lots to eat. When I finally got a chance to look at it, the book about how Mommies and Daddies fit together really was very funny and well done.

A Dream come true

One fall my 12 year old told me she had long wished she could take figure skating lessons. Possessing that hateful personality flaw that reacts to any confidence involving a problem with myriad solutions, I set to work.

Many, many phone calls later I stood contemplating my notes. Everyone I spoke to said, don't put her in a class, she'll be with a bunch of little kids. At her age she would be better off taking private lessons. Written in increasingly crabbed handwriting were fairly scary lists of costs associated with this endeavor.

I confirmed that this was a serious wish not just idle chatter before I booked a trial private lesson. Finally one afternoon we laced on her skates and sat in the stands to await her turn. Seven girls ranging in age from about 7-15 twirled, jumped, and spun effortlessly as music swirled through the crisp rink air. They wore lovely skating outfits.

I turned to my daughter expecting to see a face shining with anticipation and possibility. I did not see even an approximation of that face. The face I beheld was a mutinous face, a sour face, a face a mother dreads to see. That face said, in a tone that only a 12 year old can summon at will, "I'm not going out there!" The "you moron," was implied, but wisely unsaid.

I took a moment before responding. I knew why she didn't want to go. She was intimidated; afraid she wouldn't measure up today. These girls were really good skaters with pretty outfits while my daughter possessed only good basic skating skills and was wearing jeans and a polar fleece. I also knew this had been her dream for a really long time and that she had been so excited about taking these lessons.

I gritted my teeth. As a parent it's so easy to smooth the way for our children, to try to help them avoid unhappiness or failure. The hard road is to help them to learn to be confident and to be resilient. I smiled at her in my most loving fashion and said, "Darling, you will go out there and take your lesson or I will make such a scene dragging you out there that any embarrassment you might feel in going out there by yourself will pale by comparison! Way you go then," I caroled.

She went, but she was NOT happy.

[31]

I warned the coach, "You have your work cut out for you."

She had her 15-minute lesson, and then came off the ice. She was not flushed with accomplishment and pride although she had thawed somewhat toward the coach who had made a Herculean effort to charm her. She glared at me and said, "Let's go." We went. I bit my tongue and gave her space on the drive home.

Over that weekend we had an ongoing conversation about life choices. I told her there were two types of people in life – those who take risks and those who have regrets. I told her that if she did not pursue this dream now, she probably never would. I reminded her that the whole point of taking lessons was to learn. I talked about some of the leaps of faith her father and I have made in our lives and how doing this hard thing would be great practice for the rest of her life. I told her that if skating was a dream of hers then she should honour that dream and not worry about what others might think.

Blah, blah, blah…but nevertheless pretty heady stuff for a 12 year old entering those years when peer approbation is increasingly everything. Finally on Sunday afternoon, she came to me and said, All right, I've decided to take the lessons. But only if I can get a skating costume like the other girls." "Deal," said I.

These days, only four months later she glides across the ice, face shining, eyes sparkling, as she practices her jumps and spins. I feel pretty proud of both of us. Proud of me for remembering to support not rescue her, proud of my daughter for being willing to take risks and to try new experiences.

Teeth

What kinds of creatures grow new teeth when the old teeth are damaged or pulled out?

I knew the answer once back when my son was little. In those days, when we read together daily, he almost never wanted to read sweet fictional stories about dear anthropomorphized animals. Oh no, he wanted to read non-fiction books together.

We read factual books detailing the precise specifications of the Titanic, long tomes about the circumference, height and other details of the Sears Tower, calculations about how high speed rail transit works, whole books detailing the life and habits of Komodo dragons and many, many books about mythology, insects, rainforests, dinosaurs, road construction and the Middle Ages, to name just a few of his interests.

During those reading sessions my eyes would tend to glaze over as I read interminable statistics while his rapt face absorbed every word. Unfortunately, I learned I had to try to concentrate on taking in at least some of what I was reading as there were frequent 'class discussions' regarding what we had just read.

I will admit I never did manage to keep the Greek myths separate and clear in my mind but I did improve my general knowledge significantly, at least in the short term. Of course all that study was for naught because I'm now awash in mental-pause and information is being ruthlessly, callously and completely randomly discarded from my memory banks or re-filed with no regard for the importance of the information.

But right now, if asked what superpower I'd like to have if I could choose one, I would not ask for better memory powers, instead I'd ask for the ability to re-grow teeth.

I am at an age when visits to the dentist involve white knuckles and a gasping credit card. My front teeth are thankfully holding up reasonably well but all my molars were so neglected (by me) when I was a child that they ended up with giant fillings. Those molars are now frail perimeter shells supported by large fillings at the end of their lifespan.

This weekend I broke off a whole quadrant of a molar on a cracker! Not even a hearty healthy cracker with lots of chewing, no, just a plain old Mr. Christie cracker. A cracker, how mortifying is that! No glory in that is there! Not, I threw caution to the winds and treated myself to expensive caramels and boy was it worth it! No, I was chewing on store bought crackers.

I had to wait till Monday for my dentist's office to open. To add to my discomfort, I live with two kids who have spent years coping with sharp edges of braces in their mouths and off and on tooth and mouth discomfort as a result so they had minimal sympathy for my plight in having to wait A WHOLE DAY WITH A ROUGH SPOT IN MY MOUTH THAT IS BOTHERING MY TONGUE!

Obviously this is just a small "taste" of the indignities of old age yet to come but I am not impressed so far.

Let's Chat about phone books and water heaters and Sears catalogues...

All my life family members have teased me that I am a magnet for *characters*. Out in public among any number of people if there is a chatty or irascible character in the vicinity they will gravitate to me and begin talking.

This past summer my family was on our annual peregrination to my beloved Nova Scotia to visit family and friends. On a grey and foggy (no surprise) August Sunday afternoon we were driving along the Fundy shore when the dog petitioned for an interlude in the sightseeing to have a pee stop. We pulled off to the side of the road. While the others walked out along an old wharf disappearing into the mist, the dog and I walked down along the side of the wharf on the old boat launching road toward, presumably, the water's edge although we could not properly see the water for the fog until we were quite close. Wisps of wind started to blow away patches of fog and the dog and I stood quietly looking off into eternity thinking ourselves alone in this little quiet pocket of the world.

I was taken aback when a voice close by, apropos of nothing, suddenly said in a very loud voice, "Tanner Simpson is a big strong boy!"

Turning I saw the fog had blown away to show several knots of people standing around. Some were talking quietly but in that weird way that fog sometimes dampens sounds as well as sights I had been unaware there were people nearby. Wondering if I was being addressed or simply overhearing a conversation, I made eye contact with a very large youngish person sitting in a beached rowboat, looking directly at me.

The instant our eyes met, he immediately started talking to me."Are you from away? HELLO, what is your name?" Without waiting for a response, he continued. "Are you alone, Are you married? Do you have kids? Did you drive here or did you walk? Are you on vacation? Is that your dog? What is her name? I like Yellow Pages. I have a Yellow Pages from Hamilton, Ontario and from Fredericton, New Brunswick and from Vancouver, British Colombia and from..." (He went on and on and on listing his collection.) Do you like Yellow Pages? Do you know what Tanner Simpson is getting for Christmas? He is very excited about

Christmas. He is getting (a detailed list of gaps in his prized collection followed)." The best ones are the ones still in their plastic packages. Where did you say you were from?"

A brief pause allowed me to blurt out ,"Calgary," before he was off again.

"Calgary, home of the Greatest Outdoor Show on Earth, Home of the Calgary Flames. I need a 2009 Calgary Yellow Pages. Do you have one?" I gulped, "Well I am on vacation and 2009 is awhile ago and probably not actually..." I trailed off doubtfully.

An impatient, "Well, will you LOOK and will you send one to me?" prompted me to rashly promise that I would try and he was off again, "I want a computer. When I get a computer I am going to do *The Google*. Tanner Simpson will like *The Google*. Do you like *The Google*? Tanner Simpson also likes the Sears catalogue. Do you like to read catalogues? I like to read about water heaters. "*Quiet but efficient, same day installation, courteous friendly service, energy efficient, latest technology, guaranteed satisfaction, for all your furnace, water heater and air conditioner needs call us for same day installation*", he quoted. "When do you go back to Calgary? When will you send me my 2009 Calgary Yellow Pages, tomorrow?"

Unable to bear to disappoint the eager, smiling, trusting face, I said, "I will do my best, but I am not sure whether I will be able to find a 2009," I tried to caution. "I will be waiting," came the implacable reply.

I turned hastily away before he started talking again and I was compelled to make more unwise promises. An older man standing a little way away smiling tolerantly at the boy/man in the row boat then made smiling eye contact with me. I asked quietly, "Does he have a very large collection of Yellow Pages?"

In the thick accent of that end of Nova Scotia and the dry, sardonic gross understatement style so common where I grew up, he said, "Were our house to go afire tomorrow, my dear, it would smolder for days."

As the dog and I walked back up toward the road leaving the group behind us once more enveloped in the fog, a familiar voice called penetratingly out of the mist, "A 2009 Calgary Yellow Pages, please, in the plastic still mind you. How soon will you send it [sic]me?"

[36]

Let's Chat

Up by the road stood my family, who, of course, heard the whole exchange courtesy of fog's weird capacity to deaden sound nearby while projecting it elsewhere. They smiled tolerantly at me, shaking their heads, at my capacity, yet again, to attract a 'character' in the middle of nowhere.

So to honour my promise, I was able find an unopened still in the plastic 2009 Yellow Pages and did send it to Tanner Simpson.

Annie MacInnis

Tank's Owner

When I was growing up it was common practice among children, when in doubt about someone's last name, to refer to a friend's parent by their title and the friend's name. For example if I had to directly address an adult I might call them Mrs. Billy or Mrs. Sue (their child's name) rather than by their own first name or last name.

In my years of dog ownership I've noticed that a similar sort of system exists among dog owners. Habitually dog owners frequent a couple of favorite walking areas and often walk at about the same times so I sometimes see the same people and dogs. Yet, while often I know the names of people's dogs and have numerous conversations with the owners I don't seem to retain the owner's names and even occasionally don't initially recognize them even though I do recognize their dogs.

One day this summer when I arrived at one of my regular spots to walk my dog I saw a notice taped to the garbage bin. I veered over to see what this one was about. Typically these notices concern coyote warnings, offers for dog walking or other pet services, appeals for lost pets, petitions about off leash areas and other topics of interest to dog owners.

This notice was different. The first thing I saw was a distinctive picture of a dog owner whose face I did recognize. The picture was of Tank's owner. Upon reading further I discovered Tank's owner had been killed in a car accident in B.C. Some thoughtful dog lover had added a short note saying Tank was okay and was with family.

As I walked my dog that day my thoughts, of course, turned to how fleeting life can be and how capricious fate is. I thought about my encounters with Tank and his owner. I remembered the obvious affinity between the two. In my mind's eye I see him clearly standing in the middle of the field, drawling, "Come on now, Tank."

I hadn't known or hadn't remembered his name although I knew his dog's well. On probably a dozen occasions we happened to be walking our dogs at the same off leash area and we fell naturally into conversation.

My children and I often spoke of Tank – a huge Hounds of the Baskervilles black Newfoundland male crossed with something else really big and really hairy. My kids claimed our dog Teddy had a crush on Tank. Whenever she saw Tank she skittered around him acting silly, yipping and dancing and generally trying to attract his attention.

Tank, comfortable in his stolidness and overall charms for the opposite sex, plodded along mostly ignoring my dog while his owner and I talked.

It turns out the owner's name was Rob. He and Tank were obviously a team. Rob exerted firm, loving control over his huge dog. Both persons of strong opinions, our conversations ranged freely as we elicited details about each other's dogs, the day's news, the weather, and I'm not sure what else. I can't remember specifically what else we talked of but I remember always enjoying the sight of the pair and looking forward to another rant with Tank's owner.

I'll miss seeing Rob and Tank. Their presence was always a highlight of my walks. I'd come home and tell my kids that Teddy saw Tank and they'd tease her about having a boyfriend. If my kids were along for the walk they always laughed at the sight of my skinny little, whippet type dog trying vainly to attract Tank's regard and Tank barely deigning to notice her.

In memory of Rob (forever known as Tank's owner in my mind), thanks for the company on all those walks Rob. May flights of angels speed thee to thy rest. Know that when I walk in our spot I think of you and Tank with great fondness and not a little regret that your time together was cut short.

Annie MacInnis

Arsenic and Old Lace

She was a small, elderly lady with lovely soft, white, curly hair. She was most respectably dressed and had an admirable British accent.

During my first few days as her downstairs neighbor, I thought she was sweet. On the few occasions we met, she mentioned her two little dogs and her son, Cyril, of whom she was very proud. But as the days went by, I noticed something odd about her.

If my apartment was quiet, I could hear what happened in her apartment. I could hear her call loudly and enthusiastically to her two dust mop dogs, "Cyril's coming! Mind the door!" This was followed by scrabbling of dog toenails on the floors and frenzied barking the length of the house to the front door. After a few moments her regretful voice would say, "Oh dear, he can't come after all He's got a school board meeting." The barking would cease and I could hear the disappointed dogs slowly returning and flopping down on the floor. There would be silence for a few beats, then she'd carol "Cyril's coming! Mind the door!" and away the dogs would go again. This would go on for hours sometimes.

In retrospect, of course, I can see it was silly to let my imagination get the best of me like that, but at the time I decided she must be a bit batty. In fact, I became scared of meeting her and tried my best to avoid her. She seemed all too like one of those sweet, evil, little old ladies in Agatha Christie stories who kill off all the objectionable people nearby for their own good but in a totally charming way. I became increasingly certain her sweet face and genteel ways harboured evil designs.

One day as I was coming home she popped out her front door as though she had indeed been lying in wait for me. She was nicely insistent that I come in for tea. I felt torn. I was alone in that big city and lonely. She did seem so kind when I talked to her and a good cup of tea would be so nice and besides it daytime and, well, I said yes.

I came inside, careful not to shut the door completely in case a fast get away was necessary. I sat down edgily near the door. She excused herself to go make the tea, but continued to talk to me from the other room. I contented myself with patting the dogs. She mentioned the weather and how rainy it had been. I agreed and mentioned I came from rainy Nova Scotia. She gave

Let's Chat

a martyred sigh and said, "Rain again!" I laughed along with her then jumped up with a thrill of horror. She was suddenly beside me instead of in the other room where her voice had been coming from.

Smiling sweetly as she set down the tea tray, she said, "I see you've met Angus." I stood speechlessly, goggling at her, looking around me for Angus and debating whether to make a run for it.

Then, with a loud squawk, a black Mynah Bird stepped out from behind a curtain. I'd been chatting with the bird it turned out.

Angus perched on a nearby chair and continued to discuss the weather with me while we drank our tea. Not only could Angus imitate his mistress's voice, he could do it so perfectly even the dogs couldn't tell the difference.

Toward the end of my visit, I shamefacedly admitted my error. She laughed and chided Angus gently, saying she'd been worried that the dogs that never seemed to have any pep anymore.

Angus failed to look repentant; I did not get the impression he was going to cease and desist.

Annie MacInnis

David Suzuki and me

I was feeling a little ratty with my husband one morning recently; not enough to spit in his coffee (who would do that!) but irritated enough to be surly for a bit. Thankfully, our tiffs don't usually last long, before one of us apologizes and we forgive and forget. Once our row is over and calmer emotions prevail, I am often reminded of a lunch I had twenty years ago at a work conference.

The keynote speaker, David Suzuki, spoke brilliantly. Afterward, at lunch, sitting alone at a table, the illustrious man himself sat down beside me. While I frantically tried to think of something scintillating to say, he leaped into the breach with the always acceptable opening, "Hi, my name is...David."

Relieved, I introduced myself, complimented him on his speech, and then casting about for some topic of conversation, I asked how long he had been on tour. There was an uncomfortably long pause before he asked if I was married.

I said, "Yes."

"Then you'll understand," he said and told me this story.

He said he'd been on tour for two weeks, but the time was seeming particularly long because he and his wife had had an awful fight just before he left and although he had apologized by phone, he was anxious to go home to her.

Needless to say, I was goggling at him internally while trying to maintain an interested, sympathetic look on my face.

He went on to say that, because his wife was considerably smarter and more logical than he was (yikes!), she usually bested him in their arguments. Mostly he tried to accept this, but occasionally, in the midst of a passionate disagreement, he (like every other person in a long term relationship) would forget this basic tenet of their relationship. On these occasions he would want to "WIN" above all else, beyond any consideration of the consequences.

He explained his theory of what happens next as "reverting to the lizard stage"- a state where you have no capacity beyond basic brain stem functions wherein your mission is survival at all costs: to prevail or to succumb. In this case, he prevailed, saying

[42]

Let's Chat

something really nasty thus winning the argument but at the cost of hurting and upsetting his wife. Then he left for the airport and his tour.

I can honestly say I was so astounded by this amazing confession that I offered no helpful advice whatsoever to him. He probably went away from lunch feeling it had been a waste of time to open up to me.

I, on the other hand, have recalled this lunch on many occasions, always taking comfort in the thought that even great men (and women) are just ordinary people doing their best each day but who, in the process, sometimes screw up, make mistakes, have fights with their beloved, say mean things, and sometimes hurt those they love.

So as I begin another year already remorseful at my unwarranted crabbiness I once again remember, 'my lunch with David Suzuki': and take pleasure in the knowledge I gained that day; that love, genuine remorse and the resolve to try harder are powerful healers. Thank you David. Sorry I was no help whatsoever to you that day.

Stuffing

I thought we were friends. Our relationship had progressed to the point where we talked about almost anything. We were a buffer for each other to mitigate life's small (and occasionally looming) frustrations.

Then one day, during a relatively idyllic (no kids, no husbands, a private talk) moment, a yawning abyss suddenly opened before us.

Suddenly the comforting smells of supper cooking and the sounds of children paying happily elsewhere in the house, were irrelevant. Our mutual accord and commonality were split asunder.

I stared thunderstruck at my erstwhile friend. You think you know someone, that you are kindred spirits despite the fact that you grew up 3,000 miles from each other. Then you discover that they put raw egg in their turkey stuffing!

"Egg!?!?!" I stammer, "in your stuffing?"

Meanwhile, my friend is gaping at me and sputtering, "Potato…you put potato in your stuffing?

Now we all know there are misguided miscreants out there who meddle ruthlessly and carelessly with tradition. We have all perhaps have been stricken at some point in our lives with a holiday dinner where someone has thoughtlessly plunked down on the holiday table some walnut/apple concoction purportedly disguised as stuffing. Or, felt our expectations plummet with the gaily mentioned aside that, "I didn't bother with gravy, soooo much cholesterol" obviously heedless of the integral nature of gravy as the foundation of the meal.

For those of you who have never experienced the psychic trauma these experiences can cause, let me just say, snidely, "Aren't you fortunate!"

For those of us who approach the holiday table with reverence, having already mentally arranged our plate vis-à-vis gravy, meat, potatoes, stuffing, and turnip and carrot mashed together, I want to make this perfectly clear. We may be intrepid adventurers every other day of the year in every other aspect of our lives, but you mess with our holiday traditions at your peril.

[44]

Let's Chat

Now, I hasten to add that I am not adverse to innovations IN ADDITION to those items that must be on the holiday plate. I am even okay with small variations. We traditionalists are more than happy to look over any additional falderal you desire and consider whether it has a place on our holiday plate. But, the basics MUST be provided.

So, in case you were considering skipping the gravy this year or trying some 'nouvelle stuffing' recipe:

Annie MacInnis

Proper Mashed potato dressing the way MY Mother makes it

Tear up a bunch of bread and leave to dry on a cookie sheet on the windowsill overnight.

If you are a parent, you can torture your long-suffering children into doing the careful tearing up into bite sized un-squished pieces. This typically adds an extra nice flavour for any parents who are present.

Next day stir in
2 potatoes that have been peeled, cooked and mashed

Finely chop
1 medium onion
1 stalk of celery

Fry in butter

Season with Salt, pepper and add generous sprinkles of summer savory and sage

Mix all with your hands and shove into your turkey.

When you take your cooked turkey out of the oven be sure to scoop out the stuffing an put in a separate bowl rather than leaving it in the turkey.

I don't know what manner of ingredients go into my friend's egg stuffing. I was too horrified to ask.

Proper gravy will be discussed at a future date.

Happy birthday

It was party day and I was lightly balanced on the cusp of sanity but just managing to stay calm by dint of short, sharp barks at children, husband, dog and any household objects that strayed into my path.

In a hushed silence, I held my breath and as deftly as the most experienced brain surgeon gently eased the last cannibalized Chinese wooden bamboo skewer through the forehead of a crouching stegosaurus cake.

Amid suitably admiring noises from my family I stepped back to rest on my laurels and admire my handiwork. The birthday cake looked incredibly wonderful...for about five seconds. Then so slowly – it was initially almost imperceptible – the head started to ease down the body toward the tinfoil wrapped tray. Before I could wipe the smile of self-congratulation from my face, the head gathered speed then disintegrated from the forehead down.

I stood aghast, staring at the faceless dinosaur cake and the heap of green frosting and cake crumbs. My family quickly left the room in an orderly fashion.

As the moments ticked by, the threat of my head exploding began to recede.

I turned resolutely away and began washing dishes, my back to the disaster. I ground my teeth as I calculated still un-hung balloons and un-swept floors. My mind roiled with the thought of the as yet unplanned activities necessary to fill three hours overrun by too many four- to six-year old boys gladly abandoned by their parents for the afternoon to my care.

I wasted precious moments deciding whether the ghoulish inclinations of such boys would be titillated by a ravaged dinosaur cake. Maybe it could be the prelude to a game! We could have a treasure hunt searching for a wounded but still dangerous dinosaur. When we finally located the despicable creature we could smash it to death. Once our blood had cooled we could dismember the cake and serve bowls of dinosaur guts. We could eat with our hands while roaring as loudly as we could our favorite meat-eating dinosaur noises.

As attractive as this idea was initially, I finally concluded that there were two serious drawbacks to this notion.

[47]

One, this game might wind up the large group of young boys to such a crescendo that I might lose any prospect of regaining a semblance of control over events for the duration of the party.

Two, the thought of how this game might be gleefully described that night to other, saner parents – lucky parents not mired in giving a birthday party – convinced me to discard this option.

I bitterly recalled how blithely I had disregarded the cautionary words of my neighbour when she told me of the duck cake held together with over one hundred toothpicks and her warning never to venture into the no-man's land of 3-D cake making.

I sneered as I studied the pristine picture of the dinosaur cake that accompanied the recipe. What bag of photographic tricks had been employed to create this illusion?

In the end, I salvaged the remnants of cake scattered and drying on the counter, plastered them together with great slatherings of frosting and fashioned them into a shape approximating a prehistoric snout. I camouflaged the irregular shape with savage Chicklet teeth and fierce yellow candy eyes, and flung the whole mess in the freezer until party time.

On this occasion, disaster was narrowly averted. The boys didn't comment on the frozen cake although I felt impelled to justify its state by indicating I just unearthed this carcass from frozen tundra nearby. Other than some minor disagreements regarding distribution of green spearmint leaf spikes there were no major incidents or injuries nor damage to human psyche (other than my own). All in all, a successful party!

But if I may venture to offer one small piece of advice to those of you contemplating entering the minefield that is 3-D cake making, "Don't!"

Before you sneer at my obvious incompetence as a novice shaped cake maker and children's party planner, heed these further cautionary words. If, like me, you like to live on the edge and if your tendency is to disregard prudent advice when offered, then attempt such potential fiascoes as a crouching stegosaurus cake on the day before the party.

Let's Chat

Then if disaster dogs your frosting bowl you will have plenty of time for a frantic trip to Dairy Queen on the morning of the party if a recognizable cake is not your result.

Annie MacInnis

Happy Valentine's Day

Last year I gave my husband a Hallmark Valentine's card. It said, "A happy marriage is what happens while two people are busy trying to make it through another year ahead of the bills, on top of the chores, in sight of their dreams, in touch of reality, and always in search of brand new ways to say "I love you.""

This year I thought I'd write my own given my penchant for seeing my own words on paper.

I love my husband. I know that's not a very fashionable or oft-expressed sentiment these days. Usually people prefer to dish about what their spouse ISN"T doing right rather than what he or she is. But at the risk of boring all my readers by singing his praises, I'd like to write a few words about my husband and our marriage since Valentine's Day is our wedding anniversary.

The clear unvarnished truth is I love my husband and almost all of the time and I'd rather be married to him than to anyone else.

This Valentine's Day was our 25 wedding anniversary but being of the generation that came of age in the early seventies we've actually been living together as a couple for 34 years this spring.

Mind you, it hasn't all been sweetness and light. Our relationship has definitely run the gamut (and then some) from "for better or for worse, in sickness and in health, for richer and for poorer..."

We've had good years and not-so-good years, we've both had health problems and we've certainly been poorer more often than richer (at least in monetary terms). But in the overall scheme of life our life together has been good. The hard times have enriched us and made us stronger both as individuals and as a couple. Our hardships have taught us compassion and generosity and reminded us of how fragile life and relationships are.

Oh, we still squabble or get impatient with each other occasionally. We still hurt each other's feelings sometimes, and take each other for granted now and then. Every now and then one of us gets really irked at the other and lets them know how we feel! Ours is not a fairytale relationship. It is real and gritty and mostly lovely, warts and all.

Let's Chat

Lately it seems we have won through to a deeper understanding of our life together. We are better at leaving things unspoken, quicker to apologize or back pedal if we're at fault (and even sometimes when we're not). We fight fairer, make up sooner, are more willing to overlook each other's foibles, and more appreciative of each other's most wonderful characteristics.

Some years ago my husband said something that has stuck with me especially when life seems particularly hard or I'm feeling a little wild at him. He said, "If we've used up every bit of good luck we've been granted on having these two particular children and on your health staying pretty good and on still loving each other, how can we say we've been ill-served in life?" How indeed! On the contrary, we've been blessed.

Through our lives as a couple runs a continuous thread of understanding that we are in this relationship for the long haul. We have become texture in each other's life tapestry, an integral part of the overall design that highlights the coherence and beauty of the whole.

When I was 16 my father said something to me that I have remembered through all the years since. I think I had probably asked him some question about how he knew when he fell in love with my mother that she was "the one." He said to me, "Be sure to choose someone you like as well as love. Some years I have loved your mother more and some years I have loved your mother less but throughout all those years she has been my best friend and that has been what has carried us safely through the hard years."

Thanks for showing me what a great relationship looks like Mom and Dad.

Happy Anniversary and Happy Valentine's Day Russ. You are my beloved and my friend. May the next thirty-four years be a tad less fraught but just as wonderful as the last thirty-four have been.

Annie MacInnis

The Continuing Saga of Who Gets To Take Spike Home

It was a cold and snowy day. The school secretary was sick. I was filling in for the afternoon. As I walked toward the office, my children chattered excitedly. I took a deep breath. The phone started to ring. Students oozed out of the woodwork.

"Can I have Mrs. Foster's mail?"
"Where do I put these papers?"
"Do you know where the gym keys are?"
"Was my mom looking for me?"
"Do you know where my mitten is?"
"My ear hurts. Can I lie down?"
"My teacher wants..."

Welcome to a school secretary's world, I thought! Shortly after calm was restored, a student wandered in and announced casually, "I think I get to take Spike home. Can I call my mom to tell her?" After careful thought, I said yes.

Later another student meandered into the office saying, "Can I call my mom?"

"What for?" I asked. "It's my turn to take Spike home. I want to tell my mom to remember to come get us" said the student.

"I'm sorry," I said, in a tone intended to blend decisiveness and sympathy in equal measure, "but I have already promised another student she could take Spike home."

"Oh no, said the student, who was eminently more successful at blending authority and pity than a mere mother such as myself, "my teacher has already spoken to the other student and it's my turn."

"Let's go check with your teacher to make sure," I prudently advised. We sallied forth to speak with the teacher. (Not being as familiar with the student names and teachers as is the Secretary, this is the point where I made my critical error.)

I explained to the teacher that *another girl* had already approached me about taking Spike home. The teacher looked kindly at me and explained the situation had been straightened out between the two girls and the student destined to take Spike home was indeed standing before me.

"Great!" I said briskly, "Let's go call your Mom."(But, what I didn't know and what the teacher didn't know and what the first student didn't know and what the second student didn't know was that there was a third student who had also thought that it was her turn to take Spike home and she was the one the teacher had spoken to!)

Shortly before the bell rang Mom #2 arrived for Spike. We decided to bundle Spike out into the warm vehicle before the bell rang. I smiled complacently, thinking how deftly and efficiently I had handled this minor Spike mix-up.

Then the bell rang! In the space of a heartbeat the first student was beside me asking where Spike was. I reeled back aghast. "Your teacher told me she had spoken to you and it wasn't your turn and you understood," I protested.

"Nobody spoke to me!" she wailed. In an instant the office was chock full of students arguing about whose turn it was to take Spike home. Bystanders took sides passionately.

"Mrs. Hendrickson said...No THAT MOM told me...My teacher said...I already called MY mom...I already called MY mom...Why would YOUR teacher speak to me? It's not even your class's turn...But I missed my turn before Christmas...I missed mine too...my mom wasn't home when I called before...then I tried again and she said YES...No it was MY turn but I said SHE could because she was so sad.

I took a deep breath and tried to think what Solomon and Mrs. Hendrickson would do in this situation. Finally I ruled on Spike's behalf that given the chilly weather she would stay in the vehicle she was now in. At student #1's stricken face, I recklessly promised with no authority whatsoever, that she could take Spike next week.

As I sat down to write an account of the incident which would not make me look completely incompetent, I thought longingly how simple family disputes will now seem when compared to the saga of who gets to take Spike home.

Not that my negotiating skills are so much more finely tuned at home but it helps that at least I know everybody's names!

Annie MacInnis

Snow Quinsy

It was one of those perfect moments in parenting.

My friend and I sit on our knees looking out her living room window, her almost two year old gleeful between us.

Outside the window her husband and son and my son and daughter labour in the minus twenty snow and darkness. Moonlight gilds their laughing excited faces. Their breath streams in plumes worthy of the dragons my son is always prattling on (and on and on…) about.

They are building a Sioux snow shelter called I think a quinsy except when I looked up the correct spelling the only definition resembling this spelling refers to "an inflammation of the throat with abscesses on or suppuration of the region around the tonsils so perhaps I didn't get that bit right.

Earlier in the day snow was shoveled into a huge heap and left to sit for a few hours to cure or set. Now they are tunneling into the mound at ground level and hollowing out the inside to create an awesome place to hang out. The whole pile of snow has been poked round about with about 8-10 inch twigs so they will end up with walls about that thick. (When their hollowing out encounters these sticks they'll know not to hollow out further.)

The kids are so excited they're dancing in circles when they're not digging. Two hours go by and the structure is sufficiently hollowed out for all four to crawl inside, light candles and soak up the atmosphere. From where my friend and I sit, the snow cave glows from inside. Snowflakes fall heavily on the whole scene.

Finally they all tumble rosy-cheeked and full of the experience into the warmth of the house. They drink hot chocolate, and throw marshmallows at each other. The heat seeps into their fresh air soaked spirits and their eyes grow heavy. They can hardly summon the energy to say goodbye to each other but everyone has time to sigh with much pleasure at their wonderful evening.

We adults are filled with contentment and self-congratulation at how perfect the evening has been. All parenting and play date experiences should turn out this wonderfully.

Let's Chat

The next day is Sunday. It's another bright, cold day and more snow has fallen. My kids are psyched to build one of these structures in our yard. I convince my husband, who was enjoying his Sunday without assignment, that we should stir ourselves from languishment.

We sally forth full of the optimism that one usually summons at the beginning of such family endeavors. For the first while all goes quite well. The kids are enthusiastic and working hard. Tempers are good; the mound of snow is increasing steadily.

The dog is the first to cave and her defection is the thin end of the wedge. Moments later my husband puts his back out and hobbles off into the house mumbling apologies. Next our daughter needs to go get a hot drink to warm up. Shortly thereafter our son realizes he is working while his sister relaxes in warmth and comfort in the house and also deserts the cause. That leaves me. I soldier on for a while longer. Finally I decide we have enough for a slightly smaller shelter than our friend's shelter. I hurry thankfully into the house.

I arrive to find everyone out of sorts. My daughter hasn't gotten her hot drink; my son is working unsuccessfully at an art project marked for 15 years and up (which he purchased with his own money against my advice) and my husband is in pain and that would be whose fault?

It's obvious no one in this house is going back out into the darkness a few hours from now to hollow out our wretched snow mound and create a hallmark moment in OUR yard. Nope, not us. That snow mound will probably sit there untenanted until the next Chinook. And when it melts, since it is right outside the back door, the dog and everyone else will track mud into the house for all eternity or until I go berserk whichever comes first. I think the moral of this story is beware trying to recreate those Hallmark moments.

The Taxman Cometh

It is income tax time AGAIN. Geez it's like it happens every year! (In case it isn't obvious from the text I took a really big disheartened, martyred sigh just then.) It always seems such an ordeal to get the taxes done and I actually don't even do them.

Following my Jack Sprat theory of marriage (my theory refers to the fact that couples usually have different skills sets and it is therefore useful to have an agreed upon division of labour within a marriage), my agreed upon portion of this hateful task is to constantly collect from all family members concerned and keep track of all the little, stray, vitally important scraps of paper ALL YEAR LONG. This plays to my strengths for collecting and nagging. Come crunch time my job is to present this entire jumble in some semblance of order, stapled into appropriate groups with cover page summarizing any pertinent details (like how much we gave to charity with receipts attached and how much in eligible health expenses was not covered by our insurance).Himself has the job of actually doing the taxes and submitting them.

Given that I am a tad obsessive about not being tardy for events or deadlines and given that I would rather have bad news over with and paid for as soon as possible rather than be Scarlett O'Hara and think about it tomorrow, I usually grit my teeth and am ready to go with my assigned portion by the end of February. My goal every year has been to remember that once my bit is done, my job is complete and now I need to pass the torch and allow my beloved the freedom and space to do his bit in his own time.

But of course that's not the way marriage works in the real world is it? Because, unfortunately my beloved is one of that ilk that is happy to meet deadlines at the last possible moment.

In the early days of our marriage, I think we were both more prone to feel righteous in our opinions and more inclined to promote our way as 'the right way'. As a result we had many pointless (in retrospect) disagreements. So, many years, instead of meeting my goal of staying mum, I spent much of March barely resisting saying, "Why not just do them right now, TONIGHT, then they'll be done and I won't have to fret and you won't have to be nagged' before usually exploding at some vastly inconvenient moment and causing significant ill feeling.

[56]

Let's Chat

These days we engage is small good-natured skirmishes. One nice March day, I will put the pile of organized papers prominently near the computer, "Here are all the papers for doing our taxes. We are good to go," I will carol sweetly.

Shortly thereafter I will notice the pile has been moved to a less prominent location in order for himself to enjoy a cup of tea while at the computer. A day or two later a random newspaper article and some junk mail will be added to the top of the pile to disguise it.

Even so, as an older, wiser couple, the taxes do get done in reasonable time these days in a much less fraught atmosphere than in years gone by. We're not just getting older; we're getting better at so many things – like life and taxes.

Animal Friends Hotel

We are the 'go to' family if you have a pet that needs minding.

Over the years we have looked after dogs who growled every time we entered the room, birds that incessantly cheeped until it was difficult to be civil to them, and gerbils fresh from operations and requiring three times a day medication by mouth while holding ever so gently due to abdominal stitches.

This latest animal sitting favour seemed a no-brainer by comparison. Our assignment: look after two snails for three weeks.

Instructions were basic. Keep out of direct sunlight. Feed one small chunk of carrot every few days. Keep a very small quantity of water (not enough to drown in if said slow moving creatures were unwise enough to venture too close to their drink). Replace bedding with grass from yard if cage reeks.

Looking doubtfully at the two inert pets, I delicately inquired, "Do they have names?"

"Of course they do," came the prompt response. "The big one is Zorro. The smaller one is Ganesh." They looked indistinguishable to me. I couldn't think of any appropriate comment about their exotic names so I simply nodded.

During that first evening, my family had a lot of fun joking about how hard this job was going to be, about how you might determine whether the pets were ailing or dead or still in need of continuing care. They had not moved from the little piece of wood in the middle of the cage since arriving. Were they alive we wondered?

The next morning I spotted only one snail still on the little piece of wood. Huh, I thought, I guess they do move. I glanced casually into the cage but did not spot the second snail. I picked up the little cage and looked carefully. No sign of the second snail. Well, he must be under the wood or the water dish, I figured. I opened the cage and checked under the wood, under the water dish, and even ran my finger gingerly though the grass. No snail. I held the cage up and looked at the bottom. No snail.

Although they seemed inoffensive pets when in their cage, now I was appalled. Oh, yuk, is it loose in the house? Might the owners

[58]

Let's Chat

have warned me they are prone to escape! I looked uneasily around the vicinity. How could it have gotten out and how far could it get in, let me think how many hours since I last saw it? Was it the big one or the little one?

Just as I was about to panic I realized the missing snail was hanging upside down from the underside of the cover of the cage. My gosh, I thought, I can't believe he moved all that way.

I gave a small thank you thought for not having to explain to the little girl who owned these pets that I had lost one the first day. I mean, what does that say about you as a person! "She can't be trusted to look after a pair of snails for even one day!" Pretty damning in the eyes of an 8 year old. Thank goodness I was spared such a dreadful reputation.

Annie MacInnis

A young recruit's first posting

He was a sight to behold – clean cut, immaculate uniform, boots spit polished to a fine shine, posture ramrod straight. A city boy, newly graduated from RCMP school, he had just arrived in rural Nova Scotia for his first posting. In fact he was driving from the airport to his new detachment.

I was nineteen, alone at home while the rest of the family went on a vacation I was too snotty to go on. I was tasked with keeping an eye on a trap set to catch the creature that had been sneaking into the barn and killing birds. Cavalier when given the assignment and familiar with guns and target shooting, I had not quite thought through the 'what if an actual creature gets caught in the trap and is not immediately killed'. Although skilled at target shooting, I was not a hunter and had never mercy killed a creature.

I was the newly minted officer's first official crisis although this did not play out as a classic damsel in distress scenario. I was dressed in disreputable clothes fit for feeding animals. I ran into the road and frantically waved down his car while carrying a loaded shotgun (muzzle down, breech broken of course; I was well schooled.) To his credit (and a testament nevertheless to those simpler more innocent times), he stopped the car and got out WITHOUT drawing his gun on me.

Breathlessly blurting out an incomprehensible story about birds who were personal friends and skunks with sweet faces even though in pain in a trap I ran back toward the barn exhorting over my shoulder to "Come quick; he's suffering!"

We arrived breathless at the barn where I pointed to a skunk was caught in the trap. "Are you a good shot?" I demanded. "Here you do it," I said thrusting the shotgun into his hands without waiting for an answer.

Pushing him much closer, I admonished him, "Kill him on the first shot" even as I quickly backed away.

I was a tad shrill, pretty freaked out, and I guess the arrival of a new person was too much for the skunk. It was pretty clear the young man was also not a hunter. As he lined up his shot, he angled around so the skunk was not looking at him. Immediately, the skunk's tail shot out. Just as he fired, the skunk sprayed the well-turned out recruit full on.

Let's Chat

He reeled backward, the deed accomplished at considerable cost to his person. Skunks were apparently not in his field of knowledge, him being a city boy. He staggered about, cursing fluently, looking down at himself, clearly appalled.

Finally he calmed down to the point of standing staring bitterly at me, the author of his misfortune. He wordlessly handed the gun back to me. I gingerly accepted it then backed away from him as quickly as possible. The stench was unbelievable.

For a moment he seemed about to say something then he shook his head and turned away. His shoulders slumped noticeably as he walked unspeaking back to his car not turning or pausing as I called a belated "thank you."

I can't imagine what sort of reception he got upon arrival at that first posting but I'm thinking that, given the Maritime penchant for nicknames, he may have earned his nickname on his first day. I'm thinking "stinky, skunk, pigpen..." Something along those lines comes to mind.

Sleepover

It was 6 am on a Saturday morning. The husband and I were inexplicably awake despite all odds. I wanted coffee more than life itself. I staggered to the closet, grabbed the closest garment to suitably enrobe myself for public consumption.

Tiptoeing down the hallway, I stopped short and stood sourly surveying a room wall to wall with soundly sleeping 13-year-old girls who had stayed awake until at least 2:30 whispering confidences and giggling. They had oozed every which way in the night. In the gloom it was hard to tell what was girl and what was sleeping bag/sleeping mat/special pillows or stuffed animals.

Unfortunately, in my inner city bungalow where the original dining room has been closed off to make a third bedroom, a trip through the living room would be the only route from my bedroom to the kitchen. I blearily peered into the darkened space humming with the small, satisfied snuffles and sighs of teenage early morning sleepers. Nope, there was no reliable path from here to there. I took a moment to feel really sorry for my coffee-less, sleepless self. I struggled to come to grips enough with reality to think clearly.

Ah hah! I quietly opened the front door and slipped out. I took a quick look left and right in case there were early morning working people about. Coast clear, I slunk out in my nightgown across my front lawn and hopped down onto the sidewalk surrounding our corner lot.

I immediately realized a person on a cell phone who had been hidden by my spruce trees had turned the corner and was directly behind me.

There was an audible gulp as the person beheld my middle-aged, awry-haired, pink night gowned self hopping from among the spruce trees onto the sidewalk directly ahead of him. Refusing to make eye contact, I resolutely faced forward. I tucked my bottom in and shuffled briskly along in my cotton nightgown trying not to let any bits poke out. Mercifully the back gate hove quickly into view. I darted in.

The coffee pot on the counter was never a more welcome sight. Soon the alluring smell of coffee filled the kitchen. I enjoyed a cuppa then refilled and poured another for my husband. For the trip back to my bedroom I slipped on a longish coat and bearing

Let's Chat

two steaming mugs hastened furtively back up the sidewalk, around the corner and in the front door. A quick glance into the living room revealed all still sound asleep.

I closed the bedroom door, handed one cup of coffee to my husband and crawled back in bed to enjoy mine. At least now I would be spared the prospect of facing 10 fresh-faced, dewy-skinned (despite minimal sleep) chipper, chatty 13 year olds without the fortifying help of caffeine beforehand. I am, as always, grateful for small mercies.

Smoking Teen

My teenager was highly amused; me not so much. As the mother of two children, of course I am no stranger to public humiliation. Any brief reminder of the incident of the weeping three year old trudging behind me through the snow in sock feet (because he kicked off his boots 6,000 times) to parent teacher interviews gets me feeling anxious to justify myself to any and every one who witnessed this.

As the mother of that same child who, in elementary school, sported an extravagant 6 inch Mohawk haircut from grade four on and the mother of children who, over the years have often dressed extravagantly and unusually, I am no stranger to occasional public censure, whispered comment and judgmental glances.

But this experience was different. All the other times when I have felt judged by other adults about my children and/or about my parenting style, I have felt relatively confident in my position. My parenting style is right for me - my logical consequences policy regarding behaviour and my belief, like Barbara Coloroso, that if it's not illegal, immoral or harmful to another then it is probably okay (or at least not worth fighting about) - have left me feeling relatively unaffected by disapproval from others most of the time. When feeling the judgment of others on these occasions, it was easy to put their disapproval down to different parenting styles rather than to assume I was in the wrong.

But on this recent occasion I certainly did not feel I had possession of the high ground morally. My kids had bought realistic looking theatrical cigarettes that truly look like they are burning and which give off small puffs of 'smoke' when inhaled upon. My younger teenager (a fourteen year old) brought this 'cigarette' with him when we went to do errands and proceeded to 'smoke' everywhere we went, indoors and out.

People were appalled. Not so much to see a fourteen year old smoking but to see an obviously morally bankrupt parent condoning his smoking in the car, at her side and particularly in non-smoking areas like stores. The censorious looks were beamed my way, not his, and they spoke volumes regarding their assessment of my moral character or lack thereof. Obviously I was a slattern of the worst order, a flouter of convention, a parent intent on allowing her son to run pell-mell down the path of moral ruin with nary so much as a polite demure.

It was impractical to chase after every person and defend what they thought they saw. While I suffered the agonies of parental angst, my teenager smirked and posed, deliberately drawing attention to himself and his manky 'habit'. We accomplished our errands at breakneck speed while the teenager scoffed gently at my embarrassment. My little lecture about 'promise me you will not take up smoking because this is affording you such amusement' was received with incredulous laughter at poor deluded, out of touch Mom who has not a clue and assurances that of course he wouldn't actually smoke, eeuuww, gross.

Upon arrival at home I could hear him plotting with his sister about taking the 'cigarette' to school...okay now I'm on solid parenting ground. If he gets detention for messing with his teacher, it'll serve him right and if a letter gets sent home I will reply with appropriate moral outrage at such a betrayal of my standards.

Annie MacInnis

Theresa's skates

Theresa's skates are awesome. Even a novice skating parent such as myself can see that they are really good skates.

Theresa is about my age and was a beginning skater like my daughter. As an adult just learning to skate she approached the whole process with a deal more trepidation than my daughter then 12. She approached me one day last year and spoke of watching my daughter on the ice, hair flying, skating dress swirling, and joy radiating from her very being.

I told her my daughter had recently revealed a long held dream by starting to take figure skating lessons and that her grandparents were paying for the lessons since our single income household does not run to extras.

A few days later in the dressing room Theresa looked at my daughter's skates (which were perfectly adequate for community rink skating but I guess were not really suitable for starting to learn jumps), asked my daughter her foot size then offered my daughter a pair of skates. She said these skates were good for jumping and had hardly been worn. She said she had bought them when she first decided to learn to skate but that they were too much skate for her and she had bought something less ambitious.

After the following lessons she gave us the skates. They fit. She wouldn't take money for them. We thanked her nicely. Next lesson we brought homemade cookies prettily packaged and a thank you note.

My daughter wore the new skates. On the way home my daughter told me that her coach was flabbergasted when he spotted her skates and that most of the other girls had commented on them.

Apparently the skates were very high end. Next lesson I approached Theresa to say this was too extravagant a gift and we would need to return them. She told me a story.

When she was growing up she had longed to take figure skating lessons but was unable to. Her mother had Multiple Sclerosis and her father had trouble supporting the family. There was no money for extras like skates. As an adult she decided to fulfill that cherished long-held dream of learning to figure skate. She

Let's Chat

bought a magnificent pair of skates but after a short time realized these skates were more than she would be able to manage and got skates more suited to her. But she hated to let go of the fancy skates. They symbolized her childhood dream. When she met my daughter and learned our finances were tight and that skating had been a longtime wish for my daughter she just knew my daughter should have the skates. That was why she didn't want to take money for the skates.

As she told this story I got goose bumps and felt tears well in my eyes. When she finished I told her that the reason we are a single income family and our finances are so tight is because I, too, have Multiple Sclerosis.

Life's serendipity constantly astounds and delights me. Thank you again Theresa!

Bull, our hero

I am amazed at the differences between my upbringing and my children's. My children are so protected from the dangers of the world at large and so supervised in all their activities.

When I was young, we children ranged pretty freely through a small town world that included woods, fields and ponds. Our general rule was come home at dark. If it was mealtime and you arrived at someone's house you'd be told with little ceremony, "Go home. Your mother will be looking for you."

Although we were very much masters of our own destiny we thought nothing of being chastised by any adult in town. That was the prerogative of all adults – to berate, if necessary, any child in their purview. In fact in our small town most adults even knew what rules were specific to your family.

"Ann MacInnis, you get straight home and don't be speaking to those boys in the Co-op parking lot or I'll be calling your father!!" screeched across my town's main street as I walked blamelessly home was a not uncommon refrain from my childhood.

I often visited unaccompanied with the old tramp that lived alone in a shack at the edge of town and didn't ever consider I had anything to be uneasy about. We had a common interest - cats. He had lots of them. He, despite his shabbiness and reduced circumstances never treated me in anything less than a gentlemanly fashion.

But there was one danger in our world. We were all expressly forbidden to cross the street and the railway tracks to play in the wood beyond my house. While this rule held for a few years, we eventually disobeyed this directive one spring and almost paid dearly for it. When we finally worked up sufficient nerve as a group to enter this terrifying wood we were pretty scared. The amorphous danger there was something terrible called "sinkholes". We weren't entirely sure what these were except that we understood that if you fell in you'd fall into the bowels of the earth as near as we could figure.

As we crept through the woods that fateful day there didn't seem to be anything scary at all. But on the return trip, full of swagger and braggadocio at our accomplishment, the unthinkable happened. One moment we were walking along quite full of ourselves. The next moment George fell with a shriek into the earth. He had fallen into a sinkhole whose opening had been covered with moss and leaves and such. Although suitably horrified, we managed to stand our ground and determine that he hadn't actually fallen out of sight (yet) into the innards of the earth. He was holding onto a strong looking branch out of our reach up to his chest in what looked like quicksand. It was pretty obvious we couldn't get him out by ourselves. Our concern shifted temporarily away from saving George from certain death.

Our foremost consideration now became how to minimize the trouble the rest of us were going to be in. It was agreed the kid who went for help would NOT go to any of our own houses, which were closest. No, he would run past all our parent's houses to old Bull Nelson's house. His kid was grown and gone. He was strong and we could probably negotiate some kind of deal with him. We knew he'd come help with less recrimination than we were likely to receive from a parent and he might not tell on us.

When the breathless kid managed to blurt out his story to old Bull, Bull, to his eternal; credit, ran to his barn, and without a word grabbed a big rope and followed the kid to the scene of the disaster. Bull hauled the kid out then turned to our chastened group.

A man of few words, Bull looked at each of us individually with a fearful gaze and said, "Are you EVER coming into these woods again? There'll be TROUBLES if you do, by gollies." Absolutely cowed and in no doubt about how bad he'd make those "troubles" we all promised as fast as we could "No sir!" And we never did.

Saran Wrap

While shopping recently I found myself bamboozled yet again by the availability of too many product choices! You know the obvious ones – hair stuff, sanitary stuff, pantyhose, to name a few. The selection is so vast and so many factors need to be taken into account (size, style, colour, generic versus name brands, price per whatever) that invariably you end up buying completely the wrong item or in despair just grabbing anything or nothing.

In this case I was trying to buy plastic food wrap. I wanted the cheapest box. I did not want the super sticky stuff so that my child could turn his fruit salad upside down like on the commercials. I did not need the fancy coloured stuff to make the inside of my fridge look beautiful. I had no brand loyalty or preference other than price. I only needed wrap capable of staying around sandwiches for a couple of hours. My intention was not to preserve said sandwiches for future generations. I did my calculations and was surprised to discover that the cheapest buy that day was a name brand (NEW AND IMPROVED!) plastic wrap.

Next morning I grabbed said box of plastic wrap out of the drawer. After a few fumbles I realized there was no serrated edge on the box. Low and behold, though, further incredulous investigation turned up a bar inside the box. Instructions said to pull away the protective strip, carefully adhere the strip to the exterior of the box as indicated, and then briskly slide a cutting blade across the wrap to detach the desired amount.

Attempts to follow these directions resulted in a counter of balled up plastic wrap and such a murderous glare directed at my husband on whose behalf I was engaged in this early morning activity while still on my first cup of coffee that he wheeled about and retreated in haste to the other end of the house.

Enraged, I called the 1-800 number listed on the box. A very nice woman in frigging Alabama or somewhere, was totally sympathetic to my plight, promised a full rebate and offered to provide instructions on using this new product. Somewhat mollified, I agreed to listen.

She said, "Hold the box in your right hand, ensure the wrap is rolling from the top not from underneath, firmly pull out the amount of plastic wrap required, then close the cover. With your right thumb just to your side of the 'N' in "Product Name", tilt the box slightly away from you at a forty-five degree angle while keeping the far end tilted slightly up. You may need to anchor the end of the saran wrap on a firm surface with an available elbow as you gently but briskly slide the cutting bar across the wrap."

Lots more balled up bits of plastic. I was honestly trying to follow all these instructions until the caffeine finally kicked in. I realized I was on a 1-800 call to learn how to use plastic wrap! I hate to think how much some industry specialist was paid to fix something that wasn't broken.

The mind boggles. Caveat emptor indeed!.

The Tax Man Cometh Again

Filed your income tax return yet? My husband and I are feeling justifiably chuffed. Not only did we file in a timely manner but we did so without any major frenzy about missing paperwork, no nagging or squabbling, and no computer problems. We filed electronically and now we are reaping our just reward.

Yes, that's right. It's a frabjous day when the income tax rebate check arrives! Is there any more lovely springtime tradition than that of a government in all its generosity giving back (an admittedly very small) portion of the blood that they wring from us poor small stones each paycheck.

For the first two days we just let the check lie there on the counter and tried to think positive but not overly avaricious thoughts so as not to jinx ourselves with unexpected car repairs/dentist/new furnace type financial disasters which could more than wipe out the whole thing.

Although our family structure most resembles a benevolent dictatorship there is a patina of democracy so we began with informal discussions about what everyone would like to do if we were to consider some small family indulgence before the bulk goes to debt. I wrote down the suggestions and the approximate amounts then made a list of what was within the realm of possibility.

Although there are those in the family who would be happy to run amok with such a check I would not be among them. Having been raised by a frugal Scot and steeped in his abstemious ways when it came to debt, any potential plans for the money were firmly based on the premise of paying down debt first and foremost. Any pie in the sky plans for redoing the living room or a small winter holiday were definitely not in the cards. It was understood the bulk of the check was earmarked to clear the overdraft and to pay down the Line of Credit.

We decided that I would blow my usual $100 a week grocery budget and shop at 10% off Tuesday at Safeway with gay abandon buying all those items we normally do not indulge in and spending maybe an extravagant $200 that week..

Then we got down to the nitty-gritty. Should we set aside enough to go out somewhere for a family meal and buy a membership to the Zoo or the Science Centre? Or maybe we could get bikes for the kids? In the end the kids figured out that 7/9ths of the check went to debt repayment; $1/9^{th}$ to new computer hard drive, the extra groceries and a few small necessities. The remaining $1/9^{th}$ we used to buy one of those enclosed trampolines for the backyard.

Although the trampoline is a much bigger family treat than I'd originally envisaged, I'm not looking over my parsimonious shoulder worrying that we have tempted the fates with unwarranted frivolity. The children are ecstatic (and nicely tired out). Through our careful discussions they learned good lessons about finances and fiscal responsibility but I also think they saw that it's okay and even a good thing to reap small rewards and to indulge ourselves now and then.

Annie MacInnis

Rainy Day 'Pie

It was the morning of Sports Day at school so of course it was raining. Not just trickling a bit, I mean really pouring. I kissed my husband goodbye as he left for work, poured myself a cup of coffee and sat down with the newspaper for a couple of minutes before I woke the kids. A few minutes later as I put my cup in the sink I noticed my husband had not left. Not only had he not left, he was standing in the pouring rain seemingly talking to his work vehicle. (He was on call so his own car was still at work.)

I stood frowning at him then leaned out the back door and said, "What ARE you doing?" He replied in a fairly irritable tone of voice, "There a damn baby magpie holding onto my windshield wiper like it's a tree branch and he won't let go. I'm trying to get him to step onto this stick."

I smiled broadly and scooted into the house and grabbed the camera. He finally eased the bird onto the stick. As he spoke soothingly and walked very slowly to the bird feeder to deposit the baby under the relative shelter of the roofed feeder, I managed to take his picture.

He responded in kind, "Go away with your foolishness. Be useful and get him some bread and a drink. He's hungry and wet and tired." As I came back into the house smiling about this fun start to my day, reality intruded. The kids weren't up, we were running seriously late and I was quite soaked.

Nevertheless I took the time to tell them the story of their Dad and the baby magpie only of course I couldn't say MAGPIE out loud because our dog loves to chase magpies and I didn't want her harrying that baby. So we talked about the 'pie in the yard.

For once, the children (with the incentive of Sports Day shining in their mind's eyes) put a wiggle in it and were relatively efficient getting ready. Then we hit a couple of snags. My son couldn't find his rubber boots and my daughter announced that the zipper was broken on her raincoat. I managed to quickly substitute hiking boots for one and a somewhat waterproof jacket for the other. "Grab your backpacks and let's go," I caroled with forced cheerfulness as I reached for my keys.

The hook was empty. My husband had used my car last night to run an errand since he had his work vehicle, not his own, at home. (Now I have this theory about life. There are two classes

STOP.

[74]

of vehicle owners. Those responsible, organized drivers who ALWAYS PUT THEIR KEYS IN THE SAME PLACE and those drivers who never know where their own keys are and who have even been known, for expediency's sake, to take someone else's keys and misplace them too. Now I don't like to have to name names but I fall into the former class and my husband would be a firm resident of the latter group.)

The children took one quick look from the empty key hook to the knot in my face and thoughtfully held themselves ready for immediate departure but did not ask questions. My mind quickly ran down the possibilities – call my husband on his cell phone (can't, needs a new battery), page him (can't, keep neglecting to ask for the number of the new one), call someone to come get us.

Now that last one's a possibility that I immediately discard in favour of us walking. I think my husband will feel WAY WORSE if we have to walk to school in the pouring rain. Oh yes, that's the best solution all round. I'll gain a little composure on the walk, the children could use a little hardship in their lives to remind them how good they have it, and the guilt value for my husband will be excellent. I am more than proud of this logical consequence solution.

I shepherd everyone out the door overriding all protests and stride briskly off. The children trail along disconsolately. All was going okay until my five year old son spotted the first worm on the sidewalk. "I need to help this worm," he told me. He stopped to lift it tenderly into the grass and safety.

Finally we managed to get underway again. "I'm going to be a worm hero," my sweet son told me as he strode importantly at my side, worm slimed hand tucked confidingly in mine. I smiled down at him as I said; "You're the second hero in the family today. Dad's a magpie hero and you're a worm hero." I wasn't feeling quite so good about my kind-hearted son umpty-million worms and 30 minutes later as we still dawdled on way inexorably toward school.

By the time we arrived at school I had decided that I was also a hero today. Despite much travail I had withstood all inclinations to rail at the fates, yell at my children, or sulk, and had even managed to retain charitable feelings for the 'pie and worm heroes.

Not Perfect but precious

By most people's lights he would not have been deemed a huge success in life. In fact, no doubt there are those who would be likely to say that he never amounted to anything. He never married, he sired no children, and he never owned a home. He didn't excel in school only just graduating from high school. He subsisted over the years fixing small machinery on an informal basis without ever acquiring a shop, relying instead on word of mouth and intermittent odd jobs. He played no significant role in his community never taking a leadership role in church or coaching a kid's team or any such thing. He came from poor and stayed poor, living out his life in the same small town where he grew up.

But, sometimes heroes are hard to spot. For, in the final reckoning, this man was a true example of the idea that the measure of a person is not in what he achieves or how much he acquires but in how he lives and how he responds to adversity.

When this man was in his forties, he developed health problems. At first the problems were manageable and he soldiered on living out the modest, unassuming hand he'd been dealt in life. Eventually though, his health worsened. He was hospitalized and put on a transplant wait list. Although in some discomfort, he continued to be mobile and was not infectious although he was susceptible to other's germs. Soon he began to find his hospital stay lonely and tedious. The hospital was an hour's drive away from his small town and people there were not prone to travel recklessly or often to the big city where the hospital was located.

To help pass the time and to give purpose to his life he began to inquire about and to seek out people in the hospital that he knew (or whose people he knew) or who came from his village or neighbouring villages.

Soon he became a regular visitor to many hospital rooms. His cheerful visits helped pass many a long uncomfortable, anxious day for others. Through talks with patients and family members, he learned of others in hospital and became a fixture in many rooms over the months that followed. Other patients came and went while he remained, waiting for his transplant, failing ever so gradually as the weeks went by but never giving up on his visits to others.

Let's Chat

Finally one day his turn came. He got his transplant but his break came too late. His system was now just too weak and compromised. In the end, his body rejected the transplant and he slipped away.

His funeral was modest in accordance with his mother's means. His cremated remains sat unadorned on a table in a small, rather badly made box that he had constructed in grade six as a gift for his mother. A small plaque now graced the box. It read, "Not perfect, but precious."

Annie MacInnis

The Gander and the Cat: The Tale of A Bully and his Comeuppance (or The Story of a Gander Gone Bad)

Once upon a time, when my older brother and I were young, my brother had a friend named Leo. Leo had numerous animals. When the current guard dog died, before there was an opportunity to acquire a new dog, the gander decided to take over the doghouse and the dog's duties.

Although he seemed a perfectly nice regular gander, John had grand ambitions. Perhaps he was unaware that he was, in fact, a gander and not a dog. Perhaps he found the life of a gander boring, thankless, or lacking in purpose. Regardless, he apparently aspired to the role of guard dog and at his first opportunity; he took over the dog's house and assumed his duties.

In the beginning, John stood officiously in the doorway of the doghouse and supervised whenever anyone came into the yard. If he knew you, he did nothing. If you were a stranger, he stood and hissed threateningly and walked slowly toward you.

For those of you who are even now scoffing, being face to face with a full-grown goose neck held flat out swaying like a cobra as it advances hissing towards you is a daunting prospect.

As time went by, though, John began to revel in the power and authority attendant on the job of guard dog/gander. Soon strangers began to be greeted by a hostile gander rushing furiously toward them and driving them off the property before they had any opportunity to state their business.

But as is the case with most bullies soon the thrill of that level of activity began to pall and he craved more and greater thrills. John needed more victims, more often, more drastically frightened. Soon John began to threaten family friends who came to visit. As soon as anyone entered his line of sight he came out of his doghouse with a loud sibilant hiss and a determined tread. He advanced aggressively, relentlessly backing the hapless victim into their vehicle or off the property. Any attempts to "halloo" the house were met with fury.

For a while John seemed satisfied with this escalation of activity. But all too soon, this too became commonplace and John

[78]

Let's Chat

needed greater thrills. He began to attack family members as they came and went from the house. The other geese were completely cowed and hardly dared venture anywhere.

But John's comeuppance was nigh.

A cat lived on the property. This cat had been around the block a few times. He was a big cat, an ornery cat, a cat who rested comfortably on his laurels. One day John made the fateful mistake of deciding to intimidate the cat. When the cat put in an appearance John rushed at the cat. The cat acted as though John did not exist. John hissed. John stamped his feet. John pulled the cat's fur. The cat was impervious to John. John was flummoxed. How could the cat not be frightened and helpless? He renewed his efforts.

The battle of wills went on for days. Several times a day the cat would ostentatiously cross from one side of the yard to the other. Each time it was as though John did not exist. John relinquished all his other duties. He spent his days watching and waiting for the cat but the stress began to wear on him. He began to doubt his scarifying prowess.

In the end, John spent his days lying despondent in the doorway of the doghouse utterly defeated. He completely gave up the dog's duties although he did not relinquish the house and move back with the other geese.

I told this story to my 12 year old as I dropped her off at Junior High one morning recently as an illustration that bullies always get their comeuppance. I'm not sure the story was helpful to her situation but she went off chuckling and later told me she smiled much of the day remembering John and the cat. I did too.

Hallowe'en

My children are fortunate to attend a school that celebrates many occasions with zest and verve. The gym is "haunted" and every kid brings a jack-o'-lantern to school to help supply atmosphere for the costume parade at Hallowe'en. There are class parties for all the usual holidays and some unusual ones. We treasure individual accomplishments, celebrate class achievements, strive for school-wide goals. We welcome excuses to celebrate – charity drives, family dances, and food drives.

I love to celebrate at home too. My family celebrates our dog's birthday every year by making dog bone shaped cookies for all the kids in my children's classes at school and for as many other kids as I can manage. The dog dresses for the occasion and personally delivers the cookies. We've been doing this at my kids' school for 6 years. Nowadays all through the early spring kids come up to me anxiously checking that I'm going to do it again this year.

(Mind you, we're not completely crazed about celebrating. We do limit the gerbils' birthday to a family and close friends event with just a Dairy Queen cake decorated with a suitable sentiment to commemorate the occasion.)

Isn't this what school and family life really should be focused on? Life (and school) should be about the pleasure of the journey and learning about others and taking every opportunity to seize the day and make the most of that day. Yet, in the quest to be sure not to offend anyone, many schools have jettisoned most traditional Canadian holidays from the school calendar. Because not everyone celebrates Christmas, now we have "winter" celebrations. Many children don't even get to dress up for a Hallowe'en celebration at their school.

Isn't this just the crux of what's really wrong with much of today's society! When schools stop celebrating and people become distanced from community and church celebrations it becomes all too easy to cease celebrating joyously at home too. It happens to all of us at one time or another. All of a sudden one day you realize you are living your life at such a frantic pace of work/children's activities/home improvement that there is no time to celebrate the small (but really important) things in life.

I've heard people complain about having to plan their child's birthday party. People are irritable about needing to make

Let's Chat

Hallowe'en costumes. The joy is sucked out of holidays and they become nothing more than another chore.

Instead of reducing the number of reasons to celebrate schools and families should be looking for excuses to celebrate the events that are important to their children, their families, their communities, schools, churches and cultures?

I say, bring the celebrations on! Never mind this political correctness fetish. New Canadians should be welcomed with open arms into traditional Canadian celebrations. Just because someone doesn't personally celebrate an occasion doesn't mean they wouldn't like to learn more about it by attending and taking part in the general jollity. In return maybe these same people will teach us about and include us in some of their traditional celebrations and some of those celebrations can be incorporated into our lives.

In my experience kids love to celebrate. The occasion isn't important. What is important is anticipation of an expected celebration or the surprise of an unexpected small occasion. Even if we've only done something twice so far, I overhear my kids saying, "We always do this..." with such pride and pleasure in their voices.

Your reasons for celebrating can be rooted in your religion, your family background, your own traditions or just completely frivolous. Celebrating life's small pleasures needn't become another obligation. Celebrate Friday nights with chips and a movie when convenient. Have a backwards supper (dessert first then supper but ONLY if you have room) because it's a rainy Tuesday. Light candles for breakfast some dark morning. Let the kids eat supper while they watch television on Monday nights or have sugary cereal on Thursday mornings.

So start celebrating tonight. It's Hallowe'en. Your mantra is, "This is going to be fun. It's not stressful. It's over when I say it's over and turn off the lights. All that fresh air will combat the sugar high so bedtime won't be too onerous. If I put on a funny hat and go with the kids I'll get candy too."

As she who should not be named would say, "It's a good thing."

A Fine Romance

Her name was Perle. She was one of those small, diffident women, soft-spoken and sweet-natured. She was unmarried, a retired schoolteacher and one of my great aunts.

When my grandmother and her sisters were young, in the days before the First World War, it was common practice that one daughter, usually the youngest, would not marry but rather would remain living at home to be a comfort and support to her parents in their old age.

As the youngest of the five girls, Perle was the designated spinster. I don't think she or the rest of the family questioned that assumption even though the older girls didn't just marry and settle down in the same town but went off to train as army nurses, to marry, and one to live in exotic New York City.

But one day Perle met a young man called Percy. They 'liked' each other right away. As time went by, they spent more time together. Eventually the relationship got serious enough for them to speak to her parents about marriage. Permission was not forthcoming. She was expected to do her duty by her parents and, as was common in those days, her duty she did.

My father said Perle's mother "took to her bed" a full ten years before her death, lying in state in her big bedroom, dressed in black and banging her cane of the floor when she required Perle's presence.

I only knew Perle in her later years but she seemed to feel no bitterness about this family tyranny. In the years I knew her, she remained unmarried as her parents had decreed but she had a "beau." The "beau" was Percy, steadfast through all those many years. By the time the parents were finally well buried and Perle was free to marry, I guess the moment for marriage seemed to have passed. Or maybe that lingering memory of the withheld permission still rankled. Regardless, the impetus had been lost.

But, love and their regard for each other prevailed. Through all the years I knew her, Percy was her constant companion. Although they never lived together, they visited almost daily. They were unfailingly tender with each other.

I remember visiting when I was about 16. Mid-morning Percy arrived with a basket packed with lunch for two and invited Perle

Let's Chat

for a picnic lunch on the water. He seated her lovingly and rowed the little rowboat into the middle of the lake. Spreading an embroidered linen cloth over the middle seat, he arranged the picnic on the little makeshift table.

All that afternoon I watched as they drifted on the breeze, chatting companionably.

Another evening he came with fresh picked raspberries for dessert after supper. Served with thick cream and coarse sugar, those berries tasted of heaven.

In fact, heaven seemed to be all around us in that place of peace with those two old people whose romance spanned close to fifty years. Forbidden by her parents to marry, living their lives separately, yet it was a fine romance.

Pee Sample

It was hard not to feel bitter and resentful. It was after lunch, I was still in my robe with my hair unbrushed, and I was outside trailing around the back yard.

My dear hard-working husband had been on call for the last three nights so my sleep had been disrupted by his work calls compounded by feeling sorry for him and pointless worrying about him going out into the cold night and driving tired. So I was already a tad sleep-deprived before the vet casually told me that as part of my dog's annual checkup now that she was a senior citizen, he would like a urine sample (preferably a first thing in the morning sample).

Aaacckkkkk!!!

I decided not to ask if cleansing with a handiwipe was required beforehand and decided to cut straight to the chase. Uuuummm…and I would collect this "sample" how? He casually told me just to use any clean container and to keep said sample in the refrigerator until I was able to deliver it to his office later in the day.

Being a generally optimistic soul, I sallied forth blearily that morning when the dog scratched the door. Still in my robe, I determinedly clutched a clean margarine container in one hand as I stalked the dog round and round the yard.

At first, she ignored me and blithely went about her painstaking routine of sniffing and analyzing at the microscopic level the overnight activity in our yard. After a few circuits, however, she noticed that every time she started to squat I honed in on her. She started giving me a hunted look over her shoulder. Each time she thought better of the urgency to pee and moved on without performing.

Finally, I got quite irked and dragged her back into the house to wait until she was more desperate and would throw modesty to the winds in favour of relief. Throughout the morning, we regularly repeated this routine with the same lack of result. In between trips outside, I lay in a dispirited heap trying to catch up on my sleep and regain some energy.

Finally, close to 3 pm, we trailed outside once more. It was clear that the dog was now in desperate straits although modesty still reigned supreme. As I closed the door and fumbled with the zipper of my jacket while keeping the empty container at hand, she made a dash for the far side of the yard, slithering under the trampoline and squatting in one fluid motion.

Yelling imprecations ("STOP! BAD DOG! NOOO!!!"), I raced after her and much less gracefully crawled under the trampoline just as she straightened up and jeeringly kicked some blades of pee splattered grass in my face then trotted happily away.

As I held the door for her to come back inside, a telltale smirk definitely crossed her muzzle. "Never you mind, missy," I thought, as I slammed the door very hard, "tomorrow is another day and I'll be ready for you. We'll see who's smirking tomorrow."

Parachuting

I was in my first year of university that September feeling newly independent and brave but still only 17. Life was exciting out on my own although I was grateful that in a pinch home was only an hour's drive away.

As a gesture of my new found independence I decided to do something daring, something brave, something adult, something noteworthy (but not on the order of dating all the boys on the football team). After much thought and investigation I hit on the perfect idea. I would take a parachuting course and learn to sky-dive!!

I neglected to mention this to my parents having decided a "fait accompli" would be much more satisfactory. Once a week I met with my fellow university adventurers and our instructor to learn the basics about parachuting. We discussed aerodynamics and the critical importance of packing your own chutes. We learned how to fall on mats of the floor from a standing position and then from successively higher heights.

Finally the last class before jump day arrived. We were all bursting with excitement about the 'morrow'. Then disaster struck. The instructor passed out liability forms saying, "Just sign these forms so our paperwork is in order. I'm assuming you are all over 18 and can sign these yourselves." Eeeekkk!

Although psyched to do something daring without asking my parents, I could not knowingly lie on a form. I sidled up to the instructor. "Uh, I'm only 17," I confessed.

My instructor was completely taken aback. "Oh my gosh," he said, "Since you're in university I just assumed you were at least 18. I can't let you jump with the others tomorrow. Not without a parent's permission. I'm really sorry."

I was devastated. Desperate I ran after him. "What if I got a parent's signature before jump time tomorrow morning? They only live an hour and a half from the jump field."

"If you get a parent's signature, you can jump," he conceded. I called my parents and spilled the whole sorry tale.

At 6:30 the next morning I stood hopefully with my class on an airfield with a sky that went on forever and low lying mist burning off as the sun rose. Just then a car pulled up near us. My mother stepped out of the car and walked over to our group.

"Here's my mother to sign my form," I burbled. The instructor handed over the form. My mother quickly signed, passed back the form then wheeled briskly toward her car.

The instructor called after her, "Hey, are you sure you're her mother? I thought you lived 90 minutes away!" My mother, in one of the few moments I can recall her using profanity, replied, "Who the HELL else would drive this far by 6:30 in the morning!"

Abashed, the instructor offered an olive branch, "Well, wouldn't you like to stay and watch her jump?"

"Certainly NOT!" said my mother and got in her car and drove away.

Newcomers

My family has a favorite nature walk, a high hill overlooking the city where we live. We often talk about what we see up there (when we look at the Hill itself and the view of the mountains and ignore the encroachments of civilization).

We speculate the scenery probably has not changed much from what early settlers would have seen. This usually leads to a discussion about what sort of intrepid, hardy souls early North American settlers were.

To leave your homeland forever for the great unknown *New World*, to travel under onerous conditions with the prospect that all of you may not reach your destination, and to travel with little more than you could carry is amazing to consider. To not even know where you are going other than in general terms and to simply decide one day this is far enough, we'll stop here, and this will now be 'home'. I am filled with admiration for such people.

Twenty years ago I traveled from Nova Scotia to make my life in Calgary. I still pine for the sights of home, feel sad to be so far away for Christmas and birthdays, long to hug my parents or sit at the kitchen table with them and hear their voices. Yet I, spoiled creature of the modern world that I am, can actually pick up the phone anytime I want to hear my parent's voices, look at photographs of my family, receive and write letters regularly and fly home if the longing to be there gets overwhelming.

Those early settlers had to be content with their memory of the voices and faces of those left behind, of the comforts and familiarity of that old life. How lacking in our modern materialism they were. When I think of reducing my household to what we could carry I am overwhelmed at the thought of culling so many precious belongings to a few small portable items that would forever comfort me and remind me of home.

Looking around me as I walk I can see how early settlers would look about them at this unspoiled land and see such a pleasing prospect that they would decide here is home.

My great grandparents did almost that. They left Nova Scotia to homestead in Saskatchewan near the American border. They lived in a sod hut in the beginning. To think of spending months in such a place with small children, I rather think I wouldn't be

Let's Chat

speaking to my husband by the end of the first day in that structure if the trip had been his idea!

Yet nowadays, we have modern intrepid souls who make their way to Canada from places where, like those early settlers, they can no longer see a hopeful future for themselves and their children. Like those early settlers they come with few belongings and many memories and regrets but with their faces turned to the future with hope and faith that they've made the right decision in coming here.

In these uncertain, perilous times since September 11 it's all too easy to be judgmental of others, to blame other cultures and countries for our society's ills. But I hope that the lesson that most of us learn from this time is to value our safety, our security, and the feeling that we are all home here in Canada.

New beginnings are what Canada is all about. Why not resolve to celebrate those whose ambitious resolution is to risk all to change their family's future? Let us all go out of our way to help new Canadians feel welcome in their new home. I hope they too find Calgary a welcoming place where they can remember home and yet also learn to turn their faces resolutely to their future here.

Annie MacInnis

To Holly Ann on the Occasion of Your Birth (Ramblings on my morning walk)

The hill smells of wild sage today. Haze covers the so-close-you-could-reach-out-and-touch-them Rocky Mountains. I walk fast up the first steep hill from the parking lot. My head is still full of the mental gymnastics I employ to get my kids to school on time and in a happy frame of mind. The dog strains on the leash toward the brow of the hill where she'll run free.

My heart starts to pound satisfyingly hard and steady. I do the slow in-through-the-nose and blow-hard-out-the-mouth breathing that's supposed to help oxygenate the blood while you're exercising but always makes me think of having babies. Either way I'm distracted from my leg muscles.

The exertion feels wonderful. As my body speeds up the squirrel running furiously on that wheel in my mind decides to take a breather. The interminable internal dialogue (don't forget there's been a wash in the machine since yesterday...we're out of bread...is there soccer tonight...what's for supper...I need to buy stamps...when are the library books due...) recedes to a dull background roar.

At the crest I unleash the dog. She bounds off in that doggy frenzy of running, smelling, peeing and abruptly changing direction for no apparent reason that dogs practice so avidly.

I used to make lots of excuses in my mind and to others to justify taking this time. The dog needs the walk. I have Multiple Sclerosis and I need to walk to keep healthy. I am able to parent more patiently and kindly when I have had my walk. But the simple unadorned truth is that I love my morning walk on 'the hill.'

When my children were babies I walked daily with them in strollers and in backpacks. Ostensibly so they got fresh air but mostly for my own sanity. When my daughter started school we only had one family vehicle so I walked to and from school using one of those big exercise strollers. Once both children started school I was suddenly alone in the mornings. Lots of people started asking if I was going back to work. I was non-committal.

Instead, after I dropped the children at school I went walking. At first I felt self-indulgent about my guilty pleasure. I was not

Let's Chat

earning or cleaning up the house or getting the groceries we needed.

But my morning walk is productive, I've realized. It allows me to count my blessings, as my friend Shelly says. While I walk I put my life into perspective. My children's daily dramas, money worries, health concerns all seem less urgent after my walk. During my walk I look at my world mindfully. I spend time thinking about my life and the good fortune we have.

Today I have a special reason to be happy. I have a namesake this morning. Holly Ann was born this day at 8:09.

When I first met the babies born to my older brother I felt forever changed. Looking into those faces were moments of epiphany for me. Until then I had always thought I did not want children and would happily play the role of hands-off aunt. But my nephews changed how I felt about children.

The births of my own two children made me an eager, glad parent.

When my sister adopted a baby girl from China I was moved to look into her face and think of the miles that baby travelled to be a part of my clan.

As my other siblings had children I delighted in looking for family resemblances and quirks.

Today I have a new member in the family of my heart. Soon I'll come off the hill and start rushing around getting my kids home for lunch, hustling them back so I can grab flowers and rush off to see my friends and my namesake. But just for now I'll keep walking and thinking about babies and birthing and dogs and relatives and what to serve those sweet wretches of mine for lunch and put that darned laundry in the drier before it rots and don't forget to take the camera and find that little pink bib...(damn, the squirrel's back).

Cupcakes

So what is it with cupcakes nowadays? When I was growing up, I do not believe you could 'buy' cupcakes. Cupcakes were a humble, wonderful treat some Moms and Grandmas made. They were usually made in those cool little cupcake wrappers and had only a thin skiff of bright coloured sugar butter frosting smoothed on with a bread knife to near the edges. You might get them at a young girl's birthday party as a nod to her 'growing up'. There was a good chance of them being served at a baby or wedding shower.

Maybe in the big cities bakeries sold them, but in the town where I grew up there was no market for something 'you could make yourself'. The big city grocery store bakeries might have carried them but we would have considered such cupcakes 'not nice.'

But cupcakes these days are big business with many stores selling only cupcakes and doing very well in their specialization thank you very much. Today's cupcakes are much bigger, available in exotic flavours with equally exotic combinations of frosting flavours swirled artistically high, and surprisingly expensive.

Although I make a mean cupcake myself, these new age cupcakes looked so impressive I finally tried a couple. They are pretty tasty and they are certainly very beautiful. But I am not a convert.

The cupcakes of my childhood are most certainly the country mouse cousins to these sophisticated city ones. In fact they are a different animal completely. I still prefer the small, modest versions that I make to these new fangled trendy ones.

If you, too, love cupcakes of yore and just have a yen for old fashioned country mouse cupcakes, my favorite recipe is, of course, one of my Mom's.

Let's Chat

Annie's Mom's Brown Sugar Cupcakes with Brown Sugar Frosting

Pre-heat oven to 350 degrees.

Sift dry ingredients in one bowl,
1 3/4 cups flour
1 teaspoon baking powder
1/2 teaspoon baking soda
3/4 teaspoon salt

In a second bowl cream
1/2 cup softened butter
1 1/3 cups packed brown sugar

Beat into sugar mixture
2 eggs
1 teaspoon vanilla

To butter mixture, add dry ingredients and 3/4 cup milk, alternately, ending with milk.

Stir just until smooth. Do not over mix.

Fill cupcake papers 2/3 to 3/4 full.

Bake at 350 degrees for 18-20 minutes depending on your oven. (If you aren't sure if they are done do the finger test. Press down gently on the top of one cupcake. If the indent stays they need a little more time. If cake springs back they are done.) Let cupcakes cool before frosting.

Frosting
1/3 cup butter
1/2 cup packed brown sugar
1 3/4 cups icing sugar (add later, read instructions below!)
1 tablespoon milk

In a saucepan, over moderate heat, melt butter. Stir in brown sugar and heat until smooth.

Remove from heat. Stir in icing sugar and milk. Beat until smooth. Spread a small amount of frosting on each cupcake.

Note of caution. These cupcakes taste great straight out of the freezer.

[93]

Annie MacInnis

Spring is coming

It will soon be ducklings in peril season in our city. Every year we hear stories of baby ducklings being herded by determined mama ducklings without regard for heartless vehicles but most times there is at least one concerned citizen who steps up to the plate to help.

Last spring it was my turn to be one of those people. I was in a hurry driving north in rush hour traffic when I screeched to a halt. As we drivers craned our necks for the cause, the intrepid crosser turned out to be a self-important mother duck with a gaggle of very small ducklings trailing earnestly but untidily behind her. They, thankfully, crossed safely and continued toward the nearby park.

Relieved and heartened they had made it safely across, I drove off with the other cars. Within two blocks I turned back admitting to myself I could not leave them to the fates for two more blocks and two more intersections even if they were residential blocks.

By the time I got back the family were halfway down the first block walking in a fairly straight line in the gutter between the curb and parked cars. I drove slowly beside them and blocked the first intersection until they were safely across. At the second intersection I again blocked the way. the park was just across the street but the mama duck was not crossing.

Just to one side of the intersection was a city road crew, a large pile of dirt, a large yellow vehicle and some workers. Thinking she was unnerved by this activity I got out of my car and tried to chivvy her along. She squawked aggressively and refused to budge. The ducklings milled around in alarm.

The road crew stopped to watch the entertainment. I rounded up the ducklings and shooed them toward the mama and toward the park. The mama duck was reluctant and once on the grass continued to fuss taking a few steps then turning to quack loudly at me.

When I figured they were far enough into the park for safety I walked back to my car. Just as I got into the car I heard a tiny quacking sound and suddenly the mama duck's behaviour made sense. She was short a duckling. But where was it? I looked under nearby cars, behind a hedge and a tree, then realized it had fallen through the sewer grate. There it stood quacking for Mama.

I yelled to the workers who came en masse to help. The sewer grate looked like it had not been moved in forever. It took long anxious minutes of heaving and

straining before these guys managed to budge the grate and heave it out of the way. The duckling was out of arm's reach so one guy had to ease down with the other guys holding his legs. He scooped the duckling into his helmet, the other guys pulled him up and he delivered the duckling to his family in the park.

We all grinned at each other with relief and congratulated each other on a successful rescue. Duckling hero - yup, that's me. To the other duckling heroes - the city guys who helped - you know who you are!

Sylvia

We have a brand new member of our family! She's three years old and her name is Sylvia. Our whole family has been waiting a long time for this. Several times we thought we had found her but luck was not with us until Sylvia.

When we first saw her we all knew immediately that she was *the one*. We knew our search was over. We welcomed Sylvia with open arms. Now, only two weeks later, it's as though she has always been a part of our family.

We don't know anything about the people Sylvia used to live with except that they treated her well. Sylvia, by the way, is our new silver-coloured car, a 1997 Ford Taurus station wagon. She is a huge step up in the world for us given that my old car was a 1983 Toyota Supra appropriately named Rusty. Rusty was named for his rust-orange colour but of later years had begun to live up to his name.

Rusty was probably the most valiant car ever! He always started and repairs over the years had been minor. But he was definitely showing his years of hard service and I had begun to worry about how much longer he would keep running. He became fairly bashed up around the edges over the years so eventually we reduced the insurance coverage to liability only.

After an accident a year ago (when the idiot in front of me !!?##**++!!) it didn't seem worth major expense to try to further straighten the slightly askew headlights. They still shone but because the left headlight pointed ever so slightly to the right and the right headlight pointed ever so marginally to the left there was a tendency to feel a tad cross-eyed when driving at night. My inclination was to avoid night driving and when absolutely necessary to drive with my nose almost touching the windshield in order to spot danger sooner.

The windshield wipers began to work sporadically and unreliably so driving in heavy rain had become problematic. The left front signal light stopped working and repeated repair attempts failed to get it working again. Then the passenger window broke. Two hands to hold the window level and one more hand to push the power button were now required to close this window.

To add insult to injury, my housekeeping standards began to lower accordingly and what with two children and a dog riding with me, the inside of Rusty began to look as pitiful as the outside.

Yet rarely a day went by that one of us didn't give Rusty a fond pat. He still sits in our driveway as we look for a good home for him. The children are hoping that someone will want to buy him and fix him up. I'm not holding my breath but I'm hopeful too.

When I look at Rusty I don't see his failings. I see a storehouse of memories. I see Rusty as I first saw him - bright and shiny and new to us. I see myself holding onto the door as I sink to my knees in labour in the hospital parking lot. I see our babies strapped safely for their first trips home from the hospital. I see my husband in pain after a cornea transplant. I see our puppy sound asleep on the children's knees as we discuss what to name her. I see the love hearts and initials I draw on the frosted windows when it's a school morning and we're had a bad start and I'm trying to cheer up the children's snarky faces. (Have I ever mentioned I have a tendency to get sentimental about silly things? My husband shakes his head as I cry over *Folgers* commercials and *Little House on the Prairie* so what can you expect?)

I feel like a lucky, lucky person. Thank you to my parents who gave me an advance on the future so we could buy Sylvia and once again drive with impunity. Now if I could just get over the tendency to whip down the driver's window and fling out my arm to signal left turns I'll be all set.

Robin Red Breast

A robin gentleman is building a nest in the spruce tree outside my kitchen sink window. Every day he studies the nest intently before adding anything new. He sits in it swiveling this way and that to judge comfort. The outside is fetchingly decorated with blue tinsel retrieved from the skeletal remains of our Christmas tree. Watching him reminds me of another beautiful nest.

When I was growing up, the autumn fair in the nearest big town was highly anticipated. As Indian summer waned and school settled into routine the fair was something to look forward to.

The fairgrounds in the distance at the end of a long car drive were a sight to behold. We children would be desperate to get out as our car bumped slowly across the dusty, grassy fields to park with the other cars in orderly rows. Adults, many dressed in their Sunday best toured the barns, produce, and cooking displays, watched horse races, had tea and pie in the tea tent or a picnic on the grass and perhaps, later on, a decorous ride on the Ferris wheel.

Children ran amok through the fair, loathe to spend any of their money until they had looked at everything first. This was the only opportunity all year to go on fair rides and eat fair food; choices had to be cannily made so regrets were few.

One year one of us girls won a kewpie doll. Whether it was me or one of my sisters is lost in the clutter of my mind but I well remember the doll's fate. She was beautiful! She had a long, graceful neck and delicate arms soaring above a pink, feather dress like something out of Gone With The Wind. She went everywhere with us including the last visit before winter to our summer cottage. Somehow in the confusion of packing up five kids and the dog, the kewpie doll got left behind.

Winter promptly arrived and the cottage was inaccessible. Until she was forgotten in the bustle of winter we comforted ourselves with the thought that the kewpie doll was in a place of honor on one of the beds.

Finally spring arrived and we made a trip to the cottage for a fire and cookout. Suddenly a shriek rent the air. Hurrying to the girls' bedroom we saw an entirely bare-naked kewpie doll. Not one feather was left to adorn her. She was otherwise unmarked with nary a claw or bite mark.

Let's Chat

Usually each spring we found evidence of what a busy winter the mice had. A drawer filled with rice painstakingly carried one grain at a time from a top shelf; a pile of dry cereal carefully stored for easy (and cozy) access in a small pile under a pillow on a bed. But, as outraged as we were about the poor kewpie doll, the thought of baby mice being raised that spring in a nest of fuchsia pink feathers was a joy and still is!

Nanna's eggs

My father's mother was not a cuddly let's bake cookies and then I'll knit you something granny. She was a well-dressed let's go shopping/do lunch/play bridge kind of woman. She was a good cook and I have fond memories of her Jigg's dinner (corned beef and cabbage) (although I've never met a Jigg's dinner I didn't love) and broiled bacon and cheese sandwiches but, the dish I most remember my Nanna for is her eggs. She had a "way with eggs".

When I was young and stayed over at her house, my favorite breakfast was soft boiled eggs. She always cooked them perfectly. The yolk would be nicely runny while the white was just firm (but not too firm) and with no (horrors!) watery bits or see through jellyfish bits.

She had the most wonderful, whimsical clear thick glass egg cups that were reversible. Sitting one way up there was a nice small egg holder to eat a hardboiled egg out of the shell while a second egg (if you were so inclined) sat intact and keeping warm under the larger dome underneath.

Turned upside down, the small egg holder became the base while the large dome became a place to put two shelled, chopped up, eggs.

My Nanna always served breakfast for me at the nicely set red table in the kitchen while my grandfather ate his breakfast and read his newspaper in peace at the dining room table.

My eggs always came with toast soldiers with the crusts cut off and just the right amount of salt and real butter (not nasty margarine).

Years went by and I forgot the pleasure of perfect eggs in those amazing cups until one day I inherited some of my grandmother's glass egg dishes.

The very sight of those glass dishes made me long for her eggs and just one more morning in that kitchen with my grandfather straightening his waistcoat as he passed through the kitchen on the way to his medical offices at the other end of the house.

Unfortunately I soon learned through bitter experience that I do not have my grandmother's "way" with eggs. My eggs are tasty but usually only adequate, serviceable at best. Only rarely and inadvertently, do they approach those sublime creations made by my grandmother.

Yet, my lovely glass egg dishes do not go unused or unappreciated. Fortuitously I married a man who has a "way" with eggs. Once again on occasional weekend mornings, I have the pleasure of sitting down to a breakfast of perfectly cooked soft boiled eggs served in my Nanna's glass dishes. And yes, of course, there are toast soldiers with the crusts cut off.

My husband's eggs taste oh so much sweeter, even across the expanse of years, because they are flavoured ever so faintly with the memory of a red and white kitchen, grey hair swept up with tortoiseshell combs and a chubby kid asking for seconds. Sublime indeed.

Annie MacInnis

We've got mice!

It wasn't bad enough that the retaining wall surrounding our raised front yard fell down with a thump one day. Worse was to come that very night as, unbeknownst to us, the wall residents found a lovely new home - ours. Just as I was drifting off to sleep my daughter's voice piped up from her room with those chilling words, bound to strike dread in the heart of any homeowner, "A mouse just ran across my floor."

I gingerly crossed the hall and stood in the doorway to my daughter's room. A horror of scuttling wild things lurking in the dark made it hard to stay calm. I stood still and suddenly caught a flash of grey/brown from the corner of my eye.

Auuggghhh! We have a mouse in the house! After several fruitless attempts to capture him, I sent my daughter back to bed with repeated platitudes along the lines of, "He's way more afraid of us..."

Nevertheless, as I lay in my own bed consoling myself with the thought that in 21 years in this house this is our first uninvited rodent boarder and I guess it was bound to happen sometime, I still felt crawly and uneasy.

Next morning the man of the house was dispatched forthwith for humane traps. The traps were duly set and generously laced with cheese and seeds. I awoke in the middle of the night to the metallic SNAP of the trap door. I drifted back to sleep secure in the knowledge that the mouse had been scooped into captivity.

The next morning we viewed the tiny bright-eyed culprit. There was a prolonged discussion regarding the choices of release area where there was a chance of him not immediately being snatched as a snack by the closest predator. Finally we settled on a suitable place.

We packed him a loot bag of seeds courtesy of our pet gerbil (an acceptable rodent in a cage) and sallied forth with the interloper. We carefully released him with best wishes and words of encouragement under a low lying bush.

Back home we congratulated ourselves on a job well and humanely done but decided to err on the side of caution by resetting the traps just in case.

Let's Chat

Arriving home that afternoon I discovered another "little friend" in the trap. Before supper we all set off with a cache of seeds and gently dispensed mouse number two under the same bush to live in the great outdoors with his relative.

"SNAP" went the trap in the night. I lurched awake and went to check. Two more sets of eyes blinked up at me. I shuddered and returned to bed. We showed these two the same courtesy releasing them under the bush with the requisite seed dowry.

"SNAP" went the trap. "SNAP! SNAP"

By number eight we were flinging them willy-nilly into the bush and throwing a handful of seeds after them. I couldn't help being reminded of that movie "Mousehunt" and wondering if this was the same mouse we were releasing...but thankfully number eight was the last mouse and there was no need to destroy the house although some serious scouring took place.

Annie MacInnis

The Pet of his Dreams

We have a dog and a gerbil. My son loves both creatures but neither is the pet of his dreams. The penultimate pet would be a dragon or dinosaur, albeit a youngish one amenable to being trained up a bit. He, of course, realizes this is an unrealistic hope, hence his backup plan – maybe a komodo dragon or monitor lizard.

Whenever this is mentioned I make sympathetic, non-committal noises and immediately find something to do elsewhere to obviate further discussion. So, when I sat among strangers at the Christmas party held by my husband's work colleague I was agog to overhear a discussion regarding a pet monitor lizard.

I was admiring the obviously child free living room when a group nearby started talking about once cherished pets now neglected by their teenagers. One parent worried about a guinea pig's increasingly solitary existence; another that their snake was virtually ignored by their teenagers. Then another couple weighed in looking for a new home for their _pet monitor lizard!_ I goggled at the couple. It was every parent's wish right before me – to give our son the Christmas of his dreams, the one he would forever remember as "the best Christmas ever!!" He'd blow away all those post Christmas school braggarts with their petty Christmases in Costa Rica and play station whatevers.

I looked frantically for my husband, thinking, foolishly as it turns out, that some other parent of a small boy was going to leap at this offer. I grabbed my husband and hustled him back to the lizard couple gabbling "Son...heartfelt wishes...us covered with glory." My husband narrowed his eyes at me then took a long-suffering breath and smiled politely at the couple.

"How old is this monitor lizard?" he asked.

"Oh, only a year and a half." The other husband replied, smiling ingratiatingly.

"How big is it?" asked my ever practical husband.

"Oh only about 1 ½ feet now," replied the wife eagerly.

My husband seized on the significant qualification _now_. "How big will it get?" he asked.

Let's Chat

Shamefaced, the wife admitted, "Well, about 6 feet long including the tail."

"And why are you selling it?" asked my spouse.

The other husband hesitated. He looked at his wife, then his wife muttered, "Well actually it's kind of mean and it bites and it turns out it's carnivorous and it's getting so big we're a little concerned about our other pets and actually we recently read an article about monitor lizards eating a biologist who was studying them..." She trailed off and they both smiled sheepishly at us.

My husband turned to look at me, shook his head pityingly and walked away without another word. The lizard couple smiled brightly at some new arrivals and hurried away.

I slunk away muttering imprecations under my breath. Well if I can't be covered by glory I guess I'll just have to sacrifice myself on the pyre of the desert table as penance. Always a pleasurable alternative to any holiday setback.

Time for a Haircut

His sister was appalled. She accused us of setting him on the path to moral ruin. Our decision was the thin end of the wedge, the slippery slope, and the point of no return. From here on in we would be to blame for any accruing misfortune. Be it upon our own heads she declaimed as she stalked out of the room.

This whole kerfuffle started when I mentioned casually to my husband one evening that our son was due for a haircut and could my husband take him. My son immediately piped up to say he wanted an interesting haircut. He was tired of the same old, same old (short back, sides and top).

Over the past year he had cultivated a small queue dangling down the middle of his back to provide some variety. A couple of his school buddies had adopted this style and he wanted to join them. He still enjoyed his 'tail' but now he wanted a more drastic change.

His sister is not upset by this initial declaration. My son, whose eclectic reading taste often runs to ancient civilizations and medieval times, decided he'd like to have his hair cut like a medieval monk's tonsure. (For those of you not constantly immersed in things medieval, this would entail having his hair cut in a bowl cut just above the ears then shaving bald a largish round circle on the top of his head.)The mental image of this cut gave us all pause as we considered the prospect.

I reverted to that tried and true parenting ploy and said, "Hmmmmmm. That's an interesting idea. Let's think about that." Then I made sure to leave the room and go busy myself elsewhere.

After giving the matter no inconsiderable thought over the next few days, I sat down with my son. Although I'm a firm believer in allowing kids a fair amount of freedom when it comes to clothing and hair styles this idea at least needed careful discussion before proceeding. I said if he really, really wanted this cut we could do it but that he should consider these thoughts before making a final decision.

First, in all the pictures we've seen of this cut, the monks had very straight hair that lent itself relatively easily to this style. This boy, on the other hand, has quite curly, quite wayward hair with several quite recalcitrant cowlicks. So the haircut you see in your mind's eye may not bear a huge resemblance to what you will see in the mirror.

Second, most of your buddies are not aficionados of medieval lore. Consequently, they may not instantly grasp the inherent coolness nor the historical ramifications of your choice of hairstyle. He reverted to that tried and true kid ploy. Lowering his eyebrows, jutting his lower lip, he scowled at me and left the room.

Sometime later, he came to me and conceded that maybe a monk's tonsure was not the best choice. Anyway, he had thought of a way cooler haircut that he'd rather have – a Mohawk. This is the point where his sister reared back on her hind legs in horror.

"Not a Mohawk," she spluttered. "Only bad teenagers and gang kids wear Mohawk haircuts. They get wild haircuts, and dress weird; they skip school, join gangs and are mean to other kids. He's only 7. He's way, way too young to have a bad kid hair cut."

She and I retired elsewhere for a little privacy to continue this discussion. I pointed out that I gave her lots of freedom about how she dressed and did her hair. I asked if she thought I should boss her more about her hair and dressing style. I pointed out that her brother has always had an eclectic sense of dressing and that we needed to honour that. I pointed out that she needed to zip her lip about her opinion on this. I reminded her that this decision was "not your job." We parted company on a sort of cranky truce.

The day of the haircut finally arrived. He and his father sallied forth to do the deed.

On their return my son strutted into the living room with shoulders back and head high. His Mohawk soared above his head like a huge cockscomb, shining with green, blue, yellow, red, and white colored gels of which he had purchased an extensive supply. His queue curled silkily down his back in a long ringlet. His eyes glittered with amusement. His face shone with pride and accomplishment.

Although it was a little shocking for the first few days, his Mohawk now seems just a part of his usual self. An unexpected bonus is that taking the time to slather on today's color scheme each morning has encouraged him to wash his face and hands and brush his teeth while he's there with a few less reminders from me.

Although his sister still really doesn't approve, I think even she has to admit it looks pretty neat. Also she's having some fun with those colored gels too.

Medieval Oatmeal

It was one of those dreadful school mornings.

The morning had started out great. I'd had a good sleep or rather, since I'm a Mom, no one threw up or had a bad dream and couldn't get back to sleep and no one climbed into bed with me except for the dog and my husband so my sleep was relatively undisturbed. I woke up a couple of minutes before the alarm and didn't have to pry myself out of bed through sheer grit and willpower. I managed to get a couple of cups of coffee under my belt before I had to interact with any rugrats. I made cooked oatmeal for breakfast. The children woke up in fairly cheerful moods instead of making that horrendous, nerve-wracking whining sound as they open their eyes that tempts you to smother them where they lay. All in all there was potential for a great day.

The kids arrived at the table reasonably promptly and settled down without squabbling. My daughter and I started right in on our oatmeal but my son, although physically with us, was taking a little longer to come to grips with reality. He stared into space, one hand poised unmoving near his spoon.

I wolfed down my oatmeal and the last of my coffee, one ear tuned to my daughter's chatter while the rest of my mind ran at light speed through the usual internal dialogue in my head (don't forget to turn on the washing machine and take more bags to the car for dog walking, did I pack the kids recesses or only think about doing that, when is my dentist appointment, we need toothpaste, don't forget to bring up toilet paper when I'm turning on the washing machine, is the school assembly today or...)

As I scooted off to make beds and get dressed, I succumb to the urge to gently remind my son to, "Get a grip! It's a school morning and it's 10 after eight and you aren't dressed and you haven't even started eating!"

Moments later as I'm brushing my teeth an earnest little face appears in the mirror.

"Is it true that in medieval times spices were very rare and that explorers had to travel very long distances through dangerous places to get spices and that only really rich people usually got to eat spices?"

Mouth full of toothpaste I nod my head, yes and spit.

"Was salt a spice too or only pepper and cinnamon and stuff like that?"

I think about that for a moment, then say, "I think salt also had to be imported and like spices rich people would be more likely to use it regularly than poor people."

The earnest face considers this information then says, "What about sugar? Was it a spice that had to come from far away too?"

I take a very deep breath, reach way, way down for patience and reply, "white and brown sugar like we usually use may not yet have been available in Europe. I'm not completely sure when those items began to be imported to Europe. We could look this up later today if it's important But I think that if brown and white sugar was in Europe in medieval times it would probably have come from far away like spices did. Most likely in medieval times honey would be used for sweetening things. Again, poor people may not have been able to use it on a regular basis. If poor people were lucky enough to discover a lot of honey, I think they would consider it a luxury and sell most of it to buy more basic items like flour, seeds for planting, cloth or other things they couldn't grow or find or make for themselves. Now this is all very interesting but it is a school morning and we really do have to hustle so get cracking and get dressed!"

"But I didn't eat yet," said the somewhat less endearing face.

"I blustered for a moment before settling on "Why not?" in a slightly strangled voice overlaid with the suspicion of a whine.

"Because, my porridge tastes like medieval porridge!"

"You want more sugar on your porridge!?!?!?!?"

"Yes please."

!@#@@#$$%^#%^^&&*!!!

Going to the Chapel...

The call came about twenty years ago around this time of year. "I'm getting married in May," my sister caroled. "Will you be my Matron of Honour? Buy yourself something great in pale pink; I know you'll choose well."

My sister was getting married. I should have been thrilled for her. My sister was getting married and had asked me to be her Matron of Honour. I should have been feeling happy and honoured to be asked. My sister was getting married and I would be the Matron of Honour and I was not thrilled, not happy, not honoured.

What I was, was pregnant! Regardless of how beautiful and glowing I felt, by the time of the auspicious event I would be a hefty seven months along. "Typical," I thought, "just typical!"

Being a lifelong fan of pink, my sister probably thought she was being kind suggesting that colour and letting me choose my own outfit but I was aghast. My sister obviously had no idea of what would be available twenty some years ago in formal maternity wear in pale pink. At the best of times, a trip to the maternity department of any store was a terrible experience in those unenlightened days. Racks were filled with cutesy little kid styled clothes in pastel colours – giant pairs of overalls, enormous t-shirts with "fun" sayings, dreadful dresses with empire waists and gathers – all, it seemed to me, with the express purpose of disavowing any possible attractiveness other than innocent pre-school prettiness in the wearer.

With their puffed sleeves and high waistlines all the choices made me look like a big fat 3 year old Bo Peep with a too old face or, possibly worse, some Grimm's Fairy Tales horrifying version of the wet nurse that fed all the babies in the town during one terrible winter.

What a nice thought, to be preserved, looking like this, for posterity in all the many wedding photos, I thought as I tried on outfit after outfit and gritted my teeth at my sister. My pique was worsened by the thought that I couldn't even be irked at my sister over this imposition and call and rant at her about her timing because that would imply that I was thinking this wedding was "all about me."

[111]

Even if it was in my mind, "all about me" I figured I'd get little sympathy for my point of view. I resolved to make the best of the situation and finally managed to find an outfit that maybe if you were charitable did not make me look like a REALLY BIG preschooler.

In fact, in retrospect, I look quite nice in the pictures if I do say so myself except that in all the pictures of that lovely wedding, my expression is that of a sulky child, a put upon older sister, a martyr to family harmony. Well we all have our assigned roles to play in the family and I guess I fulfilled my role that day.

A Body is Discovered

It was a body and it was definitely dead, I'll give them that. My Dad was a local doctor and the county medical examiner. Protocol decreed he be called in the event a body was found. So when night shift workers at the local sand and gravel pit uncovered a body, they called the medical examiner to come examine the body before arranging to have it removed.

My father was awakened by the call about the discovery of a body. Upon arrival at the pit, to the general amusement of all, he was shown the body of...a Mastodon. The Mastodon had fallen into the tar pit some 60,000 years previously and was remarkably well preserved but quite definitely dead.

My father, a serious history buff, was, as the men knew, very pleased to be in on the discovery. He was also present when the museum folk came to carefully excavate the remains. As the Mastodon was carefully lifted out of the tar pit, a tree, also wonderfully preserved, was discovered beneath the body. The museum people ignored the tree. My father was surprised they not intend to also take the tree for preservation and use in the exhibit. The museum staff said that once exposed to the air, the wood would disintegrate within days.

My father, never one to be daunted by the impossible, asked if he could take a few hunks of the tree and did so. He called all his museum friends trying to discover a way to preserve the wood. Finally a friend in London advised him to paint the wood with diluted Elmer's Glue and to keep painting the wood until it would absorb no more. This worked marvelously. The wood appeared strong yet was unaltered in appearance. My father preserved one piece of wood for each of his five children. My ancient piece of wood has pride of place in my china cabinet. It is absolutely unremarkable looking; so ordinary it might easily be thrown away or burned in the fireplace with no one the wiser.

Whenever I hold that piece of wood, I am awed to think I am holding an object that is 60,000 years old. But more than that, this ordinary looking piece of wood reminds me of where my people are from and that place and time of my childhood. It was a place and time where everyone knew everyone. A place where local sand and gravel workers, upon finding a Mastodon preserved against all odds, would choose to call up the local doctor and get him out of his bed for a joke but also because they knew history is his passion.

Ordinary looking wood, worth nothing, full of Elmer's Glue, history and memories. Thanks for the wood and so many great memories Dad.

Pie for breakfast

It was a grey and snowy day. Waking up I felt a little depressed to say the least. So I confess I decided to give myself a little treat to buoy up my spirits. I had pie for breakfast. I'm not real proud of the fact but at least I'm admitting it. That must count for something.

Certainly the fact that I went for an exercise walk afterwards must provide some measure of mitigating circumstances for my behaviour. Or at least it might count for something when balanced against the first piece of pie I ate.

I rationalized pie for breakfast was an acceptable indulgence. It was homemade banana cream pie with real eggs and milk and bananas so it's healthy right? Almost like a bowl of cereal with bananas and milk really if you consider that the pie crust is a grain product almost equivalent to cereal.

Besides when we woke up to snow once again not only was I depressed but I had to shore up the kids resolve to venture out to school at all that day. They were inclined to slide into an immediate decline when they looked out the window and I was sorely tempted to declare a mental health day for all concerned. I had to scrape the car again, find the kids' boots and gloves again and my wind pants again for my exercise walk with the dog who was the only member of the family who could summon any enthusiasm for going out today.

I was only going to have one small piece of pie as a special treat to help me gird my loins for the rest of the day's chores. Well perhaps just a little bit bigger than that since it's so snowy and overcast And, of course that first piece tasted like more so I had another sort of smallish piece for desert.

But of course the pie was, pardon the pun, just the thin end of the wedge, the slippery slope down which I slid for the remainder of the day. For, once two pieces of pie were securely under my belt there was no point in concerning myself about calories today, I reasoned. Lunch was fast food with my skinny son who was only too willing to aid and abet my descent into the caloric miasma of French fries and burgers. I recouped marginally over the supper hour by serving a nutritious meal to all concerned but fell off the wagon again just before bed when a bag of chips in the cupboard called so deafeningly to me I was afraid they would wake the children.

[115]

Annie MacInnis

I woke up this morning to see snow still blanketing my pretty crabapple tree blossoms. Staggering to the kitchen for coffee and feeling dazed with sugar and fat and calorie overload and feeling definitely repentant, I resolve to once again join the ranks of sane, healthy eaters. Contrition is my name.

Tell the truth

During a visit to my parents' house a couple of years ago the dinner table discussion turned to formative childhood moments. I told a story about a clear memory I have of when I was about four.

My father is an antique gun collector of some renown. Throughout my childhood gun collectors from around the world came and went to buy/sell/trade/admire my father's collection. The gun collection took up the whole third floor of the house. That floor was completely off limits to any child unless accompanied by my father. We were welcome to look to our hearts content at any gun but only while supervised.

One day while my father was at work, a gunsmith came with a gun for my father. With laundry underway amid a baby, a toddler, my older brother and me, my mother's hands were full. Rather than traipse to the third floor, my mother placed the gun high on the living room mantelpiece out of reach of small hands. Throughout that morning whenever I walked past the living room archway I looked into the mirror above the mantelpiece at the reflection of this very unusual looking gun.

I had never actually touched or even tried to touch any of the beautiful objects on the mantelpiece but that morning the reflection of that gun in the mirror beguiled me. Finally, I could bear the temptation no longer. Fully aware that I was flouting a really big rule, I pushed the fireplace bench closer to the mantelpiece, stood on my tiptoes and stretched. I could just barely reach the gun. As I slid the gun over to the edge the inevitable happened. The gun fell to the hearth below. A piece broke off it.

Before horror completely overtook me I grabbed the gun and the broken bit, pushed them hastily back up onto the mantelpiece and rapidly fled the scene of the crime. The remainder of the day seemed interminable. I was guilt ridden.

Finally my father came home from work. After a few minutes conversation, my mother mentioned the gun the gunsmith had brought. My father walked into the living room. Moments later he came back and asked my mother if it had arrived broken. My mother said certainly not.

[117]

Annie MacInnis

My father called us children together in the living room. He showed the gun and asked if any of us had touched it. My siblings all answered honestly, "No." I too said, "No."

My father frowned at us then said; "One of you has broken this by accident. I will give you a few minutes to consider this. If whoever did this comes and talks to me there will be no punishment; if the culprit does not own up there will be trouble."

I walked away with the others but only lasted maybe a minute before I burst back into the room, flung myself into my father's arms and confessed the whole dreadful adventure. My father hugged me, reminded me I was welcome to look at any gun BUT ONLY when he was there to supervise, and then congratulated me on taking responsibility for my mistake. He talked about the importance of always telling the truth, of admitting when I have made a mistake and of accepting the consequences of my actions.

I finished my story recollecting that four year old me by saying how his words that day have stayed so clearly in my mind. I told my father how significant this conversation was for me in terms of the way I lead my life and how I parent. I smiled down the table at my father.

He, looking back across the years to those hectic days parenting five children, smiled back at me and said, "Hmmpphh. Don't remember that at all!" "No I don't remember either," said my mother. We all laughed.

I sat thinking about my own children. I wonder what moral lessons will resonate in their adult lives yet will be immediately jettisoned from the shuffle of my mind? A cautionary thought if ever there was one.

Say Please

What in the world has happened to the concept of good manners! It seems they have gone out of fashion for a disproportionate number of the population! A couple of times each day I pause my vehicle while making a left turn to permit someone to cross the street only to receive no acknowledgement of my gesture. To add insult to injury, the person is so full of entitlement they usually walk inordinately slowly talking loudly on their cell phone for the duration of my green light, completely oblivious to the fact that I am waiting for my turn too.

Recently I was at the grocery store walking with difficulty with a cane and while waiting in line at the checkout a woman pushed past me saying, "I only have three things. You don't mind if I go ahead of you, do you?"

On the bus people often seem reluctant to give up their seat to the elderly, the infirm or the expectant mother or parent with a small child. It's no longer common practice to acknowledge the bus driver with a "Good morning," and/or a "Thank you."

People veer to push through the door you have opened rather than make the Herculean effort to open the door directly in front of them. Have you held open any doors recently for someone and then they fail to acknowledge you or your gesture? How about people who consistently fail to play their part in running organizations to which they belong?

Kids who used to be considered old enough to remember by themselves have to be constantly reminded to say, "please," "thank you for inviting me," "supper was delicious," "I had a great time."

As cell phones and answering machines have become ubiquitous, phone manners have gone the way of the dodo bird. People habitually neglect to return your calls and fail to pass on phone messages. How many times a week are you privy to one side of an overly loud, way too long, way too incredibly tedious private telephone conversation? Or how about when you are dealing with a sales clerk and the phone rings? Does the clerk excuse him or herself, answer the phone, say, "Can you please hold?" then finish the transaction with you before getting back to the customer on the phone?

Annie MacInnis

Are our lives so busy and so important that people can no longer spare the time for courtesy and good manners?

Some days I feel as though the rising tide of inconsiderateness is close to overwhelming society. It behooves all of us who value good manners to do our

part in the face of this overwhelming lack of consideration and politeness. However discouraging it seems some days I urge all who continue to value this old-fashioned virtue to do your part to stem the tide by continuing to require courtesy from all children and to acknowledge good manners whenever they are displayed.

"Be the change you want to see. We will prevail."

Let's Chat about wedgies and animals' private bits and Nanna in her underwear

In the back seat of the car were three cousins - a somewhat diffident 12-year-old boy, a modest 12-year-old girl and a chatty 7-year-old girl who was more than willing to shoulder the burden of making conversation.

"I like your dog. She's very nice and quite pretty except her private parts show way too much. I don't like to look at that. My grandmother's dog's private parts don't show like that. They are all covered with fur. I like that better except sometimes there is poo on the fur and I don't like that. My grandma says animals lick themselves to keep themselves clean but her dog is not very good at it. Does your dog do that?"

"Um, not in front of us usually, she's pretty polite," says my red-faced daughter. Then trying to change the topic somewhat, "my dog had a boyfriend but he moved away."

The irrepressible little girl is off like a shot. "Well then, your dog and me have a lot on common. We both don't like to be teased about being in love. Being in love is nothing to be ashamed about. I get teased at school because everybody in my class thinks I'm in love with Richard and Jimmy is in love with me and Ben is in love with me and Joseph is in love with me…(Big breath, nanosecond pause in conversation in case others want to speak, then the spate continues) "My cat licks her bum right in front of me. I don't think that's very nice. My brother's cat doesn't do that but I don't like what he does instead. He scootches on his bum on the living room carpet to tidy his bum. My bathing suit gives me a wedgie. Do your bathing suits do that?" (Deafening silence from the boy, my daughter manages a strangled, "not really".)

And she is off again. "Want me to tell you a funny story? When my brother was little he would not poo for days and then he would have a poo day and there would be poo everywhere. One time Nanna was looking after him and my Mom said, "Watch out. Today's a poo day If his tummy rumbles get him quick to somewhere you can change him or there will be poo everywhere." Nanna said, "never mind, I'm used to changing babies." But when we came back Nanna was wearing only her panties and bra and my little brother had only a diaper and there was poo everywhere and Nanna said, "There was poo from his ankles to his chin and all over me too."

(In the rear view mirror I see the older kid's eyes boggle at the thought of poo everywhere and their grandmother in nothing but her underwear.)

Mercifully we arrive at the family cottage. The boy flings open the door and is gone almost before the car stops. My daughter is not far behind. The conversational maven looks brightly at me and says, "That was fun!"

"Yes indeed, it surely was!" I think.

Heroes among us

We are all desperate for the return of real heroes in our lives. We are tired of all the negative, horrifying, disheartening, unsettling news stories and television shows. We are tired of the ordinary, the good enough, the mediocre. We have had enough of sleazy politicians, poor service, crooked businessmen and warnings that "what you are about to watch may be offensive..." We are tired of being disappointed by those we have elected, those we have entrusted, those with power. We are tired of feeling cynical and disillusioned and ripped off. We are tired of people refusing to take responsibility, of the justice system's failures. We are tired of pushy telemarketers and rudeness.

We crave feel good stories especially in economic hard times. We crave acknowledgement that there are good people doing good things. We crave people we can admire unreservedly, people we can look up to.

Stories about the miracle plane landing on the Hudson River and the election of Barak Obama are two examples of people's eagerness to seize onto those with heroic tendencies, to welcome them into our lives.

Even though the Hudson pilot just did what he was trained to do we were thrilled that he followed through, kept his head, landed the plane and especially that he waded twice the length of the plane to make sure no one was left behind.

The election of a black US President in our time and the interest in his inauguration shows how desperately we want to believe that he is the truly good man he seems. We want to believe that goodness is rewarded, that the Golden Rule still holds true, that politicians can be honourable, that people, governments and even nations can work together for a common good.

During the Great Depression, hobos left small signs readable only to each other, indicating a good woman lives here or a gentleman lives here to designate small local heroes.

It is all too easy to get discouraged at the dearth of heroic people in the news and to disparage the media's emphasis on dissolute, corrupt, dishonourable, behaviours. These people may be talented and powerful and rich but they are not of heroic proportions. Every day our lives are filled to overflowing with a clutter of stories about inappropriate role models, rude behaviours and dishonourable actions. These types of people in the public eye are undeserving of our admiration, our attention and our trust.

Like the Depression era travelers, we all know many, many good people in our own lives. It behooves us to acknowledge them, to celebrate them. If we but look closely, if we pay attention in our own lives we will be rewarded with random acts of kindness and civility and examples of people choosing to behave well.

We cannot stop the rising tide of incivility and dishonour in our world but we can cherish the everyday heroes that come our way and let them know that we appreciate them. We can also joyously celebrate the public heroes that rise inexorably to the surface. "Yes we can."

A Gentleman Among Gerbils

He was ordinary looking, neither too fat nor too thin, with bright snapping eyes and a quick playful nature. He was about two when he developed a growth on his stomach. An urgent trip to the doctor resulted in a terrible diagnosis – the growth was a tumor. The prognosis was guardedly hopeful. The tumor was operable and there was a slim chance the patient would survive that operation.

The estimated cost of such a delicate procedure on such a tiny creature however was staggering. Not an enormous sum in the general scheme of things but perhaps a tad extravagant to save the life of a small gerbil eminently replaceable at any pet store for the princely sum of $10.

While a valued member of the family, this creature was already two thirds of the way though his allotted span. Given poorish odds of surviving the operation and that recovery was also at best uncertain, the family decided that perhaps the kindest thing was to say their goodbyes. Since he was not in pain, the little fellow came home to say his goodbyes and await his appointment with fate the following day. Once formal goodbyes had been accomplished, the mother took the dog and the kids to the cottage as a distraction for the children.

The Dad was left to spend a last night with the little friend and to take him to his appointment the following day. That night, bereft of his family, the Dad lay in his quiet house listening to the usual nighttime soft sounds of the gerbil as he chewed cardboard, shredded Kleenex and generally went about his planned projects for that night.

When morning finally arrived, Dad and the gerbil sallied forth with brave faces. The gerbil was surrendered to the vet with the instructions to "operate." Hundreds of dollars later, Dad and gerbil arrived on our doorstep. A several hour drive to the cottage to rejoin the family was not advised as post-operative activity.

"Could he ask a big favour? Could we look after the gerbil and administer his medicine twice a day while he traveled to the cottage to break the news to his wife of his vast expenditure as gently as possible? If the patient didn't make it through the weekend we shouldn't feel responsible."

Post operative instructions (obviously generic for all animals after surgery) had the kids falling down laughing over reminders not to let the pet chew or lick the stitches, and warning against running and jumping.

Despite the intricacy of seizing and dosing a reluctant convalescent gerbil twice a day without further injuring him while he was littered stem to stern with stitches, he made it through the weekend and received a hero's welcome home.

Although this gerbil walked with a distinctive stagger and held his head slightly askew as a result of the surgery, he lived for a considerable time after his operation and was fondly recalled much later by the busy vet who performed the unusual delicate procedure. For the remainder of his life, he remained a cheerful, happy, valued member of the family.

Measuring a creature's value not in terms of his size or ability to fight back, nor in dollars, anticipated longevity or guaranteed return but in what he brought to his family - now that is a life lesson to teach your children.

Hallowe'en Shmallowe'en

There was someone on CBC radio recently blathering on about how Hallowe'en is their favorite holiday because it's so non-stressful - no gifts to buy, no big dinner to cook. She waxed eloquent for some time along these lines while I gritted my teeth and muttered sharp ripostes and cuttingly witty rejoinders under my breath.

I love Hallowe'en in theory. But Hallowe'en, in practice is, at least in my household, usually fraught with the potential for at least one crisis.

There was the year of The Great Wing Debacle. My daughter decided to be a blue damselfly. Her costume was constructed from items we had in the house – electric blue leotard, antennae sprayed sparkly blue, etc. The only stumbling block was the wings we already owned. These store-bought wings were not suitable. They were too rounded and damselfly wings (apparently) are longer and narrower. I drove myself berserk trying to construct acceptable (or even recognizable) wings but my efforts were pitiful. My daughter was resigned to my failure to supply these when fate intervened. On Hallowe'en morning my daughter woke up feeling feverish and with several small red spots. By late afternoon she was quite definitely mangy feeling and the beautiful damselfly costume was set aside in favour of a large, plush Dalmatian costume, which was at least cozy. A comment about the irony of her dressing as a spotted dog in her spotted state was not appreciated. Face makeup was unnecessary; calamine lotion and chicken pox spots gave her a naturally mottled look.

Then, of course there was the Buzz Lightyear Fiasco. That was the year the Toy Story movie was so popular. My son announced in early October that he wanted to be Buzz Lightyear for Hallowe'en. I spent the next few weeks visualizing the construction of this costume. I could buy some of that accordion dryer hose stuff and spray paint it white, adapt his bicycle helmet into a space helmet, make chest logos out of cardboard, spray paint an old pair of work gloves. I assembled all the supplies and on the weekend before Hallowe'en proudly showed everything to my son and demonstrated how great this costume was going to be. My son looked impassively at the display for a little too long then turned to me and said, "But I don't want to be Buzz Lightyear. I changed my mind remember? [No, I certainly don't remember!] I want to be a raccoon."

[127]

Annie MacInnis

This was the year of the Mysterious Missing Eyelashes. My daughter was to be an autumn fairy. We had yellow flowered shoes, brown stockings, a sheer brown short skirt decorated with leaves and green sequins, a tie-dyed orange/yellow top, extra leaves and glitter spray for her hair, and wings (rounded ones were fine this time for a fairy). But the piece de resistance of the whole costume was a pair of long exotic metallic blue fake eyelashes. They really did put the finishing touch on the costume. The week before Hallowe'en she wore the whole outfit to her Girl Guide Hallowe'en sleepover party. When she came home I counseled her to put all her costume bits in her sleepover bag so she'd be all ready to take everything to school on Hallowe'en day. Of course she did not do this.

For days I kept seeing bits of her costume, particularly the critical eyelashes lying about the house. The night before Hallowe'en, at bedtime, she finally gathers the bits of her costume together but, low and behold, the eyelashes are nowhere to be found. For the next hour my husband and I turn the house upside down searching for these wretched things in between bouts of castigating our daughter. They were never found. By the time we gave up looking everyone was seriously ratty. In the end I was saved from watching my daughter learn a hard lesson on a special day by my husband using every spare moment he had in his work day to search out the last pair of beautiful metallic lashes left in the city in time for her party at school.

Of course there's also that whole treat dilemma thing to round off the holiday nicely. If you buy all the treats early on sale, inevitably "someone" starts snacking until supplies are so low you need to buy more. Then you buy way too much and by mid-November some people's jeans are too tight by midday.

So, no, Ms. Whoever you are big shot on CBC Radio, I don't think Hallowe'en is a relaxing, effortless holiday. My family doesn't celebrate Norman Rockwell style. Hallowe'en is just like the rest of my life – hectic, messy, loud, and usually fraught with strong emotions and the potential for weight gain, but I wouldn't want to miss one minute of it.

Fishnets

As if parenthood is not already chock full of ready-made opportunities for humiliation, my most recent brush with mortification was of my own making.

On a recent Saturday morning while I was trying to stay focused on the daily grind of grubby house, laundry piling up, no groceries I succumbed instead to a truly satisfying job and opted for a major cleanout of our closets.

My husband's closet was easy. "No, yes, no, no, yes." No emotional attachment (at least on my part) to hardly anything, didn't buy it, didn't give it, don't like it, gone. A really satisfyingly neat and emptyish closet was the prompt result. My closet was another matter, a daylong grind of guilt over how much I paid, how much I wish it still fit, how I'm bound to find some occasion or some matching thing to go with it. Ruthlessness comes hard when it's your own hoard.

I ended up with a functional closet, a large bag for charity, a bag for consignment and a small pile of 'think about' items. Next day, looking in the sentimental pile, I put on a shirt I had once loved.

My premonition to go shopping paid off with a huge bin of fancy coloured fishnet stockings all at 80% off. I have a daughter who loves fishnets so I grabbed a shopping basket and rummaged enthusiastically. Laden with a veritable cornucopia of fishnets I lined up to pay, chortling to myself as I calculated my savings. Holding my purse in one hand and the basket of shopping in the other, I looked around at the nearby displays, and smiled at some of the other women in the lineup. Several gave me a distinctly cold shoulder but it was not until my turn came and I dumped my basketful of stockings onto the counter and cast my eyes down toward my purse to pay that I realized the sentimental shirt was unbuttoned to my waist with an excellent view of my overly large chest available for all to see.

Of course, the wretched coincidence of me walking about showing off my 50 year old chest in my best white lacey bra while buying luridly coloured fishnet stockings was immediately evident to me. Even the salesclerk was reluctant to make eye contact with me as I hastily tried to cover up.

Walking quickly away with my shopping, I was uncomfortably aware that the clerk and the remaining shoppers were no doubt considering my departing fifty year old bottom and legs and goggling at the thought of me wearing those brightly coloured fishnets!! Even I reeled at the mental image. I may never look at fishnets the same again. And the shirt…it's gone.

Lost and Found

There is a blight on my horizon these days. Somewhere in the course of last winter my children completely misplaced their Sherpa – you know - the useful, obsequious person who trundles along behind them gathering up and carrying all their belongings. Oh, gosh, was that me?

I am aware that the majority of children in the school are quite self sufficient about their basic belongings. On television most children do travel to and from school with their knapsacks and coats and boots. I have observed that in real life this is also for the most part true. Most children remember to gather all these items as they go out into the cold car on the way to and from school. When their long suffering parent arrives to bring them cheerily home from school, these self same children oh so independently change from their indoor to outdoor shoes, put on their coats, shoulder their knapsacks and leave the school gladly and quickly and relatively efficiently. Other children do this. I've seen them.

Mine do not. They dawdle, they chat, they lie on the floor, they do not change their shoes, they forget their coats and knapsacks and inevitably the halls empty of parents, children, and belongings. Eventually we manage to gather up some semblance of what needs to be in the car. But by the time we arrive there I am laden with their belongings and at least one child does not arrive with the group at the car and has to be searched for and threatened.

I am a very organized, punctual person. I do not lose belongings. So it is particularly galling that I have children who are so blatantly careless about such things. I think these sort of challenges are just one more of those parental humiliations that strike to the quick of one's core in some kind of grand cosmic joke that carefully matches petty child-induced irritations with the parent least likely to be able to bear the burden with equanimity.

I have tried every theory I can come up with to resolve this problem. We have had Barbara Coloroso-type talks where I have outlined how stressed and unhappy this issue is making me and we have brainstormed solutions, which have worked briefly. Then suddenly one day I realize I have once again been reduced to harrying, nagging, burdened porter again. I have told them I refuse to enter the school and will wait for them in the car. This has usually ended with them forgetting all about this new regime by the day's end. I end up waiting in the car until I am steaming mad while my children wait tearfully inside wondering where I am.

I have waited patiently and calmly for them to gather up their belongings and then taken stock as we arrived at the car and calmly insisted that they return for the missing bits. In the end the parking lot is mostly deserted and we are wrung out as we leave.

The weather is getting colder and crisper by the day. No amount of wishful thinking on my part is going to stave off the return of winter and herein lies the crux of my problem. My children have begun once again to travel to and from school inundated with snow pants, mitts, hats, jackets, sweatshirts, boots and a myriad of items with great potential for misplacement. Given their penchant for dribbling their belongings around and my issues against resuming a role of laden minion, eventually one day very soon we will all be faced again with the inevitable.

One day very soon we will be critically low on hats, mitts, spare snow pants and sweatshirts, possibly even boots. Once again, our family will not be able to wait until the lost and found items are tidily laid out on long tables in the hallways for easy, casual perusal of items that we might own and have misplaced.

I will have to approach the noisome, reprehensible lost and found box alone. (Sending children to do this is pointless. They are immediately distracted by the untold wealth of cool abandoned stuff and spend their time coveting someone else's flotsam and do not attempt to recognize or reclaim their own belongings.)

THE BOX is as bad as I expect. Chock full, brimming with all manner of horrifying items like ancient teeming 42 day old uneaten lunches, damp, musty socks all balled up, always at least one pair of underwear, smelly boots and sneakers, wizened fruits, endless mittens, gloves and hats, polar fleeces, jackets.

I feel distinctly peevish as I heave the seething morass out onto the floor and start methodically but gingerly sorting. Somewhere in the midst of this horror I start locating all my children's abandoned belongings. Just as I gather up the few last items, oops, that would be my sweater and that's most definitely my scarf. Hmmm, I wonder where you sign up for a Sherpa...

Miss Little Bum

I pride myself on being an easygoing sort of person but put me in an exercise class and I'm like Goofy in the old Disney cartoon about road rage.

I am a competitive exerciser. Really the only group exercise activity I have been able to indulge in since high school is dog walking with friends. Even there I am compelled to be at the front of the group most of the time but because it's rather free form with dogs running pell mell and people veering off to do their pick up duty there's less compulsion on my part to outpace everyone.

When invited to join a group yoga class years ago, I declined, saying, "I am too competitive." My friend looked at me in a puzzled way and said, "It's yoga!' I replied, "Yeah and I'm competitive! I will outdo everyone compulsively until I am too injured to return."

So my recent decision to add more exercise than dog walking into my routine was not taken lightly. But joy of joys, I found my ultimate exercise class. The class was already underway. I smiled obsequiously and slid into an empty spot. The class was well attended – about fifty people there on a Tuesday afternoon. People seemed friendly. A few smiled at me and some chatted with each other during the class but most focused on their water workout.

Almost immediately I felt newly apprised of my potential for fitness. I felt slim. I did not feel the competitive urge to outdo everyone else in the class thereby injuring myself and never considering returning to the class. I worked happily at a reasonable pace the whole class. From my casual glances around I estimated I was the youngest in the class by about 25 years. Not only was I the youngest but, except for a few of those classic wiry ladies who no doubt could, and would, beat the $%#% out of me for referring to them this way, I was the slimmest (a relative term obviously) person there.

Now how wonderful is that! Moreover in the locker room after the class while we're all walking around in various states of undress and showering and so on, when I introduced myself to the group, one of the spokespersons, an imposing woman of European extraction, dismissed my name out of hand and declared in a decisive voice we will just call you, "Young Miss Little Bum."

[133]

I smiled ingratiatingly, feeling quite thrilled with the sobriquet. It has been a long time since anyone had called MY bum little and it's not often anyone calls me young anymore. Yes, quite a gratifying beginning to my new exercise regime. I think I may just stick with it this time.

I haven't had a decent night's sleep since...

A good night's sleep seems like it would be a modest wish but it can be surprisingly hard to come by on a regular basis. When my kids were young I remember thinking about a good long sleep with the same passion I used to think about an evening with my husband before we had kids. When our kids were very little, my husband and I would occasionally wax nostalgic about those weekend mornings pre-kids when we slept in half the morning.

On the rare occasions when I was with child free friends, I would pester them for details of their weekend, "How late did you sleep in? Did you have coffee and read the paper in bed? An afternoon nap?" vicariously enjoying the 'dream' of a good night's sleep.

When my sister came back from adopting a baby girl in China and remarked how tired they were, I scoffed unsympathetically, "Oh give me a break, you're tired after two weeks? I haven't had a decent night's sleep since the fall of '89!"

I remember weeping one day thinking that my intelligence had seeped away somehow through all the cracks and disruptions of night after night of sleep disrupted by little ones. In moments of clarity I consoled myself with the thought that one day soon the children will start sleeping through the night and I will go back to good sleeps on a regular basis. Of course this never actually happened. About the time they began sleeping through the night the kids took up the habit of having bedtime angsty moments and occasional meltdowns unloading all the anxious, lonely, unhappy moments of their day at school. During this period I went to bed tortured by tales of woe over-dramatized by tiredness that nevertheless haunted my sleep.

After too many years of this I pinned my hopes on the thought that when they go to junior high, they will go off to bed on their own. Wrong again. Those were the years of 10 pm announcements that "a project is due tomorrow and I forgot it, I need $15 cash for school field trip tomorrow with many signed pages of potential risk forms, I need to be at school 1/2 hour early and you need to drive me, I need to wear a blue shirt and none are clean, I need to bring an ethnic snack to share." Not much wonder I took up grinding my teeth while I slept.

High school years were marred by kids who became night owls, prowling around the house until all hours, eating up tomorrow's lunches and sleeping so soundly come daylight you worried they might be dead.

Just about the time it seemed there might be light at the end of that tunnel I started waking up repeatedly with night sweats and an internal dialogue so deafening I couldn't get back to sleep. After months of shuttling back and forth between sleeping in my bed and on the couch, I hit on a brilliant solution.

Talking book tapes from the library became my salvation. Crawling into bed I pop in the ear buds and drift promptly off to sleep listening to the blah, blah, blah of a British murder mystery that drowns out the squirrel in my head making lists for tomorrow and re-hashing all my conversations of the day. I have never slept so well as I do these days. Teenagers out until all hours, creeping home in the night, no problem, can't hear anything but the story and if I do wake up I just hit play and before you know it I am off to dreamland again. Too hot? No problem, flip the sheets a few time as I hit play and fast forward a couple of times and like small kids with their lullaby tape I am off to dreamland within minutes.

Unfortunately there is a fly in the ointment and he is beside me in bed. My poor long suffering husband is not sleeping well. His dreams are being frequently haunted by sibilant whispering voices talking mayhem and murder when my ear bud falls out and ends up near enough to haunt his dreams.

I guess this might be one of those 'for better or for worse' phases of our marriage for him.

He was a champion flyer in the end

The first time we saw him he was sitting hunched and alone on a perch in a pet store. His beautiful blue and green feathers belied his body language. He was not a happy budgerigar. We named him Sheldon and brought him home as a sidekick and small companion for our cockatiel, Percy.

Percy was wonderful company in those early days when we were newcomers to the city and lived in apartments where we were not allowed to keep cats or dogs. Percy lived in a big cage. When we were home we would open the cage door so he could fly. He would swoop joyfully about the room and occasionally land on our heads or shoulders and hang out with us.

I learned to be careful to remove and to put out of sight any sparkly earrings as soon as I came home as he coveted anything shiny and would sidle along my shoulder nonchalantly and try to steal them from my ears. Percy was an extrovert with a big personality. He loved lots of activity and people. He thrived on music and flying. He loved chewing things especially wood and exploring. But he minded being alone all day; hence the companion.

The new budgie seemed overwhelmed at first. Percy cheerfully dominated the cage and the little guy seemed intimidated although Percy did not appear to be hurting or bullying him. Sheldon's wings were clipped so he did not fly but gradually he began, diffidently, to explore his new surroundings and to venture along the outside of the cage using beak and feet to maneuver.

Percy was determined to teach him to fly but as the weeks went by and his wing feathers began to lengthen, Sheldon showed no interest in lessons. Undeterred, several times a day, Percy would herd Sheldon down into the cage doorway. They would stand side by side with Percy muttering encouragement and instructions out of the side of his beak then away he would swoop.

Percy would fly circuits about the room squawking all the time. It was unclear if the squawking was along the lines of further instructions or just exhortations to pay attention, watch me, watch me, you can do it!

Either way, Sheldon would dutifully sit and admiringly watch the flying lessons with small round eyes and an earnest demeanor. After some weeks he began to cheep excitedly and dance back and forth in the doorway and occasionally spread his wings slightly without leaving the doorway. One day in his excitement he swooped away with Percy and they flew laps and laps both cheeping loudly the whole time. Finally landing, they hurried into the cage for celebratory drinks.

They both flew a few more times that day and thereafter were the best of friends and flying partners. Turns out Percy was a great teacher except for one thing. Percy has always given that verbal encouragement to Sheldon when teaching him to fly so Sheldon understood that flying involved two actions - flapping your wings and cheeping as loudly as possible - both nonstop.

When flying together, Percy would swoop soundlessly, gracefully, effortlessly about the room whereas Sheldon was always flapping frantically and squawking continuously to stay aloft. He brought a smile to our faces every single time he flew!

From my kitchen to yours

It's a perfect day. I am up early as usual but not rushing. No work today. On a weekend morning like this with both my almost grown children at home, the house quiet, and everyone but me still asleep, my heart sings and thrums inside me with contentment.

I peel a pear with attention to what I am doing. I separate eggs using the tip of my clean finger to clear the last of the white from the shell. I pad back and forth across the kitchen measuring flour, baking powder, and salt with slow measured movements. There will be homemade muffins for breakfast in a little while.

The sun rises through my kitchen window spreading golden butterscotch light thickly across the floor and through the air. The smell of fresh brewed coffee wafts toward me as I look out the window at the quiet Sunday morning outside. There is nary a soul about.

Soon the house will bustle with our family plus a kid who slept over and the unexpected boon of a visiting cousin but for now the house is silent and peaceful. I am alone with my thoughts and coffee. I revel in this quiet time making a lovely breakfast for the household. Homemaking may have lost its luster out in the world but in my world I value nice meals of homemade food. Cooking feeds my soul as well as my family.

I love to look at cook books, to try new recipes and to tweak recipes. I love to hold fruits and vegetables in my hands, to smell spices, to create something delicious from my head or based on another's instructions. Nurturing is the essence of loving. In this busy world how often do we take the time to nurture those we love?

Taking baking to share at work, soup to a sick friend, making lunch for a working family member or serving them supper and leaving it for re-heating are acts of joy for me. Being nurtured makes everyone feel loved and makes the giver feel loving. I consider sharing food not an obligation but a gift of my time and my passion for good food and a way to show how much I value my friends and colleagues.

Annie MacInnis

Annie's Muffins

(originally recorded in my much stained hand written cookbook
as Diane's Grandmother's friend Anne's Banana Bread but then I
meddled over the years with the recipe)

Pre-heat oven to 350 degrees

Sift (I'm serious, sift - or you risk those little tiny concentrations of
nasty, salty baking soda bits that sometimes occur in baking
when you do not sift plus sifting is fun)
2 cups flour
1 teaspoon baking powder
1 teaspoon baking soda
3/4 teaspoon salt

In another bowl cream well
1/2 cup butter
1 cup sugar

Add
3 mashed ripe bananas (don't use under ripe ones, use
blackened soft ones)
1/2 cup yoghurt (buttermilk or, in a pinch, sour one cup of milk by
adding a tablespoon of vinegar to the milk and waiting for it to
curdle)
2 eggs
1 teaspoon vanilla

Then add about 1/2 to 3/4 cup of one or two other ingredients.
Today I am adding one peeled grated pear and one square of
grated bittersweet chocolate. This is my most popular and
requested option. (Other options are chocolate chips or skor bits,
one peeled chopped apple or 1/2 cup applesauce, berries like
raspberries or blueberries, or rhubarb).

I use aged muffin pans greased the old fashioned way with a
finger and some butter because I like a slight crust on the
outside.

Fill muffin cups 3/4 full to get a nice rounded top. Sprinkle tops
with a scant dusting of white sugar, not so much they are overly
sweet just a little so top has a subtle crunch.

Bake for about 21 minutes depending on your oven and whether
you added 1/2 or 3/4 cup of options. There should be the

Let's Chat

beginning of some browning around the outside of the muffin and the top should spring back when touched with a fingertip.

Although you should not open the oven door during the cooking process, at 21 minutes you can check and cook for another 1,2,3 minutes until the desired state is achieved.

Let muffins sit in the pan for 5 minutes while they shrink a bit in cooling for easy removal to a cooling rack.

My hero

People are so obsessed these days with celebrities and superstar athletes and public scandals. Where have all the heroes gone? I have a picture on my bureau mirror to remind me daily about one of my heroes.

The picture shows Nova Scotia artist Maud Lewis in the small (thirteen feet six inches by twelve feet six inches) isolated rural home she and her husband shared. The one room house is tiny and dark. Maud sits in a chair beside her bed. Two steps away her husband ladles supper from one pot on the stove. Every paintable surface in the tiny home is covered with a riot of patterns and with paintings.

Despite a life of considerable hardship and no formal training she is one of Nova Scotia's best known primitive artists. The vision of life she portrays in her works is joyful, luminous, innocent, hopeful and completely at odds with her own life. The scenes she portrays, for the most part, show a life she never experienced.

Born in 1903, Maud developed juvenile rheumatoid arthritis which deformed her face and hands when she was a teenager. She rarely socialized or went out in public after this time. When her last family member died and she had no means of support, Maud married Everett Lewis, a much older man, a taciturn fish peddler. The union was not a love match but a marriage of convenience, on January 16, 1938 when she was 34. Her husband earned a subsistence living travelling door to door selling fish and Maud's hand drawn Christmas cards.

She painted on every available surface in their tiny home. The home is now preserved in a permanent exhibition at the Art Gallery of Nova Scotia in Halifax. Maud and Everett were poor, living without plumbing or electricity. Maud did most of her paintings seated in a chair by the window with a TV table for an easel, using cheap house paint and painting on any flat surface including shingles and cookie sheets.

Looking often at this picture, especially if I am having a ratty day, has led me to some ideas that inform my daily life and remind me that heroes live amongst us if we only open our eyes. Maud had to quit school after grade three. She was very short with a deformed face and hands, in pain much of the time, very shy and almost a recluse for most of her life. Rumour has it that her

Let's Chat

husband was not a tender man. Yet, despite all this she found joy and hope and beauty in life and shared that with the world.

Lesson #1: Remember that I cannot control what happens to me in life but I can control how I react to events beyond my control.

Maud painted with hands which were misshapen and painful. How often do we view disability from only a negative point of view? Maud found purpose in hardship making her painful hands her raison d'être. She found and pursued her passion in life through those painful hands.

Lesson #2: This life is the only life I have. It is my job to find my own joy and satisfaction.

Maud lived in conditions that would overwhelm most of us - no electricity, no plumbing, extreme poverty, and a painful and disfiguring illness yet she still found joy and hope in her life. Despite unbelievable odds she held onto her vision of beauty, innocence and life and shared that vision with the world.

Lesson #3: Whining and feeling sorry for myself is not productive. Find joy in simple things. Possessions do not bring happiness.

Maud had way more than her fair share of hardship in life, yet she did not become bitter.

Lesson #4: Life does not have to be perfect or to be going smoothly or to be without many challenges to be rewarding, worthwhile, joy filled and fulfilling.

Annie MacInnis

Autumn leaves

It's autumn, a time of year I love. And what a beautiful fall we have had. The weather has been stellar and the colours remarkable. But that lovely hiatus is over and winter is imminent. My yard and sidewalks everywhere are full of leaves so it looks untidy wherever you go, there is a serious chill in the air and I am no longer thrilling to the sights and sounds and warm sunshine of the past months as my dog and I go on our afternoon exercise walks.

In fact on this day I am feeling downright sulky. Somehow I have wrenched my back a bit and it has been bothering me all day, I ate pastry for breakfast, can't think what to make for supper, suspect I have forgotten a load in the washing machine and the house is a tip again. I would have preferred to be doing something about supper or the messy house but can't stand the thought of an evening of reproachful looks from my canine pal. So here we are - walking. The dog is happy, happy as always and I am grumping along trying to feel more positive when I hear a loud rushing sound.

My first thought is a sudden heavy rainstorm coming in fast. I am walking on the side of a hill so would not have seen rain clouds approaching. Now I am really NOT happy. We are far enough from the car that I will get soaked so I am standing there grinding my teeth and feeling seriously put upon.

But no rain comes. Looking up the side of the hill I see endless blue sky and heavy swirling gusts of wind that are whipping all the dry leaves up off the ground and trees on the hillside in a mini tornado. Spinning very fast in an upward expanding spiral thousands and thousands of leaves are making the rushing noise I thought was heralding heavy rain. The air is completely still where I stand. There is no one in sight but the dog and me.

In this big city of more than one million people, I am utterly alone as something wonderful and a bit miraculous happens before my very eyes. I have never seen a phenomenon quite like this. It is dramatic and loud. I stand awestruck for several minutes until almost imperceptibly, the wind dies down and the leaves float lazily back to earth. In another moment other people come walking along and I step back, from whatever rift in time and space I momentarily stood on the edge of, back into my ordinary life.

Let's Chat

Except that I am still feeling such an upsurge of joy to have been witness to this miracle of nature that I feel exhilarated. Those walking nearby seem completely unaware of what I just witnessed.

Joy exists everywhere in our everyday lives if we but remember to look for it and recognize it when we see it. It's so easy to get in the habit of hurrying to the next thing on our list and not enjoying the moments of our lives that will never come again. My fall resolution is make sure I don't slide into grumpiness quite so often. Instead I will put my energy into recognizing the moments of joy all around me every day if I but chose to look and see.

Anna's Pancakes

It is a fleeting moment of outright happiness. It's nine-thirty on a spring break morning and I feel completely content. One of my children had a friend for a sleepover last night but everyone went to sleep in good time so no one is too delicately balanced this morning. The children have been playing happily (and not talking to me) for two hours.

I have had the pleasure of three cups of coffee and a leisurely look at the newspaper. The house isn't exactly spanking bright or squeaky clean but it's reasonably tidy. The beds are made, laundry is not overflowing, we have groceries and nowhere we have to go today.

Spring sunshine slants across my kitchen floor. The windows are open. I can feel the sun's heat on my back.

After a hand of Beggar-your-neighbor with the kids, the children set the table while I make pancakes for breakfast. I call these pancakes Cousin Anna's pancakes although she was my grandmother's cousin.

While I was at university, my grandmother came to stay, (ostensibly, to visit a cousin I had never heard of) but I think mainly to make sure I had a safe bolt hole in town if required. Anna was an old time minister's wife, raising a large family well on a very small stipend.

Anna served pancakes for lunch in the rectory kitchen. She made the pancakes in that efficient, practical way that experienced cooks have, measuring her ingredients by eye and by feel.

In spite of being a thoughtless, relatively well off young immortal of tender years, something about Anna and her pancakes moved me with a longing to preserve this moment. I got her to recap the recipe and carefully kept that scrap of paper for years until I managed to glue it into a little hardcover book of special recipes.

Although I know the recipe by heart, I always look at it. The recipe is splattered from much use and always recalls the memory of that kitchen, my grandmother and Anna.

My life has not turned out as I might have envisioned it on that long ago day. Like Anna, I lead a financially challenged

Let's Chat

existence and am a stay-at-home mom. Like Anna, necessity forces me to live frugally although I strive in the midst of that to live well. Like Anna, I cook by feel and touch, and take enormous pleasure in the process.

Anna's recipe calls for peewee eggs because those were her most economical egg purchase. Over the years as peewee eggs became hard to find, I determined that four peewees equal 2 large eggs. In Anna's recipe, the bran and oatmeal quantities are measured by the HANDFUL. I am not sure why, since the flour is measured by the cup. Nevertheless, I continue to honor Anna's recipe by always using handfuls. I have never even attempted to discover what that handful would be if translated into more conventional measurement.

These pancakes taste of the past and of my long gone sort-of cousin. Their flavour always summons forth memories of the grandmother I miss even now. Eating these pancakes reminds me of my young self in that kitchen and lets me take stock of who I have become. Always, always I count my blessings as I cook and eat Cousin Anna's pancakes.

Maritimers love to discuss 'where your people come from dear'. Recipes often have family tracings so merit can be judged not just on taste but also on whose kitchen they have passed through. Hence, the recipe appears like this in my book.

Annie MacInnis

Annie's Grandmother Annie's Cousin-from-Wolfville Anna's Pancakes

Mix dry ingredients
2 cups white flour
1 handful oatmeal
1 handful wheat bran
3 teaspoons baking powder
2 tablespoons sugar
¾ teaspoon salt

Mix wet ingredients
1 ½ - 2 cups milk
4 peewee eggs (two extra large eggs)
1 grated apple

Combine wet and dry ingredients and stir well.

In a frying pan, add a little oil and three small ladle fulls of batter.

Cook on medium heat until lots of bubbles form on the top.
Gently flip and continue to cook until browned on both sides.

When my children were little, I often cooked many very small pancakes and the children just ate them as-is in their hands. I always eat these as Cousin Anna served them - with butter AND syrup.

A Visit to the Dentist

I am a fan of sedation dentistry!

I belong to the generation of big families in the sixties whose stay at home mothers decreed we brush our teeth but were so busy (and so not inclined to be the helicopter parents of today) that whether we followed through or not was moot. Consequences for not brushing were imposed in the form of horrific visits to the dentist where bad results were immediately rectified with drilling and filling and multiple lectures from hygienists and dentists about moral laxness and from parents about moral laxness again, cost and chickens coming home to roost.

Thus we children of that era are all riddled with cavities from disregarding all those dire warnings plus subsisting on Kool-Aid (tastes great!), "BEEP" 'orange juice', mountain dew and coke pop, chips, and dessert with every meal but breakfast when we ate spoonfuls of white sugar on already sweet breakfast cereals.

Childhood dentists were for the most part cheerful, outgoing sadists. They did 'not believe' in freezing before drilling. You were apt to be accused of being babyish if you had the horrors. Flinching in pain earned you no sympathy and at best a stolid 'almost done' which was 'almost never true'.

Today's kids are holier than thou and invariably cavalier about dental visits with their minimal cavities. Excellent and automatic freezing has left them with no concept of the terror instilled in today's adults by the simple words, "Hmmm...looks like you have a cavity starting/filling/disintegrating/tooth falling apart. We'll need to book you in for a few hours to handle all this."

My frail perimeter shells of teeth surrounding giant aged, crumbling fillings leaking/leaching God knows what into my body holds no terror compared to the white knuckled, breath holding state I am usually in the instant that drill starts grinding. My nerves feel shredded every time. Even though frozen to the tips of my ears and unable to feel my eyes, I am fearful every moment of that jolt of pain as a nerve reacts. Like Pavlov's dog I am conditioned to dread and fear the dentist who has often told me if I will just relax the freezing will be more effective. Easy to say!

So the news that I needed a 'few hours' of work was horrifying to say the least. My face must have revealed my feelings as I

[149]

immediately started compiling a list of excuses. In the midst of a detailed explanation of how dire the situation in my mouth was I latched onto the phrase, "Of course for an extra fee you could be sedated."

I grasped this alternative with no heed for the cost, made the appointment and left clutching two pills to take one hour before arriving at 7am on an empty stomach. Be sure to have someone bring you and pick you up I was admonished. Up early on the day I took my pills and trailed about getting dressed until I suddenly realized I was veering sideways trying to cross the room.

Oops, looks like I am a good candidate for this stuff. I don't remember arriving and very little about the appointment or the return home. I do remember my kids asking repeatedly to once again be regaled by my husband's reports of arriving to take me home. He firmly held my arm when the dental assistant handed me over despite my protests that I was perfectly fine and thought I was behaving normally. Meanwhile I was lifting my knees almost to my chin in an exaggeratedly careful fashion as I walked out of the office to the car, out of the car into the house and into bed where I slept all day and woke quite refreshed and rested.

Gee, I am almost looking forward to my next dental appointment!

Have I touched a nerve?

They thought they could dance

It was immediately obvious that they had been taking dance lessons at the local legion or some such place. They took to the dance floor with little flourishes and curtseys as though to an adoring audience. It was clear they had seen way too many movies where the crowd fell back in awe of the unknown talented dancers but they were undeterred. This was their night.

Never mind they were in a rather seedy, certainly roughish bar in Nova Scotia called the Misty Moon Show Bar in a doubtful end of town. The place was renowned for great music and large crowds and that night was no exception. The place was packed and tables were strewn with drinks. The dance floor was swarming as the shank of the evening approached.

The couple were dressed to draw attention to themselves, to accentuate their new found dancing prowess. She with a swirly skirt, tight top and stiletto heels; he in dark pants and a shirt unbuttoned a little too much for strictly good taste. They began with some classic couple twirls and somewhat self-consciously executed fancy moves. He was obviously keeping up a running patter under his breath counting them through their rehearsed moves and forecasting the next bits. The music was incidental to their routine.

It was soon clear to us interested people watchers that, while showily dressed, she was a mere foil to his overweening dancing ambitions. They began to work up a sweat as the routines began to get increasingly more elaborate. Once or twice they cannoned into other couples who began to give them a wider berth more for self protection than from admiration.

Of course, they took this as encouragement. It became obvious he was trying to get her to try a move she was reluctant to engage in but he was in the zone and persistent. Finally she agreed to attempt the move. With several, increasingly elaborate, fast turns and a considerable fanfare that attracted the lighting guy's attention so that he spotlighted them, the husband wheeled them to a halt, grabbed her firmly around the waist and swung her legs to the left of his hip, to the right of his hip then using her momentum he swung her up in front of himself directly over his head.

There was a hushed moment when everyone seemed to hold their breath as her legs were spot lighted stretching to the ceiling with the band in the background. The moment went on and on until everyone realized that the low ceiling and the low hanging wires and spotlights had become entangled with her legs. She was trapped upside down while her partner struggled to hold her unable to see anything because her skirt draped over him to his waist. Luckily for all concerned (it was the seventies after all) she was indeed wearing panties. However she was quite firmly stuck and it took several guys hurrying to help the husband hold her while a couple of others stood on chairs to free her legs.

Released she stormed off with the husband scuttling obsequiously behind, all his brash showmanship gone. My guess is that was their one and only public performance and no subsequent dancing lessons were taken. Hopefully if they did venture out again they checked overhead before attempting anything so bold again. Mind you, it was a moment to remember.

Merry Christmas

There are no little kids to wake us up early desperate to see what Santa has brought them. There will be no television commercial worthy gifts like a surprise warm weather holiday and we are leaving in the morning, no car wrapped with a red bow in the driveway nor diamond ring in the toe of my stocking. One kid is working from 9-4 on Christmas Day because pay with be double-time plus great tips. The other kid is going to his girl friend's for a big chunk of the day to do gifts and dinner with her family. I have to work Christmas Eve and my husband works Boxing Day. We have no extended family living nearer than the Maritimes and our family are not inclined to Folger's coffee advertisement style surprises in the form of unexpected arrivals on our doorstep so there will be no family to swell our thin ranks.

One kid has already shopped for and been reimbursed for her big gift and is using it since it's a parka. The other kid has also chosen his big gift and he and his father have done the deed since it is acoustic equipment so no surprises there and I was not involved. We have all agreed we are scaling back on all expenditures this year including Christmas given the economy and our debt level so the rest of the gifts will be more modest than previous years.

So hmmm, where does that leave me, the mother, architect of the 'magic of Christmas'? Oh yes, the kids are older and it is time to get over all that until the grandchildren arrive, but I adore Christmas. Not the advertising or the malls, not the gimmie attitude, not the stressing about shopping frenzy/spending money/gaining weight/scheduling craziness.

I get that our Christmas traditions are evolving for the time being. The whole family helping decorate, those Christmas Eve walks through the park to see the lights on the fancy homes, the made up story for the children while we lay under the tree afterwards, reading 'Twas The Night before Christmas last thing before bed, the 'way too early' wake up with a small person whispering desperately in my ear, "Mom, Mom he came, he came!"

When my husband and I first moved to Alberta in 1981 we left behind our familiar Christmases with our families. In a one bedroom basement apartment with little money we resolved to make Christmas different so it would not be a disappointing pale reminder of what we were missing at home. We came up with a Christmas Eve sleepover party for other strays without family

[153]

that Christmas. Without a tree we all made decorations for the large dieffenbachia plant that the previous tenants had left behind. We orphans had a wonderful time eating spaghetti at midnight and sharing funny stories of Christmases past.

Yes I had some wobbly moments during long distance calls from family but we had a memorable Christmas.

When we had children suddenly Christmases became wondrous and blessed. Even though we were usually tired and often there was a sick or fractious child, their wonder and joy made those Christmases amazing.

Seems like it is time to reinvent Christmas yet again. So what do I want for Christmas this year, what's so important to me it cannot be left to the wayside in this new vision of Christmas for our family?

Most of all I want time - time to enjoy my own house at Christmas, to listen to Christmas music and to bake treats for both our house and for friends. Christmas baking gives me great joy in the doing and in the giving so that's a keeper whether others join in or are even in the house with me.

I want to continue our family charity project that culminates in a Christmas Eve spent finishing the project even if I am mostly on my own for now. Spending most of December focused on what to put in 22 stockings for people in a hospice keeps me grounded in a very real way. If this were my last Christmas what might be meaningful, comforting, or possibly just a momentary distraction from illness for me and those around me? Obviously a trip to the mall is not what is needed.

I love a tree dripping with ornaments and tinsel. No elegant tree for me; nope I want a higgledy piggeldy tree shining with tattered ornaments from my childhood, my kids' creations and tons of those vintage balls I love to collect. I choose to put it all up and take it all down because it gives me great joy.

A home cooked Christmas dinner at some point with all four of us at our little dinner table in our modest bungalow. Our dear old dog served her holiday meal the same as ours on nice china.

Life gets in the way sometimes even on Christmas but doesn't need to ruin things (unless you let it). So I'm not letting it. I am choosing a Christmas filled with what is important to me - family

Let's Chat

(when available), friends, charity for those in times of trouble, good food and some Christmas bling and Bing (Crosby). That's what I want for Christmas please Santa.

From me and mine, to you and yours, may your Christmas be merry and bright and everything you wish for.

Annie MacInnis

Isn't change hard?

Everywhere you look these days we are exhorted to change, to grow, to become a better you, the person you are meant to be, wish to be, could be. To evolve, to improve is a new religion and we are bombarded with success stories, templates for getting there, heartfelt stories about how, you too, can be a better you, find a job you love, have a more fulfilling relationship, be a more successful parent/wife/boss/employee/friend.

But when change is imposed upon us (loss of a job, a relationship ending, kids moving out, a medical diagnosis for ourselves or a loved one) the loss of control is the first devastating feeling. Change has been forced upon us whether we like it or not. This kind of change feels overwhelming.

Unlike an internal decision to change, when you spend time and energy thinking and talking to others about a potential change, the sudden change from without often throws us into a tailspin.

But whether your thought process occurs before the change (you decide to make a change) or as a result of the change (change imposed by another) the process is the same. A weighing up of possibility, an opportunity to examine life as you know it, a chance to make deliberate choices is now offered to you.

Some of the most important lessons I have learned in life as well as some of the best parts of my life have been the result of pivotal moments in time when change was forced upon an unwilling me or when I took a leap of faith and made a change, for better or for worse. Isn't that true for most of us?

We can chose to grow and to adapt regardless of whether we desired the change or not. We can chose to accept the change and to find the lesson we are meant to learn. We can choose to make the best of a bad situation and find the small blessings along the way. We can choose to find our way back to happiness and balance and a life worth enjoying and celebrating again.

These moments are the moments where we demonstrate resilience, when we show our mettle, when we rise to the occasion, when we prevail despite the odds and we mine deeply to find joy, to find purpose, to find value in our new, changed circumstances.

[156]

Let's Chat

Change is a part of life, yet so often we fight it. We agonize over why me, why now, and is this the right choice issues instead of trusting that small quiet voice inside each of us that knows what is right, that knows what is important. That voice if you but listen will remind you, "This is just another new beginning, we have done this before."

Many years ago my husband gave to me a rhinestone broach of a bird walking, head down, one foot raised, walking forward with these words of advice, "just keep your head down and keep putting one foot in front of the other."

I wear the pin when I need to remember his wise words and eventually, one day I look up from my angst or sorrow and the change is finished. I have evolved. Joy and peace have returned to my life

Embracing change is probably one of the hardest aspects of life, but new beginnings, along with fear, doubt, and unhappiness offer new blessings, new opportunities, new vistas, new friends and a new, different you.

So if your life is in flux, in you are in the trenches of change, if joy and balance and serenity are gone for the moment from your life, please heed the immortal words of Christopher Robin to Pooh. "Promise me you'll always remember you're braver than you believe, and stronger than you seem, and smarter than you think."

One day soon you will look up from putting one foot in front of the other and life with all its imperfections and beauty and laughter will be all around you once again, touched with the piquancy of what you have just been through but no longer overshadowed.

This is a new beginning. I am always and forever becoming the person I was meant to be - filled to the brim with memories of life with those I love and have loved, with all my triumphs and all my failures, and with a wonderful world filled with new people and experiences all around me waiting for me to seize it with both hands.

Annie MacInnis

Welcome Home

We were beyond proud - our first house! A modest, inner city bungalow, but all ours and the bank's. A housewarming party was in order. We had only been in Alberta for 5 years and had no family to help us celebrate but, with gay abandon, I invited my friends from work and he invited his friends from work and we invited the few old friends from the Maritimes who were in town. An eclectic group to be sure, with his oil company computer and technology guys mixing with my University of Calgary academics, stirred with random Maritimers and hangers on.

The house was choc-a-bloc with people, the air fizzing with music and animated conversations. My husband and I smiled at each other across the room. Our party was obviously a hit. Everyone seemed to be enjoying getting to know someone new and different. We basked in our success for all too brief a time.

One moment I was chatting mindfully with a lovely woman who was my husband's boss' wife. She and her husband were a bit older than the rest of the crowd and were devout Mormons. From our brief conversation I learned she had married young, had a grist of children and stayed home minding them while her husband worked. Today's party was a rare foray into the world away from home. I cannot remember what we were chatting about when the whole conversation went sideways, but sideways it went when another young woman joined us.

One of our old Maritime friends had brought his new girlfriend. We had met her a couple of times. She was a colourful character one might say and although she and I would never become close, I enjoyed her refreshingly unusual take on life. Keeping in mind this was the mid-eighties, she had multiple ear piercings and visible tattoos. This was not commonplace in those fashion forward days of big hair, workout inspired day clothes, big shoulders and neon colours when your fashion choices gave some indication of your personality and interests. In fact only sailors, veterans and a certain type of girl sported tattoos. And only that certain type of girl would display multiple piercings in public in addition to a significant, eye-catching bust on display at an afternoon housewarming party.

Fatalistically, I introduced the two women to each other. From across the room I could see my husband frantically sending telepathic messages to me with his eyes the gist of which was quite obviously, "What are you doing?!?!?!"

[158]

Let's Chat

For one long moment I thought all was going to be okay as the conversation idled along on the lines of, "Isn't this a great house...how do you know..." small talk until suddenly I saw it go awry when the boss' wife politely asked, as one is wont to do at these sort of things, "And what do you do?" Our friend's girlfriend answered frankly with a large smile as she looked at the prim corporate wife , "I'm a stripper."

During the long (or so it seemed to me) pause that followed I racked my brain for what to say but the boss' wife, with a quick look to ensure her husband was safely involved elsewhere in the room, beat me to it with a rapid fire series of questions. She was clearly VERY interested in knowing much, much more and our friend's girlfriend was happy to share. When asked about the novel piercings (three in each ear!), the answer was a laconic, "Yeah I have nine piercings."

Without volition I could feel my head following the boss' wife's head as we visually counted 'one, two, three' in the left ear; 'four, five, six' in the right ear then glanced questioningly, 'where are the rest?' Before either of us could voice the thought, she lifted her shirt saying, "I have a belly button ring."

The wife and I goggled, never having seen or heard of this before except in books and National Geographic. I glanced up to see my husband staring aghast at me and the boss' wife, who was bent slightly to better peer at the girlfriend's stomach.

Of course the next question was, "And the other two piercings?"

"Come to the bedroom and I'll show you," was the reply and she turned and started for my bedroom followed closely by the wife and by me. The door was hardly pushed to when she lifted her shirt revealing no bra and two nipple piercings. "Did that hurt?" asked the wife. "The piercings didn't but the three needles per...sure as...did."

"My goodness, well I never..." was the faint reply. She looked at the girlfriend, then at me, we all smiled, then she politely thanked the girlfriend for a very interesting conversation and we rejoined the party all going our separate ways.

When the boss and his wife came to say goodbye and thank you for inviting them, the wife took my hands in hers and held them tightly as she fervently said, "Thank you so much. I had a WONDERFUL time!"Yes, I believe you did.

[159]

Annie MacInnis

A Bad Day

I was having a bad day the moment I opened my eyes. I detected a sinister tickle at the back of my throat as I cast a hostile look at the germ laden husband lying beside me. Determined not to be ill I went about my morning dosed with extra vitamin C but by mid afternoon it was obvious I had caught himself's cold.

I dragged in the door from work with thoughts of hot lemon tea then bed. But when I opened the door, there at the top of the kitchen stairs, like nemesis herself, was my happy, happy dog ready to go for our usual afternoon walk. "Anyone home?" I called forlornly but there was no sign of a teenager to be assigned that chore.

As appalled as I was by her excitement and the thought of more driving and exercise one look into those Siren eyes and I was lost. Shoulders slumping, I changed into at home clothes and grabbing a tangerine for hopefully a little energy boost set off.

As we set off on our walk I did actually feel a tad better and resolved to try to enjoy the walk. A bouncy young Shepherd immediately joined us quite enamored of my female and oblivious that she is nearing 15. He tried everything to get her interested in playing while his young owner sucked away obliviously on the teat of his cell phone. My old girl resolutely ignored all the young dog's entreaties. Finally in a last ditch effort to win her favour he bounded over to me and leaned hard against my leg. I reached to pat him and sympathize that she was not interested only to realize he was peeing on me!

I yelled in outrage. The owner came running in alarm but I was not appeased. "Not your fault," I said civilly but decided the walk was over.

When I tried to drive away, the car did not move. I got out to access the situation. I was parked on a slight incline with my front wheels in two small puddle sized ice filled depressions and the back wheels on sheer ice. Parked very close to my rear bumper was another vehicle. A few cautious attempts to ease myself out resulted in me sliding perilously closer to the vehicle behind me. I would have to wait for the owners to return.

As the minutes ticked by I repeatedly tried to relax and enjoy this quiet interlude but my dear dog kept leaning repeatedly into the

Let's Chat

front seat area wrinkling her nose as she pawed inquiringly at me to ask why I smelled so exotically stinky. A half hour passed with me almost pacing in the front seat in irritation.

Finally a car came from the upper parking lot and drove past me. My window was open and we made eye contact but by now I was so irritated I had a knot in my face of fearful proportions and a grimace instead of a smile. Amazingly this brave guy drove past me, then stopped and backed up to ask if I needed help.

I was properly grateful but said I was too close to the vehicle behind me for him to safely push me. But my hero was not deterred. He produced a tow rope, shimmied under my car and hooked me up. He decided we would need to wait for a 'work truck' as his vehicle did not have a lot of guts and 'ta da' one appeared. My hero flagged down the driver who did a quick turn, hooked the rope to his truck, gave a gentle pull and I was free.

Oh frabjous day! To my two saviours who 'turned my frown upside down' in that parking lot, thank you , thank you for helping me. A special extra thank you to the first guy who certainly risked getting his head chewed off by a very irritate, smelly, sick woman.

Annie MacInnis

Jack the Knife

He was only five but he was desperate to have one. His Dad had one. In those days most men carried one in their pocket. His mother wondered if perhaps he might be too young but in the end the father bought him a very small jackknife.

When his Dad presented him with his beautiful shiny new knife the small boy was filled with pride. He turned the small knife over and over as he tried to listen carefully to his father talking about responsibility and being careful. They discussed what sort of things the boy could use his knife on – not on living trees but deadwood was okay and any scrap wood from the workshop was fine.

They talked about safety issues. When using the knife always cut away from yourself. Think about where your fingers are before you start cutting. Do not open the knife while playing with friends. Never threaten anyone with the knife. Do not dig in the dirt with the knife. Satisfied that all the bases had been covered and that the boy was clear on safe and appropriate knife usage, the Dad went off to work, the boy's shining face as he held the knife remained in his mind's eye throughout his workday.

The boy had a wonderful day. Everywhere he went and everything he did involved his knife. He was the object of envy and admiration when he displayed his knife to the boys next door. He strutted through his day confident that he could master any eventuality now that he was suitably equipped like other big boys.

It's hard to say at what point in the day his perception of knife usage rules lapsed. Was it simply that the knife was so beguiling and that chipping away at an object was so satisfying. Or was it that he had exhausted all other different things for carving? Was he so bereft of some object to sacrifice to his ministrations? Did he think no one would notice? Or was he simply so caught up in making his mark that he got carried away?

Regardless, when the father came home at the end of the day and asked the boy how his day had been, the boy was full of glowing reports of all he and his knife had accomplished. He displayed all manner of objects that he had worked on – a block of wood from the scrap pile, a dead branch from the orchard, a box he had poked holes in, some paper he had cut up. He told of all the fun he had had and he and the Dad had a quiet moment

[162]

considering the pleasures of being jackknife owners. Then the Dad patted the boy on the head and strolled off to watch the evening news.

At that time of night the sun slanted in the west windows directly onto the television screen so the Dad crossed the room to close the curtains before switching on the set. As he reached to close the curtains his eyes fell on a small neat wedge cut out of the edge of the windowsill. He flicked his eyes to the adjacent windowsill. There, too, a small neat wedge was cut from the sill.

The dad's voice reverberated through the house. The boy's heart pounded in his chest as he skidded to a halt in front of the Dad who face now looked like a thundercloud.

Under questioning the boy shamefacedly admitted a considerable error in judgment when using his knife on the windowsills. They reviewed the rules of knife usage again. The boy was respectful, contrite, fully resolved never to make such an error again. The Dad was forgiving, wryly remembering the mother's hesitation about whether the boy was old enough for a knife. The boy ran off to play.

The Dad decided that he could sand down the sills and the damage would be fixed. Smiling to himself he walked over to the lovely big new floor model television he had recently purchased. He reached out his hand to turn on the set and there on the front of the wooden cabinet was cut a small neat wedge.

The Dad's voice reverberated through the house...

Annie MacInnis

When mice fly

My father was returning home from a busy day at work. He was tired and ready for his supper. As he drove into the yard, he was just in time to see small white objects being chucked out of one of the third floor windows of our house. As he watched a gaggle of kids leaned out the window jostling each other and cheering on our particular favorites. Little bundles opened out into what appeared to be small homemade parachutes with something attached to each of them.

Closer inspection revealed that the *somethings* attached to the parachutes were in fact our pet white mice. It was clear to my father that this was not the first time the mice had made this jump. The mice appeared to be instinctively refining their technique for softer landings in the grass below by spreading their bodies very widely like flying squirrels in order to glean a smoother descent. My father gathered up the reluctant paratroopers, cast a long, speculative look up at us kids, by now lurking in the shadow of the window, then strode toward the kitchen door.

We hurried downstairs with some trepidation, stumbling over each other's words in an effort to mitigate the incriminating circumstances and lay any blame at someone else's door. Neighboring children immediately distanced themselves from any further involvement and hastened, heads down, past my parents and away to their own homes quickly rehearsing possible alibis in case they were needed later in the day.

After much patience on my parent's part, what with five children still remaining to tell the tale, the whole story was revealed. Our explanation went something like this and was we thought, perfectly reasonable. We had been talking about airplanes and thinking about how they fly and trying out flying different designs of paper airplanes from the third floor window.

In a completely logical progression, we then got thinking about other sorts of flying, like rockets and parachutes, and about how these kinds of flight were accomplished. We all agreed that rockets needed fire and explosions to work and that project was best left for some day when Dad could supervise.

So naturally, we decided to try to make some parachutes and we wanted to test our theories. We spent much time experimenting with different designs using small inanimate objects like green

[164]

Let's Chat

plastic soldiers, berry baskets and those small troll dolls with the standing up hair. Once we had achieved a workable design *of course* we wanted to progress to the next logical phase of our endeavor.

We needed LIVING SUBJECTS.

We had all agreed that even the littlest kids were too big for at least this initial phase of the project. The dog was also definitely too big. The cats were nowhere to be found and were probably too big anyway so it wasn't worth wasting too much time trying to track them down. The birds could fly anyway so they wouldn't be reliable test subjects. That left...the mice...who seemed ideal participants in every way.

Before my parents rendered any judgment, we hastened to add that we had gone out of our way to explain the project to the mice prior to ANY jumps. Comfortable, safe harnesses were a key design aspect of all the parachute models we had constructed and tested. We had been reassuring and supportive to the mice throughout the process. During the experiment, we had expended much time and effort rewarding and praising the mice for their intrepid, adventurous spirits and we felt sure they were enjoying themselves.

My parents were, as always, kind and amazingly calm regarding our latest slightly out of control project. We weren't bad children or even cruel or thoughtless children. We were children with a lot of space indoors and out in which to play. We had huge imaginations and much freedom in which to explore our world. We fought and played fiercely. We took risks and got hurt often but always protected and helped each other when it counted. We learned much about life and creatures and how the world works and enjoyed life enormously along the way.

Thanks Mom and Dad for a great childhood.

Hello siblings. I miss you all but have many fond memories to pull out and treasure in the light of a lonesome day.

Annie MacInnis

I blame the bank

I know that is a commonplace, knee-jerk reaction. It is so predictable and so easy to blame those money-grubbing cash greedy monolithic entities for our all woes that it's almost a cliché. Nevertheless, in this case they really were to blame.

My son had been invited by a family friend to stay with her family in Japan for 2 ½ weeks. When I agreed to let him go, I was already feeling I might be a tad judged by a society that treasures sons above all. Allowing our 12-year-old son to travel alone to Japan, even though at their invitation, seemed cavalier. Worse, upon his arrival, I was certain his skinniness would lead the family to presume that not only was I casual about the safety of his person in sending him alone halfway around the world but obviously I never bothered to feed him.

As if all this wasn't enough fodder to judge me as barely a fit parent for this sweet boy, the bank's advice really landed me in the soup. On the sage suggestion of no less than three bank employees on three separate occasions, I sent my son to Japan armed with a debit card with large daily limits and a small amount of cash.

One week into his trip, I was aghast to arise one morning to a brief cheery email from my son the gist of which was, "I'm having a brilliant time and, oh, by the way, my debit card isn't accepted over here not even at the banks. I'm borrowing spending money from my friend and her family and they're paying for everything else."

"AAAAUUUUGGGGHHHH," as Charlie Brown was wont to say.

So not only does it probably appear to the traditional Japanese family he is staying with that I am careless with his personal safety sending him traveling alone so far away and not only do I apparently not bother to feed him but I am so feckless and so irresponsible that I send him halfway around the world with no money and expect them to pay for his trip! How mortifying for someone who prides herself on being organized, feeding my children home cooked meals, and doing my share.

Never mind the carefully chosen hosting gifts and thank you cards sent in his suitcase, never mind the admonitions about wiping the sink after himself and making his bed, being polite and blah, blah, blah. All that careful coaching and shopping paled by comparison with my obvious, demonstrated inadequacies as a parent.

I had nightmares where I was kindly informed via email that the family had decided I was not fit to be the mother of this lovely boy. Further, since he was obviously an inconvenience to me and since they would love to have a nice boy like him, they would just keep him. I took out my ire on everyone who crossed my path at the bank. They were obsequious; they were apologetic; they would investigate; they paid for a wire transfer. I was only slightly mollified and did not relax until my son was once again under my roof on this side of the world.

A moment in time

A woman passes me carrying a little boy in her arms. The boy is maybe two, obviously hers. She is smiling at him with a brightness in her face that instantly thrums my heartstrings. His small, chubby hands cup her cheeks as he leans in close telling her something important.

I know his sweet breath is fanning her cheeks. She has been away from him all day and now she is drinking him in, reveling in the sight and sound and feel and smell of him. His cheeks shine. His eyes sparkle. His eyes are intent on her. His legs twine around her as he leans into her.

Ah, mother love. The sight of it transports me immediately. I remember those days with a sharp edged intensity. I remember the feel of my young children in my arms as they told me everything. I remember the intimacy of that relationship where they trusted me implicitly, utterly in all things. I remember how it felt when I had been away from my babies (even for only a little while) to be returning to them. As much as I probably enjoyed the time away doing some exotic grownup thing like sitting and drinking a whole cup of tea while it was hot or having a conversation with another adult where I completed sentences and thoughts, I would hurry once I was returning to them.

Suddenly after that short time reminding myself of my old self pre-kids, I would feel desperate for the feel of their cheeks on mine, long to hold them tight in my arms, secure in the knowledge that THIS is what's really important right now. This relationship, this connection is the point of everything else I do in my life.

When a moment occurs like today, when I see two people connect intensely, I am reassured by my sense of commonality with the world. Those moments in life when we are privy to intimacy - a mother and child, an old couple holding hands as they walk down the street, a couple embracing at the airport...these are reminders that we need to remember to cherish those who are important in our lives. The moments in time when you connect, truly connect, with another human being are the moments to value.

Fostering good feelings in those around you costs nothing. Taking time to reflect on what makes you happy, making time to

Let's Chat

do something nice for those around you; these are cheap pleasures with great returns.

As Christmas and the pressure to spend spirals we would do well to remember that many, many people live through tough financial times and yet live rich lives. I may have lost investments but nothing truly important like my health or my vision or my family has been taken from me.

Annie MacInnis

A Day in the Life

Is there a more hateful feeling in the world than being awake at 4 o'clock in the morning with some hateful kid's television show song bouncing around in your head? (Well except for if the song were the *I Love You, You Love Me* Barney song or the Disney *It's A Small World After All* which would be equally bad.) I'm lying in the dark, but all the lights are on in my head. I should get up and do something useful but calming and boring until I'm tired.

Unfortunately tomorrow's not a weekend and the kids aren't on a sleepover until lunchtime, so tomorrow I'm going to be bagged. The chances of factoring a recovery nap into tomorrow's day are probably zilch. I grit my teeth at the thought of what my husband would say if he were awake.

He always says the same thing in this situation. "Is your squirrel loose again?" "Yeah," I snarl in my head, "He's on the loose and he's on his way ALONE to warm, sunny Mexico on that little exercise wheel. C'mon guy, let's hustle, head down, good foot placement, run away while they're all asleep!"

Being awake in the night always seems ironic and particularly frustrating to me since I've been sleep deprived so many days since becoming a parent. I heave a long-suffering sigh and trail out of bed to make myself useful. I clean out the Tupperware cupboard and once again resolve to keep it tidier. I also tackle the drawer under the stove (yikes) and I read for a bit. Then the alarm goes off and the day starts.

Ahhhh, Coffee, coffee…maybe I'll survive. But, the gods are not smiling on me today. I have a sick kid.

Okay I can do this. I get the healthy kid protesting the injustice of a sibling getting private time with me to school. The trip home with the inconvenienced, complaining sick one and the disappointed dog that is missing her walk is trying but thankfully short.

Unfortunately, while this kid is sick enough to be home from school, he is not sick enough to be quiet and lie nicely in a heap on the couch where I can nurture him. No indeed! He feels well enough to chat. In fact, he talks non-stop all day. All day long, everything I do, is with a small, flushed, feverish child talking, talking, talking following closely on my heels. He resists sitting quietly with me to read or rest and just trails around talking and

[170]

Let's Chat

talking. I struggle to pay attention but my mind resists the topic. I spend the day hearing way more than I ever wanted to know about Pokemon and Digimon and their individual characteristics and fighting abilities and blah, blah, blah.

By the end of the day my head is roiling with the need for sleep and an overload of unnecessary data. I'm ready for bed immediately after supper but manage to soldier on until close to bedtime.

Meanwhile the children have gotten their second wind after their nice healthy supper. Sensing a vulnerable overtired parent they go inexorably into overdrive. Their energy soars and crackles as they wrestle like puppies, shrieking and bouncing off the walls. After several fruitless attempts to calm down the hooligans I know I do not have the patience for this tonight. Any minute now I'm going to snap and it ain't going to be pretty. If I start ranting when I'm this tired I know I'll regret what I say and how I say it. Going to bed guilty tonight will just be the last straw. So, to heck with them, I decide. I brush their teeth under protest then say I'll read to you when you're ready - if I'm awake. I retreat thankfully to my bed leaving them to their own devices.

It's a good solution. I get to lie quietly, completely stretched out in my own bed for about five blissful minutes. When the hooligans meekly join me books in hand. The sick one reads out loud to me for a bit while I lie with my eyes closed. Then I read briefly from each child's book. I'm the first one asleep. Lucky me!

Annie MacInnis

Temper, temper

I guess days like this are just some kind of cosmic payback. All those childless years when I inwardly sneered at the mothers in the mall with flipping out kids and thought to myself, "I would never countenance such behavior in a child of mine!" Such sanctimonious judgments always seem to come back to haunt one.

I don't even know what set my kids off that day. Before school my kids squabbled. When I brought them home from school for lunch, they bickered. After lunch while playing in the yard the disparaging comments were reaching dire levels.

I watched their confrontation from afar (just as all the parenting manuals suggest). My daughter, the older by three years was unfortunately out arguing himself at every turn. I debated about intervening. Before I could act she mocked him for being little, smirked and sashayed away. My sweet, little, non-violent son erupted. He grabbed the first thing to hand, which happened to be an old, fortunately dull, axe he'd been playing caveman with and flung it at her retreating back. Luckily it missed. He was immediately aghast at what he had almost done and burst into tears.

He was sorry. He apologized to everyone concerned, even the dog. He promised earnestly never to behave in such a fashion EVER AGAIN and believed that he never would. His big eyes welled with tears.

I took a deep breath and consulted my inner parents. The only ones available were the one without the backbone that just wants my children to be happy and to think of me as the loveliest mother that ever was and the snarky harridan who pleases herself by ranting at every opportunity.

So I was on my own with this one. Fine, how typical. All right, revert to that most basic of all parenting tools – take a deep breath. Think calm, good parent thoughts and hope for inspiration.

I called the school secretary and said, "My children will be late returning to school. My son has just thrown an axe at his sister and we need to debrief before I consider returning him to interact with other people's children."

[172]

Let's Chat

I sat my children down and told them very briefly how the day felt from my perspective. I acknowledged that we all have bad days and cranky days and days where another family member really rubs us the wrong way. But I also reminded them that these days are usually hard on everyone and that those in a bad mood must, nevertheless, curtail this behavior somewhat for the sake of other family members. We agreed that they would both make an effort to minimize bickering and that throwing maiming type objects at any sentient being was beyond the pale. We also agreed that perhaps for the well being of all concerned we would take a mental health afternoon and endeavor to regain some sense of equanimity and charity in the house before we ventured out into public again.

Annie MacInnis

When I Grow Up

My heart pounds hard and slow in my chest. My mouth is dry. My chest feels tight. I watch from the window as the small, ramrod straight back walks determinedly away from me, alone, absolutely unaccompanied, toward the corner store a mere two blocks away.

My firstborn had insisted on this small measure of independence as her just due. I had reluctantly agreed after days of pestering. In the end I had conceded that since it was only two blocks in a straight line from our house she could walk alone to our corner store. After some investigation I decided that if I was discreet I would actually be able to watch the whole time. Unfortunately I had not counted on my less than stellar long distance vision nor on all the parked cars which meant she was repeatedly, if briefly, out of sight.

I would have run downstairs for the binoculars if only I wasn't too frightened to leave my vigilant post. When I realized she was also about to walk past many large spruce trees behind which could be lurking Gods knows what perverts, I rushed outside, so panic stricken by this point that I was uncaring if I was seen to be watching, my word broken.

I was ravaged with fear. Why, why had I ever agreed to this unbelievably risky venture! Who gave a crap how much freedom and independence other children have! Who cared how many other children wait for the school bus, walk home alone, stay home alone, go to the corner store alone. What if she forgot to look for cars as she crossed the alley, what if someone grabbed her before I could reach her, what if...my mind simply boggled with the possibilities for a terrible, terrible outcome.

What was I thinking? What would I tell my husband if something happened? How would I explain I caved to the nagging of a child when I am the parent and supposed to be in charge and making good decisions? How would I explain my misjudgment; how would I live with myself? My mind reeled with horror. Ahhh, I think I'm going to throw up! Can I throw up without taking my eyes off my child?

Okay she is in the store. I take a deep breath. The clerks are nice. She is fine for the moment but the moments tick by so slowly. I peer down the street. I will her small face to appear. There are some cars parked in front of the store so I can't

[174]

actually see the door but surely she will come out any moment, any moment, any moment.

Finally there she is, face shining with accomplishment, carefree and proud as she walks unscathed up the street. I scoot inside to await her triumphant return. She was obviously ready for this small measure of independence.

It is equally obvious that I was definitely not ready for this small measure of letting go! Maybe when I am a little more grown up I'll be ready to try again.

Annie MacInnis

Warning, the following program may contain…

My family watched some television over the holidays and I am sick and tired of sitting with my young teenage kids watching yet one more inappropriate movie, music video or television show. I happen to be an open minded, easygoing parent but in recent years, I have been offended so many times by cheap sexual innuendo and disgusting visuals that I've lost track of the movies and shows I would consider warning another parent against. I'm not a prude but it is so hard to find shows and movies that we can watch as a family.

The programs on television before 10pm that are completely beyond the pale are astounding. The shows that purport to be fun family entertainment but contain really uncomfortable moments are legion. I don't understand why most of these moments need to be included; they are rarely central to the plot; they are usually just cheap shots.

I fondly remember my whole family, parents included, watched Sunday night Walt Disney movies. I know for sure, there was never a moment when my parents had to turn down the volume or take time to discuss a sexually inappropriate interlude in the show. The only time I can ever recall any debriefing being required was after we watched Dr. Zhivago. The next day at lunch, we older kids were talking with my parents about the Depression and my little sister burst into tears and ran away from the table. She thought we were going to end up bereft and hungry in the snow.

I am mystified why society is so accepting of the amount of trash on television and in movies. Oh, I know there are ratings and we can choose not to go to certain movies and we can choose not to watch certain shows but this stuff is so pervasive, it's hard with teenagers to find good shows that aren't too juvenile and aren't too sophisticated. Maybe the problem is society has stopped assuming families with teenagers sit down together to watch a show. Today so many people listen to their own music on iPods and MP3s instead of the local radio station. Kids and parents have televisions in their own rooms so everyone can watch what they want instead of sitting down together.

I fear society and families have lost that sense of connectedness that came from everyone knowing the words to Marg singing at the end of the Don Messer show "Smile the while I kiss you sad adieu…" and everyone watching the newest hot music on Ed Sullivan and everyone knowing who Chitty Chitty Bang Bang was and how to say Super-cali-fragi-listic-expi-ali-docious.

Everything we instinctively know about parenting behooves us to keep connecting with our teenagers on every level possible. It's too bad the movie and television and music industries are unlikely to desist in their quest for cheap laughs and titillation at the expense of moral sensibility. Maybe consumers need to start voting with their wallets and start looking for common ground in what music they're listening to and consider watching television and going to movies together but I guess that's another rant.

Annie MacInnis

Home Economics class

In the days of yore (when I was in high school) girls took Home Economics and learned to cook and sew. Boys took Woodshop and learned to build. Never mind that I was already a quite competent cook or that I had no interest whatsoever in learning to sew. Home Economics classes were not optional for girls. It was assumed that most girls would get married relatively soon after graduating from High School and would henceforth run the household even though they might also hold a job.

There are only two lessons I clearly recall from those years of home economics classes. There were those where we learned to make Popovers. Much time was spent over several classes discussing how critical it was that we all learn to make excellent popovers. We all understood the implicit messages behind these discussions. Only a future trollop, a poor housekeeping slattern in the making would not be able to produce perfect popovers by the time our teacher was finished with us. It was clear to everyone that popovers were an integral part of any morally upright young woman's civilized aspirations for a genteel, gracious existence. If one day our husband brought home his boss for dinner and we served substandard popovers our husband's career could very well be jeopardized let alone our marriage and our reputation within the community in which we lived. Funnily enough I don't really remember precisely what popovers were like. I seem to recall thinking they were like little Yorkshire Puddings without the beef drippings except that I think they were meant to be a dessert or possibly an appetizer. We had never eaten popovers at my house. Since high school I have never had occasion (or inclination) to make popovers and low and behold did not slide down the slippery slope to moral ruin.

My memories of the sewing component of home economics are scarcely much better. My one clear memory of those classes is the first item we were required to sew – a dirndl skirt. For those of you not privy to this term, this style of skirt has a waistband that buttons and a skirt that is gathered into many, many small folds before being sewn to the waistband. For egalitarian reasons we were not permitted to buy our own material. We had to choose from school-supplied material - stiff, unattractively patterned cotton (like what aprons, which coincidentally I love, are made of). In that era of miniskirts all our project skirts had to be knee length.

Let's Chat

Between stiff material, the dowdy length and myriad gathers at the waist everyone except the stick girls looked frightful.

I was definitely not one of the stick girls and was aghast at the sight of my somewhat pudgy self in my finished project as we suffered the final humiliation – the fashion show!

So I tell my lucky daughter as she hems and haws over the wealth of wonderful and interesting option choices available at her school, count your blessings; you could be making popovers and dirndls.

Annie MacInnis

A clean house

The house looks so beautiful this Christmas. A cut above our usual state of affairs but enjoying my tidy, sparkling, festive house reminds me how much I enjoy a clean, orderly house. For many years, while a stay-at-home-slash-spend-life-in-car parent, I suffered through the housecleaning that was my lot in life. I did not enjoy this aspect of my non-earning existence.

Being a stay at home parent was mostly balm to my soul. The low key life style was a perfect fit for me. There was time to volunteer lots at my kids' school; time to read, time to walk my dog, time to enjoy shopping for groceries with my kids, long walks to and from school through the park, energy left to cook a nice supper most nights and to read with the kids at bedtime. The flexibility of most days suited me.

With only one wage earner in the house money was tight all the time. Not only couldn't I justify the expense of paying someone else to do my cleaning, there was no money to spare anyway unless we all agreed not to eat. I loved my lifestyle and didn't long to go back to work except for one thing. I envied those working Moms in my circle who could afford to blithely pay to get their houses regularly cleaned. What bliss to come home to a clean and tidy house, I'd think.

Now that I've returned to work, albeit only part time, the state of my house certainly reflects the reduced hours spent trying to keep it socially acceptable. At the best of times, when I had hours that could potentially be allocated toward cleaning, my efforts were more a matter of "a lick and a promise" rather than a vicious eradication of germs, dust and grime and taking pleasure in working up a good healthy sweat to do a really good job.

Last winter I came up with a brilliant scheme that would allow me to have a cleaner house at minimal cost and inconvenience to myself. Here in my house, underfoot as it were, were two feckless teenagers with hands out all too often for cash. My frugal soul thrilled to the idea. I would assign tasks with the balm of a cash reward (but not as much as I'd have to pay a professional cleaner) nor would I have to tidy before their arrival so I wouldn't be judged a slattern.

The kids even liked the idea. I told my husband excitedly. He smiled politely but derisively. I defended my idea; he rolled his eyes and wished me well.

[180]

Let's Chat

The first weekend, one kid borrowed money on Friday in return for vacuuming, sweeping, floor washing and bathroom cleaning. The weekend ended without the work actually being done.

I was quite cranky as I spent Monday and Tuesday evening cleaning while the culprit attended already paid for after school activities and did homework.

The next weekend that child did the cleaning - all of it.

The following week I was duped yet again with a promise that was not fulfilled in a timely fashion when a kid advanced the money and the cleaning did not get done. Since then the kids have been evasive and non-committal whenever I mention housecleaning.

I guess unless I make a New Year's resolution to become a good housekeeper or to pay a professional, any day now the house will gradually ooze back to its previous status of piecemeal cleaning attempts whereby the whole house is never clean all at once. Ah well, I guess if my house looked this lovely every day, Christmas wouldn't feel so special.

Annie MacInnis

Home again

Like many Canadians, I live far from where I grew up. The pull of home is never stronger than in the summer when like a salmon irresistibly fighting their way upstream, I long to return to the Maritimes for my fix of home.

I have lived in Alberta for 25 years, own a home here, and am raising a family here, yet still, after all these years, I continue to feel as though I have two homes: Alberta, where I live my life happily and fully; and the home of my heart, Nova Scotia.

I am privileged to continue to return most summers to the home where I grew up. My parents still live in the same house, I sleep in the bedroom where I was a child, waking up each morning to the same sounds and same views out the windows. Each morning when I come down the stairs the same familiar kitchen, albeit having gone through several decorating versions, still awaits me. Outside the fields still beckon me. Wind rustles through the leaves of the trees, dew and spider webs sparkle on the long grass, time seems suspended as I stand in this place and among these people that pull so strongly on my heart.

Every year I bless the fortune smiling on me, affording me another year to cherish and once again fill myself with the sights and sounds of this place and these people. I try to drink in the experience, to fill myself with this place, to store all this as balm against the day that inexorably approaches, as my parents get older, when all this will be only a sweet memory.

I know I am luckier than most to have been able to return for so many years. I mind the advice my father gave me when I first was moving to Alberta, "to say everything I wanted to say" to my elderly grandmother before I left. Then, if I were unable to see her again, I would have no regrets for words left unsaid.

As the years pass, each visit is beyond poignant as I try to cherish each moment, carefully store each memory, fix each face and voice firmly in my mind's eye. Each summer as the day of departure comes; I resolutely turn my eyes away once again from my past toward another year in the west. I give thanks that for one more summer I could bask in the balm of my family and the land that draws me like a beacon in the fog. Once back in Alberta, Nova Scotia retreats once more to a fond memory, a bearable separation.

[182]

Let's Chat

The threads of my wonderful life here entangle me immediately.
My modest home on my city lot is home too. I touch my things,
call my friends, turn my thoughts to work and another school
year and feel so fortunate, so blessed, for another year, to have
two homes that fill my heart with gladness.

Annie MacInnis

Don't worry, be happy

The media spends an inordinate amount of time focusing on whether people choose to pursue wealth or happiness. The perception seems to be that it's an either/or choice and one oft-cited conclusion is that you are more likely to be happy if you are well off, healthy and/or in a relationship.

I believe we can choose happiness regardless of whether we are wealthy, healthy or in a relationship. Society and the media so often encourage us to compare what we have, what we want and what we value with what others around us have and want and value. We are often led to feel that we are somehow 'settling for less' while others 'have it all'.

If we choose to stay at home with our kids, we worry about what taking satisfaction in a homemaking life says about us, about missing out on work opportunities and getting ahead financially.

 If we choose to work, we worry about what that implies about us as a parent and how our children will be affected.

If we choose to pursue material possessions because they represent security for us, why should that imply we are more shallow than the person who chooses to 'settle for less'?

If we decide not to have children or are not in a relationship why should that suggest we are less loveable than those who are in relationships? If we are in a less than perfect relationship are we settling? If we have health problems that limit our activities does that make the life we have of less value than the life of a healthy person?

The idea that what brings us contentment and happiness is of less value because of what others choose is a false but common comparison that often makes us unsatisfied with our life. Our satisfaction with the choices we have made in life is often eroded by the judgment of others or by our own perception of others' judgments. That satisfaction is often further eroded by whether we feel our choices were made freely or whether circumstances have forced choices upon us.

Too often .people allow their happiness to be affected by the knowledge that they have not freely chosen the path their life is following.

Let's Chat

Yet choosing happiness anyway is still an option. Happiness is a conscious choice each day when we wake up.

Each day we can choose to seize the opportunities that come to us to take pleasure in our life.

Each day we can choose to be happy in the midst of financial hardship, ill health, a job we don't enjoy.

We can choose to make the best of what we have.

We can choose to enjoy the good days.

We can choose to take delight in the small daily pleasures that life brings us.

Nobody's life is perfect even if they are sickeningly wealthy and blissfully married.

Look for the silver linings in your own clouds. That's where you'll find YOUR happiness.

Annie MacInnis

I have a guilty secret

I suspect many parents harbour a similar guilt but we all hesitate to talk about it. This habit is mostly indulged in the privacy of our own home although it is occasionally practiced during play dates or at close friends' houses.

My secret is this. My children spend more time on the computer than the experts recommend. Oh, it's mostly educational games that require some thinking but nevertheless there they are all too often pecking away at the keyboard, their faces bathed in the glow from the screen.

I fear my children are techno-junkies - addicted to computer and I am their enabler. Hardly a day goes by that someone isn't in a snit because she had more time than me, but he got to play this morning, but she had more time yesterday, or he won't get off so I can go on. It's hard not to get impatient with the seemingly endless negotiations, the cajoling for extra time and the length of time it often seems to take before the player is in a position where they can 'save' their game and stop playing.

Without vigilant supervision and strict limits they would be wild-eyed, red-eyed burned out, exhausted addicts. Oh, I know, I've read a gazillion parenting articles about setting limits and the dangers of too much computer, but I just haven't come up with a workable plan for our family.

How much is too much? What is safe computer? Is it okay to play a little bit every day? Should play be restricted to weekends only during the school year? Should I allow them to play if they're ready early for school/their sibling has a friend over and they don't/their homework is done/they've had a bad day at school? Should play be allowed during play dates? Is overindulgence on the weekend okay or only the thin end of the wedge? If computer privileges are lost should this also include television privileges? If a child has used up his/her allotted time should they be allowed to sit and watch and advise another child or does this constitute extra time at the monitor? Should the time limit for computer time also include television viewing or should that be negotiated separately? Can allotted times be carried forward to other days?

Even if rules can be agreed upon these rules need to be applied. Enforcing an exact amount of time results in timers being set and reset, a timer being paused for bathroom breaks and constantly trying to keep track of how much time remains. All regulating systems other than, "That's it. You've been on that thing for ages. Get off this instant." drives me crazy.

Some days I flirt with the idea of banning computer and television completely for a month. I read regularly about families who've done this and who extol the virtues of rediscovering other pastimes. But do you think these articles represent real life or are they like those articles about the family who are living on next to nothing and managing so beautifully only you find out at the end that Daddy bought their house for them and they won a brand new car and received an inheritance last year?

Maybe I'm just addicted to the computer as a mainstay among my parenting tools. Because my children love to use the computer, the privilege to compute has become a powerful tool for negotiation and coercion. Loss of computer privileges currently constitutes the worst possible punishment in our house.

Maybe because I have no inclination to play computer games myself, I can't understand the lure of these games and worry about their possibly insidious nature. Would I worry so much if they were watching this much television? All I know is I am tired of feeling guilty that they spend too much time on computer, tired of nagging my children to get off the computer and do something else and tired of negotiating new strictures.

Maybe I should spend some time on the net researching this a little more and see what the most up to date advice is...I wonder when the computer will be free...

Annie MacInnis

A soupcon of guilt

Do you suppose pioneer mothers ever sat down at the end of a June day and felt guilty about not spending enough time with their kids or having enough money for "extra" activities or a really extravagant summer vacation?

Or is this sort of angst some modern problem my generation has dreamed up so we can all feel equally guilty, whether we work outside the home or not?

Most days I feel glad and privileged to be a stay at home Mom even though bill paying causes month-to-month anxiety. I love the freedom of knowing that if one of my children is even only a little bit sick, they can easily stay home with me. I love that they come home for lunch most days. I love that I volunteer in their school, that after school they can invite friends home and I can make warm muffins for a snack since supper is already underway. I love that most evenings I have time to read and sit with my kids instead of having many chores to do. I love that my children are free to dream up summer adventures we can do together for the next two months (as long as those adventures cost no more than a pittance).

But often I also feel anxious when I think of all the extras we don't have money for. Fancy somewhere warm holidays that many of my children's friends went on for March break and weekend cabins nearby are not in our budget. Expensive activities like movies, new clothes and takeout food are rare treats in our house.

I grew up in a family privileged to enjoy all those extras – a big family in a huge house with lots of land, big vacations, a lakeside cottage nearby and all the freedoms afforded by enough money for extras and a small town in a more innocent time.

So some days, like today, with our very modest summer vacation plans in place, I struggle with what I can't give my children instead of focusing on what I am giving them.

But, I know in my heart of hearts that I am giving them many of the wonderful aspects of my childhood because what really made my childhood so memorable was not actually the trappings of a well-off family.

Let's Chat

Rather it was the sense of being cherished and listened to, of my feelings being important. I learned about the big, important aspects of life up close and personal – my mother feeding the town drunk, always driving with a carload of extra kids wherever we went, and doing everything with such kindness and love and panache; my doctor father getting up in the night when someone was hurt or ill, immediately stopping whatever he was doing when 'duty' called and yet always living life out loud with great enjoyment. I don't ever remember either of them being too tired or too busy if I needed to talk.

Most parents, whether they work outside the home or not, strive to give their children the best that they can. Our job as parents is not to provide our children with a perfect world where no one ever feels slighted or envious. Our job is to teach them to make the best of the choices life gives them, to be resilient, to make good decisions, to take responsibility for their actions, to be forgiving, to practice tolerance and kindness, to give of themselves to others and last, but not least, to save the best of themselves for their family and their loved ones.

So during this summer's holidays I resolve to remember that my job as a parent is not to regret what I can't give my children or envy others for what they can give but, rather, to value what I am giving my children.

Our family journals in which we draw pictures and write about our adventures, our fires and occasional fireworks in the back yard, too seldom trips to visit family in Nova Scotia, walks with the dog, time to sleep in, to stay up late, to read and to think and carefully selected treats, these are my gifts to my children.

Surely one of the hardest aspects of being a parent is the uncertainty about whether you're doing the right thing for your child. It's so easy to get bogged down in worrying about whether to let your child crawl into bed with you if they wake in the night, whether to let them cry it out, when to wean, what about thumb sucking and eating junk food, how much computer/television time is too much, and how many bites of vegetable constitutes the bare minimum.

Parenting advice is ubiquitous. Magazines, books, and television shows all tout their version of how to be a parent. Well meaning grandparents, family members, in laws, friends, neighbours, and meddlesome strangers are all too willing to expound on their version of how you should treat your child. This constant

[189]

bombardment of "how to parent", some of it great but much of it contradictory, out-of-date, unworkable, ridiculous, and sometimes downright silly leads a parent to sometimes doubt their own ability to make a judgment call in any given situation.

Regardless of what you decide in any given situation the outcome will be unknown for years to come. Will your grown up child resent you because you didn't work, threw away the soothers when she turned two, insisted she play

team sports even though she hated every minute and forbid television on weekdays? Or will he be tormented as an adult because you worked, allowed him to suck his thumb until he was ready to stop and then needed braces, didn't insist on team sports so he never became athletic and is a television addict?

Parental guilt is so insidious and searing that it's easy to let yourself feel overwhelmed by all the information out there. In all situations whether immediate (as in your child runs into the road) or long term (what about the thumbsucking) we need to strive to take at least one really deep breath then trust our gut instincts, our intimate knowledge of this particular child, and be prepared to respond differently next time if necessary.

There are few absolutes in parenting (other than letting love for your child guide you). Very few hard and fast rules can be applied in all situations to all children. Instead of looking for parenting absolutes think of all the sources of information available like the pirates in the Walt Disney movie Pirates of the Caribbean. Reference to the Pirate Code of behavior is followed by a comment along the lines, "The code is more what you call 'guidelines' than actual rules."

So next time you doubt yourself trust that whatever decisions you make as a parent are the best that you could make at that time in that situation. Parenting is somewhat like home renovations: if you knew at the beginning what you know at the end how much easier it would be. Hopefully your child will eventually understand that you made the best decision you could at the time. And if not, there's always my father's parenting disclaimer "Once you're twenty-one your neuroses are your own."

Young girl

You run pell mell – arms and hair and heels flying. Then, suddenly conscious of your dignity, you slow to a more sedate pace. You are on the cusp of becoming a young woman, tall and lithe, more grown up looking than your years.

You delight in new small freedoms. I drop you off at gymnastics and let you walk in alone while I wait in the car to see you safely inside the doors. At first you walk a little self-consciously, your pride in being unaccompanied visible in your shoulders and nonchalant face. But soon you are skipping as the joy of your momentary freedom overtakes you. You whirl more gracefully than I ever could, ponytails flying, face shining. You flick a wave to me then twirl again, long legs flashing, t-shirt floating, oblivious to everything but your joy in the moment as you sail away to class.

In everything you do you radiate enthusiasm and confidence. You feel everything so intensely and live so passionately. You love "powerful" books, strong opinions and intimate conversations. You are endlessly curious about what motivates adult behavior.

One moment you are a perceptive well-spoken young woman, the next a fretful child in need of comfort only I can supply, then moments later engaged in bathroom humour with your younger brother.

Your favorite spot to sit and read is the peak of the doghouse roof. In the morning you sit there, a frilly parasol shading your eyes, waving cheerily to me. Later you are elegant in black slacks, hair piled high and long swan neck inclined toward me as you suffer politely through my conversation.

I catch glimpses of the young woman you will become but I also get tastes of the battle of wills we may endure on the way there.

I have loved every stage of my children's development. Each time I see my children enter a new phase I have a small passing regret for the behaviours left behind – nursing, toothless smiles, the rocking horse walk, first words, learning to read, first day of school, first night away – but, always, always the new skills more than make up for those charming discarded behaviors. Watching my children blossom toward the adults they will become is surely one of the greatest pleasures of parenting.

But I'm a little nervous about this next stage you're about to enter. I read articles on puberty and pre-teens and listen with a kind of fascinated fear to stories of friends' battles with their pre-teens hoping to glean that magical tidbit of wisdom that will allow us to sail through this period easily.

You and a good friend plan to attend a weeklong overnight camp this summer. You are entirely psyched for it. I am full of trepidation. Not that you won't have a great time. I know you will. You are ready to spread your wings. It's me I'm worried about. I know I'll pine for the sight of you twirling into the room talking a mile-a-minute, the sweetness of your cheek against mine, your eyelashes sweeping your cheeks in sleep.

I'll prop Kahlil Gibran's words where I can see them daily: "You may give them your love but not your thoughts, for they have their own thoughts. You may house their bodies but not their souls, for their souls dwell in the house of tomorrow…you are the bows from which your children as living arrows are sent forth. The archer sees the mark upon the path of the infinite, and He bends you with his might that His arrows may go swift and far. Let your bending in the archer's hand be for gladness. For even as He loves the arrow that flies, so He loves also the bow that is stable." (from the book, The Prophet)

And I'll hope that the you that comes home from camp has not grown too terribly far away from me. If you have changed a lot I promise I'll work hard to catch up and to adjust to our new relationship.

I console myself with the thought that I remember very few battles of wills with my mother. I hope I can succeed in modeling myself on her example so that your adult self and I will enjoy the close, candid, loving relationship my mother and I do.

[192]

I am grateful for...

I find I spend a lot of time lately thinking about gratitude and living in the moment. Maybe this is a sign I'm getting old or getting wise or maybe I've just got too much time on my hands.

Regardless, with Thanksgiving only days away, my thoughts turn inexorably to the blessings in my life. Although I'd like to talk at length (when don't I) during our Thanksgiving meal when we do our little go around about what we're grateful for, I'm usually (thankfully) brief because I spend some time whittling down my thankful thoughts to a succinct sentence or two.

I am not thankful that no one in my house has a green thumb or a tidying gene and as a result my yard is still full of debris from the retaining wall project and the house is less tidy than I would prefer. I am not thankful that I still have not managed to get the living room repainted and that I still need a new couch and these items keeps falling to the bottom of my ongoing list. I am not thankful that my car is still grubby because I haven't managed to make an appointment to get it cleaned even though my husband kindly gave me a gift certificate to have it detailed. I am not thankful that as a feckless child I was a careless brusher and now I have ageing teeth that are fragile hollow shells filled with giant fillings that are on their last legs...Ooops, that's the UNgrateful list...

I am thankful that my two dear children are happy and safe with us for another year.

I'm thankful that those two children are grateful kids who 'get it.'

I am thankful that I continue to have the support and love of my husband and that we are in sync and in sympathy with each other most of the time.

I am thankful that my Dad still has some of those nine lives in his back pocket and is on his way back to hale and hearty yet again.

I am thankful that my Mom is the strong, kind person she is.

I am thankful that I have friends who understand when I don't manage to return their calls or deliver their birthday presents on time.

I am thankful for my beloved dog, Teddy.

[193]

Annie MacInnis

I am thankful that my Multiple Sclerosis remains under control and that I can go for a walk with that dog.

I am thankful that I have M.S. because it has allowed me to realize that each day that I wake up feeling energetic is a blessing.

I am thankful my husband has a new car with a heater that works.

I am thankful the retaining wall is almost finished and that we had the wherewithal to get that job done (or rather the ability to access a Line of Credit…).

Last but by no means least, I am thankful the mice in the basement are finally vanquished and we upstairs have managed to prevail.

Happy Thanksgiving to you and yours from me and mine.

Oh look, a gopher...

There are countless parenting moments I would gladly relive - to see once more that first smile or step, to once again feel that thrilling rush as I held my babies in my arms for the first time.

On the other hand there are some moments I'd just as soon never have to think about again. I had one of those moments recently.

My daughter and I had driven outside the city for 6 more weeks of skating lessons now that the ice had been removed from her usual rink. We left with ample time to spare and arrived ½ hour early. I suggested we explore for something to do. Within 5 minutes we had seen all there was to see – roads, fields and impressive McMansions littered everywhere.

We were sitting companionably in the car chatting when I decided we should take the dog for a walk since fields surrounded us. We pulled into a lay by. A little way into the field were two gophers."Oh look," caroled my city-bred daughter, "Aren't they cute. They're like my gerbils only bigger."

I agreed they were very sweet looking as they stood on their hind legs looking with surprise at our car. In retrospect I probably should have blown the horn or something to send the gophers on their way but I just assumed they would be wary. I stepped out of the car. The dog barreled out and took off after the gophers. My daughter screamed, "NNNOOOOO!! Don't hurt the gophers!!"

"It's okay," I blithely reassured her, "They're smart wild creatures with safe holes dug everywhere here. They'll not let her catch them."

The words were hardly out of my mouth when our dog reached the 1!#!@:K$<@!:$stupid gophers who were just standing there, grabbed one, shook it briskly like she does her sock when we throw it, then dropped it and stood looking at it in puzzlement.

My daughter screeched and cried as though the banshees of hell were upon us.

The dog slunk guiltily back into the car.

I walked out into the field to make sure the gopher was dead then I tried to calm my daughter. I tried to talk about what had

[195]

happened but skating was a grim experience. The drive home was strained.

The dog sat chastened in the back seat, flinching slightly every time my daughter muttered "killer" over her shoulder. My daughter sat in the front radiating anything but forgiveness.

I scrolled endlessly through the disorganized mess in my head for words to 'make it all better'. She would have to make it all better in her own mind.

That night after much talk and thought, she could look at the incident from the dog's perspective and forgive her. Learning about love and death and forgiving those we love for something that seems unforgivable are part of growing up. I sure don't like reliving that incident but I recall with pride how my daughter dealt with it.

Thank goodness for coffee

I usually get up half an hour before my children. This is a matter of self-defense rather than a mission to be an early riser. I like to have the opportunity to get at least one cup of coffee (and ideally a second) under my belt before I have small humanoids in my face chattering relentlessly the moment I open my eyes. If I manage to achieve this goal, there is a much greater likelihood that we will all have *a good day*.

If I *do not* get my cup of coffee, quiet read and trip to the smallest room in the house prior to little feet hitting the floor there is a greater chance that someone is going to *lose it* before school.

When my children were babies their neediness was balm to my soul. I craved the touch of their cheeks on mine, the tinkling sound of their laughter, and the warmth of them sleeping in my arms.

With school age children, although I still love them immensely, some days how much I like my children may be tempered by how easy it is to get out the door to school.

The all-consuming love for my perfect young babies has become tarnished by their tendency to dawdle when leaving the house despite repeated lectures about the importance of punctuality.

Like most parents I have a deep dark secret that I hide from much of the world. There is sometimes a considerable discrepancy between the image of the parent I present to the world and the real life parent I am at home when the world isn't watching.

When my daughter first started school I felt mortified to arrive at school after being impatient trying to get my daughter and my two-year-old out the door on time. At school it seemed every other parent and child looked hurried but serene – as though they had some secret for how to get to school on time without the stress and unhappiness and downright meltdowns we seemed to be experiencing.

My first new friend at my daughter's school was a fellow Maritimer. Being sharing sorts of people and recognizing in each other kindred spirits, we began to talk about real life to each other. One of the things we often talk about is how our day has gone so far. We often greet each other with, "Okay, we've had a frightful morning so far" or "I was impatient" or "I didn't yell once, I was a model of propriety!

If you had an unsuccessful start to your morning, we commiserated and related. If you were an ideal mother, we offered congratulations.

The group of mothers with whom I share my parenting successes and failures has widened over the years but the sentiment remains the same. We share problems and successes and solutions (however temporary). The opportunity to talk about *in the trenches parenting* with parents I trust and whose judgment I value has been an ongoing boon over the years.

No matter how firmly we resolve to be a better parent tomorrow, reality doesn't always pan out that way. Life interferes with unset alarms, cranky children, unexpected changes of plans, hormonal swoops and peaks, lack of the only edible cereal in this city. Sometimes life's day-to-day stresses prompt us to be less than charitable (and even downright wretched) to the ones we love.

The kids and I have gotten better at getting out the door (at least some of the time). Sometimes we go for longish periods when we are doing great and very proud of ourselves. Then all of a sudden we slide down the slippery slope into horrid mornings full of squabbling again.

On those days when I realize that I have become the parent in the mall I once considered calling the authorities about, I look for support from my friends.

For better and for worse

How often, when you hear of a couple divorcing do you think, "Who would have guessed? They seemed such a happy couple."

I think a good marriage doesn't necessarily look beautiful or easy from the outside. Absence of conflict is not a prerequisite. Managing to stay connected, charitable, forgiving, and willing to compromise and sacrifice for each other is important. Adversity doesn't hurt either.

When I inquired about a friend's husband's health recently she said if he had not suffered ongoing health difficulties over the past decade they would probably have divorced. From the outside, their relationship looked idyllic – beautiful house, lovely children, no money worries yet adversity remade their marriage by allowing them to recapture intimacy.

Over the years my husband and I have had vexing health problems, financial hardship and lived far from the support of our parents and siblings. Yet, maybe these very factors, which I often regret so much, help us to be strong and resilient for each other in the face of adversity.

Like all couples, sometimes we irk each other and regrettable words are spoken. Often this happens with an audience of two children. At night sometimes I torture myself with the thought of what lessons my children are learning as they watch us occasionally be angry or unjust with each other? I hope they are seeing it's okay to occasionally be angry with or unfair to someone you love and to be forgiving of those we love.

When we do get cross with each other I try to remember my father's sage advice about marriage. He told me when you realize you're in a conflict try to quickly step back mentally and decide whether you feel strongly enough about the issue to upset your mate in order to have your way.

Like when your child yells at you, "I hate you!" words spoken in anger are often less about the meaning of the words than about feeling briefly unhappy or unappreciated.

Sometimes the small irritations of life get overwhelming. Hopefully most of the time we deal with those feelings in a healthy way – going for a walk, talking with a friend, taking a bath, having a nap – rather than taking a bite out of our nearest and dearest.

But when tempers do flare we try to diffuse the situation with sympathy, a hug, or an apology then move on, like you do after a spat with your children. Sometimes just saying, "Wow, gosh, I really lost my mind there. I behaved badly and I'm sorry" accompanied by a hug is enough.

Truly and often forgiving each other for large and small things is part of really loving someone for better or for worse, for richer or for poorer…

(N.B. Writer's husband's disclaimer: Any or all references to any negative behavior on the part of the presumably fictional husband referred to above should be understood to be simply a product of my wife's imagination and not applicable to any person in real life.)

Gerbil Rescue Unit #1

'Twas a dark and stormy night thankfully nowhere near Christmas Eve. Not a creature was stirring not even a mouse (or so I thought). The laundry was folded and put away with care (yeah, right!)...

However as I went about my after supper tasks chauffeuring children, at home a duplicitous gerbil was scheming a trip to that great big chewable world called my house.

Unbeknownst to us the escape artist formally known as Ember had decided on a breakaway. Never mind she and various of her cronies had tried this on past occasions with limited success. Never mind they all received subsequent earnest lectures from their owner about the perils of the big, hungry, dangerous world outside their cages. Never mind this gerbil had a clearly implied obligation to stay in her cage. Never mind the girl who lavished endless amounts of love, attention and time in this gerbil's direction even though she was occasionally an ungrateful small gerbil who scorned said girl's entreaties.

Equally unaware of the best-laid schemes of mice and other such creatures was my husband. On his way to an appointment, he hurriedly stopped by the house. While standing in the littlest room in our house he spied something in the periphery of his vision. His first thought was there's a mouse in the hallway. Then he realized this was a member of the family who, while valued for her contributions to overall harmony, nevertheless did not possess the freedom to roam at large.

The gerbil stood on her haunches, front paws neatly folded across her chest, eyes wide, ears up, whiskers twitching, agog at the many splendors of the world outside her cage.

Suddenly she spotted my husband. BUSTED!

She took off into our son's room. My husband hurried to organize himself and capture her before she hastened further afield. Recapture might have been a relatively simple matter if this were a gerbil that my husband held often. Unfortunately while my husband did not dislike this gerbil and in fact daily said a cordial hello to her when she was presented to him, he rarely held her.

Recapture might also have been a simple matter if the gerbil had fled into a room without TOO much debris on the floor. But the gerbil had fled into that sinking morass of small objects and horrendous clutter usually referred to in generic terms as a boy child's room (and not a tidy one by a long shot not even with the incentive of a weekly allowance were any effort whatsoever at neatening to be detected during the weekend).

Alas this gerbil fled into our son's room, which is quite definitely in the sinking morass category most days of the year. All my husband would say subsequently was that my daughter says she is a hard enough gerbil to catch in her little cage sometimes so use your imagination when you picture her loose in that bedroom!

When the children and I arrived home, our first clue that 'an incident' had occurred was an obsequious dog who, despite her terrier heritage had been no help to my husband whatsoever during the whole recapturing episode. She led us guiltily to the hallway where the light was on and a stool had been moved from the living room I had a thrill of unease before I spotted the note written in my husband's hand and taped to our daughter's bedroom door.

A terse description of the breakaway incident and cautions about opening her door and checking the cage for means of escape followed. The note was signed *Gerbil Rescue Unit #1.*

We all had a great chuckle. (And, of course, there was a short, contentious discussion about who was gerbil rescue unit #2 based on past performance about which, of course, there was some disagreement due to selective memory.)

The gerbil in question suffered through a series of lectures spanning several days from all family members.

As I went to sleep that night I sent up a small thank you to the powers that be for the timely arrival of Gerbil Rescue Unit #1. Good karma has indeed returned to our house!

For generous figured women everywhere

My family was privileged to be able to go on a March break vacation to Cuba a few years ago. This was our first exotic warm weather holiday as a family and it was a revelation for all of us.

Fresh from affluent Canada with all our attitudes about appropriate dress and body image intact, we were delighted everywhere we went to see crowds of generous figured women of all ages dressed with panache and whimsy and a lot of skin.

The remarkable thing from a Canadian point of view was that all these women carried themselves with pride. They didn't cover themselves with loose clothes; they didn't assume they were less attractive because they were less than perfect.

We were immediately conscious of how our attitudes about how women should look and dress were irrelevant here. The Cuban women were unfettered by our North American urban notions of imperfect bodies. They wore belly shirts, short skirts, short shorts, low cut tops and figure hugging dresses. They walked as though they expected admiration and they received it because their joy and pride in themselves was so self-evident. Their inner beauty and joy de vivre shone so brightly it was unmistakable.

In this country where poverty is endemic and consumer goods are rare, I saw such joy and pride in the people that I felt ashamed of our glut and humbled by their careful care of old items we crass Canadian consumers would never bother to try to keep operating. Cuba is poor but not backward.

As a generous figured woman myself, I was charmed and inspired by the Cuban women and vowed to view myself with a little less judgment. Of the many things I learned on this vacation, having a more forgiving attitude about my own body will be one of the most enduring. I have a new determination to celebrate how good I feel about myself these days as I grow older.

I'm a tad thicker around the middle than I'd like to be and a little saggier here and there than I'd wish and possess feet that no longer enjoy high heels for any length of time. Despite all that and more, I am healthy and happy and still love to dress to please myself and to garner my husband's admiration.

[203]

I don't look young. I look like who I am, a woman of experience with my life writ large upon me.

The world sees a mature woman holding up reasonably well but if I look closely I see a young adventurer, a twenty something with a capital "C" career, a thirty something young wife, a proud mother of two babies.

If I look closely I see a hint, hear an echo of those amazing Cuban woman whose beauty was borne on so much more than a perfect body. Their beauty shone from their eyes, sparkled with the light off their skin, and radiated around them.

I celebrate those women and aspire to emulate them.

If the rest of the world only sees an older, not slim woman in bright red that is their loss.

The Mysterious Case of the Missing Fruit Basket

She called long distance to a flower shop she had used before. Could they deliver a bouquet to her sister-in-law in hospital? Could they also at the same time assemble and deliver a fruit basket to her brother-in-law in the same hospital?

The following day during conversations with family members on the scene, the bouquet was mentioned and greatly admired but no mention was made of the fruit basket. "Odd," she thought.

The following morning she called the flower shop to confirm both flowers and fruit had been delivered. "Oh yes," they said, "Both were delivered at the same time."

She called the ward nurse on her brother-in-law's floor. Had he received a fruit basket? The nurse checked and returned to say, "No."

She called the flower shop back. "Are you sure the fruit basket got delivered yesterday because the brother-in-law didn't receive one?" Consternation at the flower shop, followed by confirmation that they delivered to the named person at the named hospital.

Another call to the brother-in-law's ward. Could the nurse check to see if basket was perhaps delivered to someone else possibly with the same last name?

Next call, the nurse confirms that no one else with the same last name had received the basket in error. She ended by saying that, mind you, she had not checked the dementia ward because it has tight security and it was unlikely the basket was misdirected there but she would check there as well. Please call again tomorrow.

A follow up call the next morning revealed that, in fact, the lovely fruit basket had been delivered, in error, to a veteran in the dementia word. The veteran had the same first and last name as the brother-in-law. Further confounding the laws of coincidence, my friend's name on the card was also the name of the veteran's granddaughter AND the basket had arrived on the old gentleman's birthday.

The old gentleman was pleased to tell the nurse all about his thoughtful granddaughter and what a lovely fruit basket she had sent and what a great birthday he'd had. The $60 basket had one apple and three grapes remaining.

The nurse confessed to my friend on the phone that she hadn't the heart to disillusion him. She mentioned not a word of the mistake, simply congratulating him on his birthday and his sweet granddaughter.

For the recipient and the granddaughter to have the same names and to have the serendipity of a mistaken identity and a delivery on the old gentleman's birthday beggars the imagination but offered a sense of hope and humor and wonder to my friends during an otherwise stressful time.

Letting go

I am the parent of a teen and a preteen and gone are the days when I was the reassuring center of my children's world. Gone are the days when I could make almost anything better with a silly song, reading to them, making cupcakes, or taking a walk together.

Sometimes I miss those days with an ache that comes close to breaking my heart. Usually this happens when I have had a confrontation with one of my children and seen the swirling emotions in their eyes and the expression on their face as they look across this new gulf between us. I can see that I am being measured and that, once again, I'm falling short despite all my efforts.

In those halcyon days when our children are young, we fool ourselves into thinking that when OUR children become teenagers we will not be among those parents for whom the teenage years become harrowing. We imagine that we will be the parents that aren't un-cool, the ones that don't nag and fuss, the parents who aren't disparaged. We imagine that we will never hear "I hate you"; never see contempt in their eyes.

Then our children grow up and begin to pull away no matter how strong the foundations we have laid. Overnight, it seems, they no longer want to be hugged or kissed in public, they jettison once precious rituals, and they stop sharing everything with you or expecting that you will be able to help solve their problems.

I know rationally that distancing themselves from their parents is a natural, normal, even necessary aspect of growing up but the reality is so much harder to bear. Many days the affectionate, enthusiastic, wonderful children I know and love are there loving me back. I cherish those days and try to treasure every moment and not feel sad when next day it all unravels.

But the days when these new older children and I butt up against each other remain difficult. I see scorn for me, impatience with my reminders, questions and rules. I know intellectually that their distain is nothing personal but that knowledge is not comforting.

I try to remind myself that my parents and I are very close as adults. I could not love them more, value their opinion more, or wish more often that we lived closer to each other. I can only hope that I do as good a job as my parents did raising me. I can only hope that when my children are satisfied they have distanced themselves far enough from my values and my person, they too will come back to a new closeness and a new relationship of ease and comfort.

In the meantime I try to remind myself to appreciate learning more each day about the adults they are working on becoming and to minimize the opportunities for being regarded as beneath contempt by not caroling "Did you remember your lunch, honey?" and "Are you dressed warmly enough?"

I don't think the fear ever leaves you

When my children were babies I would slip into their room and lean over their crib to make sure they were breathing. If they slept through the night, I would wake in the morning with my heart almost pounding out of my chest. My first thought was never that sleeping through the night would be a good thing. No, my mind always went to dark thoughts. I would be frantic in my haste to reach the baby. The soundless, screeching stress rocketing inside me undoing any possible good the extra sleep might have done me. Thankfully, I was always lucky to have that moment of nameless horror and dread disappear as sweet baby's breath washed over me along with relief.

News stories of unrest and disaster and tragedy elsewhere in the world hit me particularly hard once I became a parent. Thoughts of those families make me endlessly grateful to live in Canada where I have the luxury to let my imagination dwell only occasionally on nameless horrors and the potential for accidents and disease out there. My imagination fails me entirely when I think of living somewhere where my family's personal safety was daily in peril.

The journey away from constant fearful vigilance practiced by a parent of young children has occurred slowly. As my children have grown older I have learned not to instantly panic if they sleep in or have a long bath. Nowadays, I can blithely watch my children go off with friends for a day and see my daughter off to sleepover camp without pacing the house like a caged creature during their absence. I try to limit myself to only twinges of worry if their return is overdue.

But this week when my son was really sick with a bad flu his long, so sound sleeps reawakened old fears but nowadays instead of obsessing with the worry I remind myself that such worries are a natural part of being a parent.

I try to welcome those feelings and remember that worry is our mental reminder not to take life for granted. To suck out the marrow of life, to savor life's sweetness to the last drop, to remember until eternity claims you, the sound of your child's laughter and the feel of your child's sweet breath as it fans across your cheek, to recall precisely the sweet relief that floods through you as your child walks safe and sound through the door, as your hand lightly touches their warm skin when they are sick before you tiptoe back out of their room.

[209]

Annie MacInnis

Fear affords us moments that give life depth and meaning. Fear prompts us to be mindful of those parents less fortunate this night. Fear reminds us to be glad we are blessed with safety and our children near us this night and to spare a thought for parents everywhere who are not so fortunate.

Let's Chat

December 6, 1917

Each year as early December approaches my thoughts turn to a particularly Nova Scotian anniversary- the Halifax Explosion.

The Explosion occurred on 6 December 1917. It was the largest manmade explosion until Nagasaki and Hiroshima. The explosion was so big that people in the town I grew up in some 40 miles away, felt the impact. Dishes fell from shelves and pictures from walls. Much of downtown Halifax was destroyed by the explosion. More than 2,000 people were killed and more than 9,000 injured.

The Explosion devastated Halifax long before I was born but I recall this event for much more personal reasons. The stories surrounding the explosion resonate with me each December because I grew up hearing family stories about the explosion from my grandparents who were in Halifax at the time.

My paternal grandfather was a young army doctor working at Camp Hill Hospital in Halifax. His boss was in Boston and the second in command, an elderly doctor, was home ill so my grandfather was in charge that fateful day.

Pictures of my grandfather then show a man I never knew, dashing and achingly handsome and stalwart in his uniform.

His broad shoulders carried a heavy load that day. All the hospital windows shattered in the aftermath of the explosion. The initial sound of the explosion sent many people throughout the city hurrying to their windows in time to receive the impact of shattering windows full in the face so many of the injuries that day were due to glass.

The young army nurse who would later become my grandmother also worked in the hospital that day.

One of her patients was the engineer from the small Halifax tugboat that was escorting the munitions ship out of the harbour before the collision. The engineer had the top of his skull blown off but, miraculously, survived the explosion. My grandmother was his nurse. Once when I asked her if he was okay mentally, she replied, with her usual wry humour, "Oh, he was fine but he did tend to have terrible nightmares!" I don't doubt he did.

[211]

In one of the twists so typical in small Nova Scotia, one more connection to the explosion exists in my family. My other grandfather, my mother's father, owned land on the Noel Shore where some of Nova Scotia's oldest and largest trees are located.

After the explosion the first city to send help to Halifax was Boston. As soon as news reached Boston of the explosion, a train was dispatched with doctors, nurses, medical supplies, and food.

Nova Scotia has never forgotten the help sent by Boston that day. For many years the huge Christmas tree in downtown Boston was harvested from my maternal grandfather's land and sent by the Nova Scotia government as an enduring thank you for the timely, desperately needed help sent in Halifax's hour of need.

Family stories are a treasured legacy. Too often stories are not preserved, not passed down in the family. Our personal experience of events is what connects us to the past, to our forebears, that marks our place in time and memory. If you have family stories to tell make sure they get told and passed on.

A cautionary tale of paying your own way, trying to save a buck or two and the perils of decision-making and growing up

My daughter's friend had just had her thirteenth birthday and decided she wanted to spread her wings a little now and then. Her mother was happy to afford her an increase in responsibility and independence.

The girl and a friend prepared to indulge in a little freedom. The plan was for them to be dropped off at a leisure center sans a supervising parent. Her mother made plans to take the younger sibling on a four-hour outing and arranged to pick up the 'big' girls at a specific time.

After pestering the daughter in question about whether she had all the items she might need (bathing suit, towel, money) and receiving long-suffering responses the mother finally sallied forth and delivered the girls hither with one last reminder about pick up time.

The girls carefully perused the admission prices like the canny consumers they were. Now that they were thirteen and babysitters they had their own money to spend and while they would no doubt often spend frivolously they did not intend to ever spend unwisely.

Our young friend checked out the price differences based on age ranges then in a quiet aside to her friend our savvy spender commented that last week (when she was 12) it would have cost her $2 less to get in. Hmmmmmm, she thought.

While her friend opted to pay the full amount, our intrepid girl decided to save herself an easy $2 for a snack later on and when her turn came up, she unblushingly said, "One 12 year old admission, please."

The cashier smiled at her and looked over our friend's shoulder then back at our friend.

"Do you have an adult accompanying you?" she asked.

Our frugal friend gulped, then rallied and said, "Yes, my friend, she's 13."

"Ah," said the cashier, "unfortunately your friend must be at least 18 to supervise someone 12 or younger."

Momentarily stumped, our young friend, decided in the end to opt for candor. Smiling winsomely at the cashier, she laughed self-depreciatingly and confessed her small fabrication and the happy news of her recent birthday.

The cashier smiled back at the lovely young girl and said, "Have you any proof that you are, in fact, thirteen?"

She did not.

The cashier said no dice. The girls whiled away the four hours sitting and talking and spent more than the admission price on snacks as they waited for pickup time. Luckily they were thirteen and possessed of an endless supply of chitchat with a friend.

Was a lesson learned? Hard to say. On an outing the very next weekend, she forgot her money entirely and had to be temporarily bankrolled by the kind accompanying adult that day-me.

What does being rich look like to you?

Living in boomtown Calgary, examples of rich are flaunted in our faces every day – flash cars, humongous houses, high end stores. Most people would answer me that being rich means having lots of money, more than enough money to do whatever you want.

Despite the fact that my husband and I moved here in the early eighties, we have not made our fortune here. I stayed home when the kids were little. Living on one income meant a big financial sacrifice. I don't regret that decision but the upshot is that for most of our married life we have not had quite enough money.

I don't mean we've been homeless or hungry; we've been fortunate to have been spared that. I do mean that many months have been a tight squeeze the last few days before payday. Many years there was almost nothing left once the bills were paid. Many years our bank balance sank slowly but inexorably toward the red despite all our hard work and all our efforts to tighten our belts and to be frugal.

For many Canadians this is reality.

As the cost of homes, gas, parking and more continues to rise, the working poor remain. They work hard. They have a mortgage if they're lucky; a rent payment if they're not. They may have cars and dress well, but have little in the way of cash; little in the way of savings. Each month is a struggle to pay the bills; each unanticipated expense a small disaster.

My husband and I feel lucky these days. I have returned to work and money is not so tight. Despite critical home repairs and replacing my car we are making progress paying down our debts.

For me that feels rich. For me being rich means having some wiggle room, finally, in our budget.

All those years of penury mean my standards for feeling rich are lower than most. To me being rich is making enough money to be able to pay down my debts a little each month while still having some left over to have some modest family treats. Having

<u>Annie MacInnis</u>

a family dinner out at a restaurant once in a while, buying new runners when the kids need them instead of making do, not pausing before reaching the grocery till to estimate if I need to return some items, now that is rich.

Maybe those Canadians living so "high off the hog" these days would do well to remember where most of us came from and where many of us still live – that hard working, frugal, desperately trying to save for a rainy day middle class.

Green eggs and ham

We thought it was one of the most brilliant, most outrageous pranks ever, a prank to end all pranks, a prank of epic proportions.

I can't remember who first came up with the idea. I can't remember if refinement was necessary or if the idea appeared full blown, ready for implementation. I can't remember if anyone needed persuasion or whether everyone was in from the get go. I do remember the ferocious glee tinged with horror than accompanied our many secretive planning meetings.

Charitable people would have called us high-spirited. In our defense, we figured the reaction to our prank would be good-natured. We were, after all, children suckled on Dr. Seuss.

Drastic consequences, like poisoning or illness, were not considered. Any inkling that this object might not be entirely fit to eat was mitigated by the fact that our father was a doctor. I guess we just assumed he could deal with any small intestinal problems that resulted. In retrospect I guess the fact that he was also the intended victim was not properly taken into account.

You see, my younger brother raised birds; not for eating or their eggs, but rather for showing at local fairs. He had ducks and chickens and exotic birds like Canadian geese and chickens with feet that looked like fluffy bedroom slippers and heads that looked like pompoms with beaks. There was also one that laid ostrich size eggs with lurid green shells.

Although we had never eaten any of his weird bird's eggs, I guess, we just assumed, with that careless childhood certainty of immortality, that all creatures' eggs were, in theory, edible, regardless of size, colour or parentage.

After several false starts, the day finally dawned when we had a fresh egg plus a father for whom we, out of the goodness of our dear sweet hearts, offered to cook a lovely breakfast.

That beleaguered father of five horrid children, tired from a night out delivering a baby, sat at the table drinking tea and reading the newspaper while, with fitfully suppressed giggles, we made his delicious repast.

Annie MacInnis

We were aghast when the one egg filled the frying pan. Fortunately, on the inside the egg was a normal colour although the yolk alone was the size of a normal egg. The cooked egg filled the plate.

We watched with barely restrained horror and bated breath as he lifted the first bite toward his mouth.

He chewed, swallowed and continued to read the newspaper. He ate the whole egg and some buttered bread without comment, thanked us for our efforts and left the room.

Throughout the morning, we watched him carefully for signs of impending illness but he appeared to suffer no ill effects.

Somewhat deflated we eventually trailed off to other pursuits.

To this day, I don't know if he genuinely didn't notice that remarkable egg or if he was so diabolical that he aced us by calling our bluff. Knowing my Dad, I suspect the latter.

Thinking back on the incident, I don't think you could really justify calling us evil children

I prefer to think of us in those halcyon days as high-spirited, full of zest for life, full of mischief. I like to imagine we were always ready at a moment's notice for high jinks, like the kids in those 6 pm Sunday night Walt Disney movies we watched while eating pancakes and bacon on TV tables in those pre VCR/DVD days.

But in these days of bland political correctness and "use your words not your fists, dear" and zero tolerance for any sort of violence against a person's person there might be those who would consider my brother and me to be horrid little children and wonder how my mother, in particular, survived our childhood with her sanity intact.

We had gone to bed like good children. The summer cottage had open rafters so we could hear snatches of the movie our parents were watching in the living room. Not wanting to disturb them, we elected to crawl along the rafters and watch the movie from there.

It was a murder mystery. The bad guys had captured the good guy and were arguing about how to dispose of him. The good guy had his hands tied behind his back and his ankles tied together with the same piece of rope. Finally the bad guys agreed to disagree and simply heaved the good guy off the boat into the ocean.

After the bad guys left, the good guy started rocking forward hard enough so that on the backswing his face would come out of the water enough for him to gasp a breath before his face went under again. He did this until finally another boat came along and rescued him.

The next day my brother and I argued over whether this feat was physically possible. Funnily enough (well at least I think it's funny but this column portrays my sense of humour as slightly warped version) I don't actually remember whether I thought it was or wasn't possible.

Regardless, we eventually decided we were at an impasse. The only solution was to test the theory and here, perhaps, is where

[219]

some might say we segued from mischievous pranksters to outright wretches.

We snatched our little brother from whatever innocent pursuits he was involved in, dragged him down onto the wharf and tied him.

We instructed him on what he had to do, admonished him that he could do this if he didn't panic, conceded we'd come in and get him if it looked like he was actually going to drown, then heaved him off the wharf into about 10 feet of water.

At that moment, our mother glanced out the kitchen window. An excellent runner and swimmer and a dab hand with knots, she had our little brother back on shore and freed in no time.

I seem to have blocked from my memory what followed but I suspect it wasn't pretty and most probably involved a serious tongue lashing from here followed by the words, "Wait 'til your father gets home!!!"

Let's Chat

(Saskatchewan, a small town, names have been changed to protect the innocent and particularly the witness…)

She was short to begin with, sturdy of body and shaped like an "L", bent almost double with osteoporosis as she struggled with her cane to get out of the car with his gentle help. She was in full spate from the moment he opened her car door and offered her his strong arm. "Peter, don't talk when we get inside! Do you hear me? Don't tell me what to do! I'm telling you, Peter, don't talk!

"Yes, darling," replied a patient, loving voice.

In spite of her seeming frailty, she spoke forcefully and with an obvious expectation of unquestioning, uncomplaining acquiescence. They moved in tandem, slowly, inexorably, toward the door of the drugstore. Once more her authoritative tones rang out, "Peter, get the door! Peter, are you there? Peter, are you listening? Peter, I'm telling you, when we get in there, remember, don't talk!"

"Yes, darling."

Once inside, they made their way, her cane thumping rhythmically, to the pharmacist who took his turn bearing the brunt of her diatribe. Her voice was muffled somewhat by the shelves but could be heard at the edges of your consciousness like distant rumbling thunder, not of immediate concern but requiring some wary attention.

Some short time later she came back toward the cashier moving through the aisles slowly but with infinite determination. Like some unstoppable force of nature she continued her refrain, "Peter, I said don't talk! Peter, don't crowd me! Peter be some help!"

Everyone got out of her way anxious not to end up swatted by the flat of her sharp tongue.

"Yes, darling," came the reply spoken yet again with no hint of irritation or impatience. Then his eyes flicked sideways and he smiled and winked ironically at those around him.

[221]

There was a moment of surprised silence then a struggle not to giggle, to remain respectful of this fierce old woman. The battle was lost; one small, muffled snort of laughter leaked out.

The response was immediate and directed, of course, at the nearest culprit. "Peter, are you talking? Peter, don't talk!"

"Yes, darling," was followed by a more exaggerated wink at the assembled company. More snorts of suppressed laughter.

She swung about irately, still bent double, but forceful nonetheless, "Peter are you on stage again? Why do you always have to get on stage? I told you don't talk! Peter are you talking? I said don't talk!"

"Yes, darling." came the ever patient reply.

The cashier interrupted with a request for payment and suddenly from that small irate woman issued the dulcet tones of a kinder, gentler possibly loving person. "Peter can you pass the Mastercard?"

Moving toward the door, her voice rang out predictably, "Peter, get the door! Peter pay attention! Peter I said..." Peter gently held her arm and her bags and the door and smiled once more over his shoulder at those watching.

Mercifully for us, the door swung closed on one last patient, loving "Yes darling," and we were spared further strident tones.

Love is a many splendored thing and comes in many guises.

A Day like no other

It is a day like no other. After days of rain and grey skies the sun is shining and the sky is a high clear blue (crystal blue persuasion).

The house is a tip; the kitchen floor particularly nasty. I need to do a few hours work today and my perennial "to do" list has grown beyond all imagining. I SHOULD be doing many other things this morning but instead the dog and I are playing hooky for awhile, enjoying a nice, long walk.

A slight wind blows, just enough to cool my brow as the day warms up. The dog's tongue is lolling as she trots around checking out all the smells (reading her newspaper as my Mom would say). I worry sometimes about how many years we have left together but I'm not worrying this morning as she runs with a young dog's legs, face split wide in a grin.

Right now I am trying to cup this morning gently in my hands, to hold this moment in time in my memory, ready to take out at a moment's notice, on a day when I need a good memory. Life is so full of moments brimming with promise; moments when life is thick like honey with its sweetness.

We all have occasional dark days; times when life is stressful or unhappy, those times when we feel overwhelmed occasionally come to all of us. Days when a simple "How are you?" seems quite beyond responding to, these are the days when you need beautiful memories to hearten you.

Memories of days like today when your soul sings a pure high note and your spirit responds with recognition to an old friend.

A day like today when my beautiful daughter is planning to cook a delicious supper for the family.

A .day like today when my handsome teenage son smiled so sweetly at me as he left the house; the smile of that four year old I remember so well.

A day like today when my first thought on waking was the memory of a kiss on the cheek and a soft "have a nice day" from my husband as he left for work early.

Annie MacInnis

A day like today when I don't feel my age, when I feel everything is possible, when I feel life's richness is spread out before me.

All I need do is pause and look around me and seize these moments of pleasure, of walking through dew laden grass with the sun shining on my face, the breeze twirling past my brow and my dear four legged friend at my side .

I'll take up the reins of my today soon. I'll cross an item or two off that unending list, I'll get some work done, I'll give a 'lick and a promise' to the kitchen floor and through it all today I'll hold this feeling that life is good and today is a miracle I am glad to behold.

The Dancers

My husband and I are not big dancers, never have been. Oh in my younger years I danced as most youngsters do and loved going to dances but dancing is not high on my list of life skills or on my "to do before…" list.

Don't get me wrong. I love the feeling of waltzing with my husband. After thirty years together we fit. But mostly I prefer a waltz in my own living room in my bare feet to dancing in public.

So during the after dinner dance portion of the evening, we mostly sit at my husband's fancy Christmas party, me in my extravagant dress, he tall and handsome in a nice suit and we mostly watch other dancers. We appreciate the music, we enjoy people watching and before the night is out we will no doubt enjoy a waltz together but we will not turn any heads with our style.

As dancers approach the dance floor we like to speculate about who the dancers worth watching will be.

There are always a few guys that clearly fit into the Dirty Dancing/John Travolta/lounge lizard genre. This group is usually immediately recognizable by their flashy suits, the prime location they choose on the floor and the flourishes with which they arrive. Their companion is a mere accessory and the dance floor a means to an end.

There are always lots of serious dancer couples. They are there to work up a serious sweat, are having a REALLY good time and are there till they drop or the band takes a break. These dancers are dressed for action, suit coats discarded, dresses chosen for movement, drinks close to hand.

There are always a few couples who fit into the "we have taken dance lessons and look what we can do" group. For them, the dancing seems less about enjoying the music and each other's company and more about the invisible teacher grading their performances.

By far our favorite category is the ringers. They are hard to spot by their dress, their demeanor or their chosen floor location. One clue is that often they are unprepossessing and frequently the least likely looking to be incredible dancers. Typically they are middle aged or older. They are nicely dressed in a classy understated way; not the gorgeous young things you might otherwise be inclined to watch. There is no flash, no obvious technique. The man holds his companion's hand as they walk onto the dance floor. He doesn't look especially fit and maybe walks without grace but the moment he reaches the dance floor and takes his partner into his arms he morphs into Prince Charming. You can't take your eyes off him. He moves easily, smoothly, confidently. His companion follows him effortlessly. Their grace makes them a delight to watch. She is definitely Cinderella as she twirls about the floor dress sweeping gracefully around her legs.

If life was a movie the other dancers would fall back to the sidelines to watch in awe as the Prince deftly steers her around the floor. It is obvious they are meant for each other. It is obvious they have done this for a long time and know each other intimately.

After a couple of dances, they leave the dance floor and like super heroes once again return to their everyday selves – an older man slightly balding with a small paunch and a well groomed, somewhat stout matronly lady. Who would guess looking at them that they are "the couple to watch."

So you think you can dance?

Let's Chat

Math Class circa 1969

It was the first day of grade seven at my junior/senior high school. There were a few familiar faces in the crowds but many, many strangers. The day was exhausting and frightening but I thought I had made the first inroads towards some new friends.

I sauntered to my last class, math. Not my favorite subject by a long shot. The teacher, a Mr. Brown, had a fearsome reputation. My older brother, although typically not wont to spare me any passing pain or humiliation, had deigned to warn me to 'keep my head down' in Brown's class.

Mr. Brown was an older man, white haired with a brusque manner. He started roll call. I was debating the inherent coolness of a nonchalant "here" versus the absolutely correct 'present' when suddenly he paused, goggled at the sheet and shouted, MacInnis? Ann MacInnis!! Where are you? YOU! Do you have an older brother John? Oh my gawd, I taught him last year! You're Anthonys! Aren't your people from Kennetcook? Yes, your mother's the one that married the doctor over this way. My Gawd, when I taught the last of your mother's brothers and her sister math I swore I'd never teach another Anthony math ever again. And now here YOU are!! "he bellowed as he advanced down the aisle toward me. "WELL, how many more of you are there?!?"

I dared to hope that the floor would open up and swallow me then mumbled, "Three more after me, Sir."

He grimaced dramatically at the class. The rest of the class tittered ingratiatingly; glad his ire was directed elsewhere. He stalked back to the front of the class and the rest of the roll call was without incident.

I was mortified. When I got home I burst into the house and wailed at my mother, "Who is Cyril Brown and what did you ever do to him?"

My mother reared back in dismay at my first words. "Cyril Brown! He's not still teaching! Goodness he taught ME math!" Then she regaled me with some horror stories about when he was teaching at her school.

As always the problem seemed less insurmountable once I had talked about it with my Mom. Our talk didn't solve Mr. Brown's dislike of teaching math to Anthonys and their progeny nor did I trade teachers or get great at math that year.

The teacher and I toughed out the year in mutual dislike and in the process I learned a bit about enduring what you cannot change, doing your best under adverse circumstances and trying to see the humorous side of life whenever possible.

Thankfully such teachers are usually the exception to the rule. Although Mr. Brown dampened any spark of interest I might have had in math that year, I also had one of my favorite teachers ever. My English teacher was young, cool, smart, funny and nice. She more than made up for the curmudgeon in the math room.

Creamed peas on toast!?W#$%##^#^

Not nice fresh home grown peas in a beautiful béchamel sauce made with real cream; oh no! Not even frozen peas which would have at least lent a pleasing green shade to the whole confection; oh no! No, these were canned peas of that particular hue of greenish, grayish, brownish shade sometimes referred to as 'swamp green' (or worse).

A sauce made from powdered milk and flour added a particularly glutinous pasty texture to the sauce. Served on marshmallow-like Wonder bread that is prone to gluing itself tenaciously to the roof of your mouth unless, as in this case, it is toasted. But lest you think this made the meal more alluring, I can assure you the texture and consistency of the creamed peas and sauce only exacerbated the tendency of the bread to stick to the roof of your mouth.

This was my first job, living for one summer month about an hour's drive from home, boarding with a local family Sunday evening until Friday afternoon. In the days when 25 cents an hour (75 cents after midnight) got you a babysitter, I was earning the princely sum of $35 a week! It was a near fortune. For that magnificent salary all I had to do was be responsible for 135 elementary school children for eight hours a day while I taught them to swim!! Gee, sounds idyllic doesn't it?

As if that wasn't enough fun, the family I was boarding with served creamed peas on toast regularly. To this day I don't know if it was their favorite meal, or that they couldn't afford anything else, or they were trying to make enough money for a vacation out of what I was paying them. Although I lived with them for 4 weeks that summer I was fourteen, I don't remember their name, their house, how many kids they had only that execrable meal that we had too many times.

Maybe the harrowing days spent all alone minding those children within a few feet of a large lake just sapped my mind of all ability to retain information. Maybe the unfettered thrill of collecting all that wealth each Friday allowed me to forget the work week. Maybe the horror of those creamed peas suppers forced me to instinctively block out everything else that happened in that house.

Regardless, as this holiday season fast approaches, I have resolved that this Christmas all these years later, I will forgive and forget the appalling creamed peas on toast meals served me by that nameless family. So, to that long lost family that took me in, wherever you are I'd like to wish you PEAS ON EARTH (but definitely not creamed on my plate), AND GOOD WILL TO ALL MEN.

Secret Weapon

I had a blast from the past recently. I was visiting my friend and her new baby. When I accepted her offer of tea, she made me lovely tea in her china teapot. She made herself decaffeinated instant coffee in a mug.

As she poured boiling water on her instant coffee granules, a memory surfaced in the teeming morass that is my mind. I was whisked back through time to a morning when I, too, was subsisting on decaffeinated coffee.

On that fateful morning when I decided to kick over the traces of self-sacrificing sleep-deprived decaffeinated motherhood, the noise is deafening. The house looks a complete fright. I am all alone except for two small children. Saturday cartoons blare on the television. My daughter screeches with laughter as she pounds on a toy piano. The dog is barking in protest. The dishwasher thrums. My hair is awry and my face unwashed. Laundry and small treacherous toys surround me. Any minute my sick baby will wake up and want to nurse and puke again. My husband, lucky fellow that he is, long ago fled gladly to work.

I stand stock-still in the midst of this bedlam. I recognize all the warning signs. I am teetering on the brink of an unsightly meltdown. Suddenly, as I am striving for some semblance of self-control, I turn a corner in my mind. I am immediately calm. I am now undeterred by the prospect of another day filled with a cranky baby and an energetic toddler.

I have just realized I have a secret weapon and today I'm desperate enough to use it. It's not a grandmother or other family member or nanny or even an insane friend willing to temporarily take my place. It is not illegal drugs or even prescription help. It's not unlimited long distance phone time and a cordless phone. It is not Oprah or any other talk show. I haven't decided to run away or lock myself in the bathroom until my husband comes home.

My secret weapon is a small thing really. Something much of the world takes completely for granted. But to those of us who have been denied this everyday comfort for so long it looms before us like a mirage, tantalizingly out of reach. It is a boon to other people's days. It pours salve on bruised souls. It provides sustenance to sleep-starved bodies. Yes, *it* is caffeine-laced COFFEE!

Today I have decided to chuck 7 years of pregnancy and nursing induced caffeine-free sanctimoniousness and healthy living. That straw has broken this camel's back. This morning I will reenter the guilt-free ranks of those fortunate enough to kick start their mornings with real honest to goodness caffeine.

In mere moments, it seems, I hold in my hands…nirvana. Opiate of the tired parent, savior of a poor mother wakened to such a Saturday morning…a hot, fragrant, caramel-colored cup of coffee laced with extra cream, chock full of lots of caffeine and served in my best china mug now rests securely in my hands.

I savor the moment but not too long in case the baby wakes up. I raise the cup, inhale and take that first wonderful slug. AAAAHHHHH!!!!! Once again life flows in a rich thick stream as the bedlam in my house and in my head fades into the background.

Like the very best of Folgers and Juan Valdez, the Colombian coffee picker commercials I am effortlessly transported to ANOTHER WORLD. Petty, mundane things like so many mountains of laundry to wash, dry, fold and put away you'd think I was washing for a small country fade into unimportance.

I lean back in my chair with a large sigh of satisfaction as the caffeine races pell-mell through my body. I smile a world-weary, sympathetic smile for all those poor, harried mothers still soldiering on in the ranks of the caffeine prohibited, unheralded and unrewarded and without the comfort of even one cup of real caffeine to brighten their day.

Our children will never know the extent of the sacrifices we mothers have made on our children's behalf. To those of you still mired in the ranks of the caffeine-free, I salute you.

Clue

It was the sort of conversation that sends a shiver down a parent's spine.

My daughter had a friend over for her first sleepover at our house. The friend is a sweet little girl being brought up in a strict, very conservative household. It is clear to me that we are a family 'on trial' as suitable friends for this child.

My daughter, 11, her friend, 10, and my son, 7 were all in the living room watching the movie Clue. My kids had watched it a couple of times.

It's a fun movie, based on the old board game with all the classic characters, Mrs. Peacock, Miss Scarlet and Colonel Mustard. Murders occur, but the emphasis is on the murder weapon (the lead pipe, the noose...), the room (kitchen, conservatory, library) and the mysterious circumstances. There's no gore except for a little blood on Mr. Boddy's head. There are few adult references that might make another parent uncomfortable. In my opinion there's only one line that might engender further discussion for younger children. This occurs when one of the characters confesses that he is being blackmailed because he is a homosexual and works in an important government job. There is no further discussion and no attention is drawn to it.

The first time I watched the movie with my kids, I was prepared for questions regarding this line but the moment passed without comment from either of my children. My kids loved this movie and the many funny scenes in it. Over the next few weeks, they watched it several times. Never once did they raise the issue of why someone might be blackmailed for being homosexual so I had no occasion to give my delicate explanation to my children.

Never once until the night we had this child (in the midst of a very sheltered upbringing) visiting our house for the first time.

I was sitting relaxing at the kitchen table while the children indulged in those sleepover pre-requisites – chips, pop and a movie. I was reading a really good book (and indulging in just a few Friday night chips myself) when that part of my mind, which was unconsciously monitoring the activity in the living room, came suddenly to attention. With the movie on pause, the conversation was as follows:

[233]

"What is a homosexual?" asks the visiting child.

My son answers authoritatively, "it's someone who's not a man and not a woman. It's like a...a worm."

Silence in the living room. Aghast silence in the kitchen.

My mind staggers at the thought of discussing homosexuality on any level with this young visiting child from such a very religious family present.

I take the cowardly way out and stay sitting in my chair hoping they'll just put the movie back on.

Forlorn hope, of course.

After a moment's silence his sister's voice loudly and derisively says, "Not it's not! It's a man or woman who doesn't want to have children. If it's a guy, he'd rather live with other guys. If it's a girl, she'd rather live with other girls."

"No, it's not!" my son retorted passionately.
"Mmmmmooooommmmmm! Tell her."

I briefly consider slipping away to do laundry, but in the end do the responsible adult-in-charge thing.

I make myself walk into the living room but I go oh so reluctantly. I can't think of what to say and my mind reels at the prospect of having to report this conversation to the visiting child's parent tomorrow. "The girls had a good time and went to bed at a reasonable hour. They've had a good breakfast and, oh, yes, by the way, we all had a little talk about homosexuality and why, in the not too distant past, that lifestyle was not considered completely desirable by some sections of society." Yikes!!

Three eager little faces look toward me as I enter the room. My two children are waiting for me to settle the disagreement, the visiting child for illumination.

"Mom, tell her!" my son pleads.

I look at his passionate little face, his pride on the line in front of the older girls.

Let's Chat

I use a classic parenting technique that has stood me in good stead over the years. I stall for time.

"A worm?" I ask.

"Yeah," says my son, "or a creature like Godzilla. Godzilla doesn't need a mate to reproduce."

"Aaaaahhh!" I say, "Ahh, that's asexual. You're right Godzilla and worms are asexual. And you're correct, a creature that is asexual is a creature that doesn't need a mate to reproduce."

My son leans back smiling happily, vindicated before the older girls.

The girls sit, nonplussed, diverted by the unfamiliar notion of myriad Godzillas recklessly reproducing without benefit of marriage or romance.

I remain standing in the doorway in case required to answer more questions but after a moment's contemplation, everyone decides to resume watching the movie, the original question long forgotten.

Well, that seems to have gone well, I dared to hope.

I heave a very quiet, very grateful sigh as I slink back to the kitchen. I decide to reward myself for this quite stressful parenting moment with lots of chips and decide not to mention this incident at all to whichever parent does the pickup tomorrow.

[235]

Annie MacInnis

Good Housekeeping

I'm quite certain my mother never reeled in horror when an unexpected guest asked to go to the washroom or followed her to the kitchen. Her bathrooms and her kitchen are always well within acceptable cleanliness limits.

I'm not sure why housework seems such a challenge for me and much of my generation. Maybe because my generation spearheaded feminism and a renegotiation of household roles most of us now live with no clear assignment or acceptance of chores in families.

Feminism was all about choice, about women being able to choose a career if they so desired. But when so many women went out into the work world, housekeeping became a less respected role in life.

A well kept, well ordered, lovingly appointed house filled with the smells of home cooking in many cases became less a labour of love and instead became a matter of assignment or contracting out or family squabbles. Housekeeping became a burden relegated to evenings and weekends, a daily bone of contention in families.

When I decided to stay home with my children most people seemed to assume either I had no education that would afford me the opportunity to 'aspire to more' or that my husband earned so terrifically that we could afford to have a single wage earner.

In reality I willingly gave up a good career and we lived below the poverty line for the duration. I did not consider this lifestyle a sacrifice. Rather I felt blessed that we could manage (just) and that I had the skills to help us do so. I cooked from scratch, pinched pennies until they squeaked, shopped thrift, made do, reused, was creative and loved most every moment.

Yes, life would have been much easier if we had had more money but its lack did not make us miserable. During those years I developed skills that are second nature to me now. I'm good at economical grocery shopping, enjoy making meals from scratch and am an accomplished thrift shopper.

Cutting back this fall was not as frightening for me as for some. I know that we can live happily on much less than we have been

Let's Chat

in recent years. I know I have the skills to do this plus these days I am back to work and helping contribute financially.

I am already enjoying challenging myself to cook more frugally, to be more conscious about what needs to be used up and to cook creatively with what is in the house. But it is likely the cleaning part of housekeeping will continue to challenge me. I like the house to be tidy and clean but never felt I could justify paying someone else to do it nor seem to find the motivation to keep up completely. My mother would say I give the house "a lick and a promise" most of the time (as opposed to a proper cleaning).

I guess the lesson we all need to embrace these days is playing to our strengths (like cooking economically for me) and forgiving ourselves for our failings (living with a less than pristine house).

Clay Feet

This has been my year of clay feet and his summer of discontent.

I have a fourteen year old boy. Some days I awake to the dear little boy that has been a part of my life these many years but increasingly I wake up to a relative stranger. My every word is debated, dissected, disregarded and discarded. He doesn't go so far as to roll his eyes but I know he's doing a mental eye roll on a pretty steady basis when around me.

Every request is quibbled with. All in a relatively respectful but nevertheless somewhat patronizing attitude that indicates a passive forbearance overlaid with a lingering fondness for poor old, not very technologically adept, kind-hearted but not very in tune, Mom.

Seems only yesterday that I was his world and our days were spent with his small, warm hand curled tightly in mine as he gazed at me with those big brown eyes and talked to me about every important thing in his life. Only a heartbeat since his sweet breath fanned across my cheek as he lay limp with sleep in my arms, one small chubby arm looped around my neck. Only a moment since he was first laid in my arms after those long months, a son, my son. Only the blink of an eye since he first took steps toward me, since I hugged him goodbye the first day of school.

Now he is a young man. Sweet and loving as he mostly still is I can see I have fallen in his eyes. Or rather the scales have fallen from his eyes and he sees me now as fallible.

I am no longer omnipotent. I can no longer make it all better. Even worse I have discovered that I may not even be able to think of a helpful or useful comment when his heart is breaking or his life has gone awry or he has a big decision to make.

Sometimes I long for the old days when I had the power to banish mean children from our lives, to cure a bad day with a cuddle and some reading time together, to spend the day together from morning until dusk.

But most days I remind myself that like all moments of transition in life, this one is uncomfortable and unsettling. Nevertheless

Let's Chat

these moments of transition are also an opportunity for growth and change, if only I seize the chance.

So I struggle to find the new me (the mother of a young man; no longer the mother of a biddable little boy), to find and keep my balance in this new role, to adjust to the new him. I know in my heart of hearts that I'll love the new, more grown up him as much as I loved all the younger versions of him. I believe that this next phase of life as a parent will be as rewarding, as challenging, as illuminating as all the previous ones have been. I'm up for the job because it is my job – to keep loving him no matter what.

Cinderella

I'm sick and tired of picking up after everyone else in the house.

My daughter, who admittedly has never been excellent at picking up after herself, had a brief episode of keeping her room tidy after we bought new-to-her bedroom furniture last summer. We reorganized her room, turfed a lot of debris, and for an all too short yet happy hiatus I enjoyed the illusion that my lonely solitude as the sole tidier in the house had finally ended.

Alas, she has once again been drawn back to the dark (and predictably untidy) side by the duplicitous remainder of the household.

My son's room has long been (let's be real here, forever or at least since he was marginally mobile) a sinking morass of small precious objects, miscellaneous drawings and jottings now discarded and useless but not having actually made it as far as the conveniently placed wastebasket.

My husband, the other grown up in the house and, in theory, my obvious ally in the boons of keeping a tidy house and certainly the first to lose his cool when he can't find something he needs NOW is one of the worst offenders in the household. His coat rarely makes it to a hanger in the closet by the door. Instead he walks past this closet and chucks his coat on a chair in the living room. (Do you think that's like a prerequisite for becoming a husband? Is it in a secret codebook known only to guys?) He is also guilty of leaving phone books on the counter when finished with them and emptying pockets full of odds and ends onto counters or bureau tops and leaving the detritus there in perpetuity.

In the early days of our relationship long, long ago I let these habits slide as a gesture of how much in love we were. Then for many years I withstood these habits for the sake of marital harmony.

Had I but known that his offspring would follow in his footsteps and I would become Cinderella to their wicked ways I might have spoken up sooner.

The last straw however was one day recently when I was picking up clutter and preparing to sweep now that the others had left the house. As I trailed unenthusiastically about the house

Let's Chat

returning stray items to their designated spots I suddenly realized I was being subtly yet insidiously undermined in my efforts.

The dog, who usually takes my side in all family disputes knowing who shells out her food and provides regular walks, was carefully replacing her toys about the house as fast as I tidied them away.

What's a poor, beleaguered wife and mother to do? Shut up and forever tidy the bed I've made for myself while the rest of the family continues to swan around the house oblivious to the clutter?

What I wouldn't give for a fairy godmother with a wand and some "Bippity Boppity Boo" magic.

Church

It is Sunday morning. I am in a beautiful church with my wonderful daughter. The choir is singing. I should be happy it is a lovely spring day. I should be feeling grateful and blessed to have a daughter who wants to go to church and who wants me to come along.

I do not! I do not feel grateful. I do not feel blessed. I certainly don't feel prayerful or reverent or even calm. I am standing stony faced. I can feel my mouth has a grim set and I am holding the bulletin in a death grip. I am surprised people aren't staring at me and that my hair isn't crackling and sparking with electricity because I feel so irritated and put upon.

It has been too busy a week. The house is beyond messy; it is a fright. There are almost no groceries so I need to go shopping after church and laundry has piled up to epic proportions and the beds need changing and...

My husband came home cranky from work last night and said something snarky to me and instead of letting it go and waiting for him to get a grip and apologize, I stewed all evening and woke up feeling furious and...

I am radiating irritation and my family scuttled around me this morning with hunched shoulders and that definitely did not help and...

The dog petitioned me repeatedly to take her for an exercise walk instead of going to church and part of me really would have preferred to go blow off some steam in the fresh air but I was just too irked to try to make myself feel better yet and...

My daughter couldn't find one of her favorite earrings and consequently we were late leaving the house to go to church and I HATE being late for anything and...

The other child did nothing to irritate me other that he was a slugabed and hadn't even gotten out of bed by the time we left (and we're talking Protestant church not early morning mass!) and...

On the drive to our downtown church, the road with no warning is blocked off due to construction and our usual lot is completely

[242]

Let's Chat

inaccessible so I have to trail around downtown trying to find another lot that won't cost me a fortune and...

When we finally get to church we are scandalously late and I can hardly hear the choir because the internal dialogue in my head is DROWNING OUT EVERYTHING.

It is definitely one of those days! Thankfully, I don't often feel this way - where everything seems irritating and hateful and designed to add insult to injury.

I look around the church and try to absorb some of the serenity. I remind myself that this angst is in my head, that there is no conspiracy between my husband, my children, the dog, and the Calgary Roads Department (to name a few possible culprits) to irritate and to frustrate me today.

I take a long deep breath and recall my daughter's wise words as we race walked to the service "You seem kind of stressed today, Mom. Just tell us what you want us to do and we'll help."

I take one, more, deep, cleansing breath and remind myself that no one enjoys a martyr. I consciously let all the irritation and self righteousness go, gently squeeze my daughter's hand and smile at her in apology. I turn my attention to the uplifting music and the minister's always thought-provoking sermon while making a short mental list of chores for everyone except the Roads department.

Annie MacInnis

Yum, chocolate

The chocolate fountain was awesome. This was the first one I'd seen close up. No one else seemed as amazed and intrigued as I did. In fact, they were downright blasé.

Oh well, maybe they all travel in these rarified circles all the time, attending soirees nightly where wondrous buffet tables are run of the mill. I, on the other hand, have just reentered the working world from a long sojourn in the land of Rice Krispie squares.

Well, a pox on all these strangers for their mundane approach to life. Their nonchalance didn't faze me one iota. I've never been shy of making a bit of a fool of myself. I believe in grabbing life experiences with both hands to ensure maximum enjoyment. Mind you, this time I did hang back and watch for a bit to determine the general protocol regarding usage.

I made a couple of circuits of the buffet table sampling all manner of delicious small treats while observing the chocolate miracle and it's usage only honing in on the fountain when I had the drill down pat.

Take a wooden kebab stick, spear a piece of fruit, dip it briskly into the bottom segment of the fountain until coated generously with dripping chocolate, enjoy.

So, clearly, the key issue here, was not getting a trail of chocolate down my front in the process. Otherwise, the whole thing looked a cinch.

I speared a piece of pineapple, drenched it with chocolate, zipped a napkin underneath and ferried the fruit to my mouth without incident. Excellent! Definitely tastes like more.

Several pieces of fruit later, I'd taken the edge off sufficiently to be more intrigued now by how this contraption worked. When you dipped your fruit into that bottom compartment, you could see inside that part of the waterfall of chocolate. So the question was, could you poke your fruit in the upper waterfalls? Surreptitious experimentation revealed you could not.

Just then, I noticed a child watching the fountain. A little girl, maybe five, very neatly and properly dressed.

Let's Chat

I turned to her with enthusiasm, "Isn't this chocolate fountain so cool? Have you tried it yet?"

The little girl looked silently (and possibly a bit disparagingly) at me, then turned to her also very properly dressed, obviously capable of sucking the fun out of any experience parents and said, "That strange woman is speaking to me!"

"That's alright dear," said the mother, glaring at me as though I had touched her daughter inappropriately, "It's always okay to talk to a stranger if Mummy and Daddy are here."

The father followed up by drawing the child carefully away from the chocolate fountain and from me as though drawing their coattails away from a noisome spill, saying, "Here you are, sweetheart, here's some lovely blue cheese on a nice cracker."

God spare me from the naysayers in life. What is the point of having a child who goes into ecstasies over blue cheese?

I guess the whole experience harks back to my mother's words to live by, "If I weighed 20 pounds less, I might be cranky!"

Annie MacInnis

Chicken for lunch

My father sat down at the table for lunch. He took a long, grateful draught of his tea then commented how good lunch looked. My mother began serving the rest of us.

My younger brother called down that he'd be right along, that he was just finishing feeding one of his baby chicks. (He raised birds and competed at shows with them.) This was either an orphaned chick or one who was doing poorly and needed "building up", there were lots of both.

My father asked us what we'd been up to all morning and we competed to tell him. He managed to get a couple of bites under his belt before a howl came from my brother's room. My brother came thundering down the stairs skidding into the kitchen with a baby chick in his hands, gasping, "Dad, Dad, this chick just aspirated a bit of bread and milk! It's choking! It can't breathe.

My father, the doctor in a large rural practice, did not turn a hair. He swallowed his bite as he held out his hand for the chick. After a quick assessment of the situation, he gave a few quick taps on its back to no avail, then laid the chick down quickly, pried its beak open and gave it several careful little puffs of air. The chick coughed up a small spec of bread, gave a small, shuddering ragged breath then struggled to stand up. It stood ankle deep in mashed potatoes and blinked it's eyes at all of us then stepped delicately over to the edge of the plate and into my brother's "Are You My Mother?" hands.

My brother hurried off back to the nursery with his charge. The rest of us returned to our meal and conversation. All except for my father.

My father looked consideringly at his lunch. There was a small indentation in his potatoes where the lifesaving procedure had taken place bracketed on one side by small bird footprints leading to the edge of the plate. He pursed his lips, gave a very small sigh then picked up his plate, passed it to my mother with a rueful smile and asked, "Is there any chance of fresh mashed potatoes?" We all laughed and luckily there were extra potatoes.

I wonder whether the thought that without my father's fortuitous presence that lunchtime the chick might not have survived affected my brother's choice of profession? Nowadays that

Let's Chat

brother is a Stars paramedic who can resuscitate his own chicks were the need ever to arise!

Annie MacInnis

It wasn't my fault

Yes, I was the driver of the car and yes, I had promised faithfully to be very careful, as this was a brand new car (less than two weeks old).

I will also admit that I was the driver of my father's old car two weeks ago when it was involved in a bit of a dust up. Well, actually more than a little dust up as, actually, the car was totaled. However, on the up side we now owned a nice new car that I was driving on that fateful, but lovely summer evening.

Left to my own devices, I'm certain that I would never have considered driving on a beach. However, my boyfriend's mother was taking an art class and she specifically asked us to go get her a bunch of beach stuff for a still life or some such arty thing.

We drove off to the nearest beach and you know how it goes with teenagers. The beach looked such a long way away. Moreover, we really were not very keen on being sent on assignment when we had places to go and a life of our own to pursue. It seemed completely reasonable to drive down onto the beach to save time. It was quite safe and practical to drive on the firm packed wet sand and it was sure a blast zipping around there with the Atlantic Ocean going on forever just past our windows.

But the charm of the ocean so near at hand quickly paled when I veered a little too close to the dry sand and got stuck. Attempts by my boyfriend to push us out failed but the whole outing still seemed a bit of a lark.

Then we noticed that the tide was coming in and fairly quickly at that. We ran a long way down the beach to some distant people and brought them back to help push. By that time, in that unpitying, relentless way that oceans have, the water was lapping at the wheels.

I was beginning to feel a bit panic stricken when finally we managed, with the extra manpower, to get the car moving. With water spraying high to one side of the car we raced the tide the length of the beach and got onto the dirt road back to civilization.

We grudgingly delivered the beach bits and bobs to my friend's mother and borrowed all manner of cleaning supplies to remove the evidence of our beach adventure.

Let's Chat

Although the story made for amusing telling among our friends that night I was pretty sure that even my easy going, usually understanding father would not take kindly to the thought of how close I came to trashing a second car in two weeks.

Compounded by the thought of how close I came to having to explain how this car was NOT JUST DESTROYED but, actually, LOST AT SEA, I was certain this story was best left untold until now.

Hopefully the statute of limitations has expired on this story, Dad.

Annie MacInnis

I yelled

Well, all right, I yelled a couple of times.

The children had been endlessly hounding my husband and me to go camping. My husband was in a busy phase at work and (lucky him) had a great out to say he could not possibly go camping.

I'd been trying for some weeks to fob the kids off with the prospect of our upcoming vacation with grandparents, and, in the meantime, a steady round of fun activities with Mom like swimming, Science Centre, etc. etc. All to no avail in the end.

Finally, one evening, beaten down by the children's long-suffering faces brought on by the knowledge that most of their friends had already gotten their camping fix, I succumbed. I announced I would take the children camping myself.

Now, while I consider myself to be a competent person and have taken the children camping solo on several occasions, I admit that camping is not my thrill and our camping ventures have not been without minor calamities.

Once I forgot the tent and we had to sleep in the car. Once I forgot the axe and my husband had to fetch it so we could have fire.

On this trip, I was determined to have everything I needed. I made lists all evening. (On every previous camping trip, I had resolved to make a comprehensive list of camping prerequisites upon returning home but had never actually followed through.)

The next day I laid out the supplies for a visual check. All morning I packed and schlepped to and from car, basement, bedrooms and kitchen.

I harried the children "Get dressed, eat breakfast, brush your teeth, wash your face, pack your own stuff, get dressed, eat breakfast, brush your teeth, wash your face, pack your own stuff..." For the most part, they ignored me, preferring to let me remind them later while they focused on more important tasks.

Camping in my rather ancient '83 Toyota Supra with two kids and one largish dog must of necessity be minimalist. Making room even for critical items becomes an exercise in 3-D visualization coupled with serious cramming.

Finally, we sallied forth after a really fairly small meltdown on my part when I called, "Let's go!" and found unwashed, undressed, unfed, unpacked, unhelpful, unrepentant children. That's when I yelled.

This minor set-to cleared the air nicely. I felt quite refreshed and the children were subdued so the drive to the campground was pleasant.

Unfortunately, this harmony was relatively short-lived. At the campground I discover I have forgotten the axe (again!), bathing suits, towels, raincoats, a paring knife, dish pan and bug spray. I grit my teeth and start scrounging abandoned kindling from empty campsites.

By early evening, it is raining lightly. I try to keep the children occupied with books and card games under the tarp over the picnic table. They repeatedly find reasons to venture out and cavort in the rain. I get testy about damp clothes with them; feel guilty about spoiling their fun, and then grizzle to myself about how little I like camping.

The next morning I am over the trauma of our foray into the wilds. The dog and I enjoy the fire in peace as the children sleep on. I have two cups of coffee with cream. I am a happy camper!

We have a lovely day. The children spend the morning foraging for beer bottle caps and negotiating trades amicably. They swim. We explore. Meals are eaten without complaint. We are a harmonious family.

Then, just after supper, a massive hailstorm virtually covers the ground with white. Luckily, this only lasts about 20 minutes. Unluckily, the hail is replaced by heavy rain. After 2 hours huddling under the tarp listening to me whine about how much I hate camping in the rain, the children concede and agree that we can go home.

By the time I manage to gather up all our supplies and stuff them higgledy-piggledy into the car there is very limited visibility from within but even the dog climbs chastened and grateful into her considerably smaller allotted space.

On the drive home, we are rewarded for our disappointment with an hour-long double rainbow display well worth the trip.

Upon our return, I think with renewed resolve about making that comprehensive camping packing list. I'll do it in just a minute. Although maybe I'll wait until…

Let's Chat

Camping reprise

I hesitate to say this in the land of, *"Well of course we're still going camping! It's the May Long weekend [Labour Day weekend/or anywhere in between]. We always go now. We have reservations. We're meeting friends. Snow/rain/cold weather is immaterial"* but actually I don't love camping.

Oh there are aspects of it I do like somewhat – like lots of time with the kids and the dog gets really tired out but for me the sheer drudgery of the packing/unpacking the car casts a pall on the experience.

Although I am usually an organized person I can't seem to develop a workable system for going camping. Although I aspire to being a minimalist camper and make lists in secret (in case I decide to bail due to bad weather or whatever) on departure day I am always having to jettison items for lack of space and still have a car that's packed to the scuppers yet always missing small critical items.

On departure day my children sense my stress level rising and ratchet up their silliness/bugging each other/impervious to requests for help meters until they are driving me berserk and I'm considering screeching, "That's it! I'm not taking you wretches anywhere! You can drink coke and watch videos and play computer until your eyes fall out and I could care less! !!?@#$?*!!**!!" Then, just as I am about to reach critical mass, like the accomplished children that they are, they power down, act chastened and help just enough so that I continue to schlep.

Camping isn't really my husband's thrill either so between work and convenient weather excuses he usually manages to weasel out of most camping trips. I, on the other hand, usually end up going out at the behest of my children who pine to be 'out there' way more often that I do.

Mind you, I have gotten marginally better at this camping thing. I've only forgotten the tent once and now that I have a really good axe life is much easier out there.

The axe is courtesy of my dear husband who, on his first trip out with us, reared back in horror when I suggested he might like to cut up some wood with the small rusty hatchet I handed him.

"Where's your axe?" He demanded.

"Well I've been making do with this hatchet I found," I said.

"You've never been cutting wood with that!" He declared.

"Well no," I admitted, "actually what we usually do is scour all the empty sites as soon as we arrive for any leftover kindling and split wood others have left behind and we use that. And if anybody packs up their site and leaves while we're here we scoot right over in case they left any kindling.

"What?!?!?!?" he yelled. "What kind of unreliable, ridiculous, furtive way to operate is that? Not much wonder you don't like camping! What other foolishness am I going to come across out here?"

So now I have a lovely sharp axe to take with us and we are quite self-sufficient wood-wise.

When camping I always try to focus on the positive aspects of being there in the hope these will obviate the deficiencies. But somehow eating the nice meals I've planned, spending extra time with my kids and being closer to nature never quite seems to make up for the noisy neighbors/bad sleeps/bugs/cold mornings/lack of nice bubble baths/rain/hail/cooler of melting ice.

I keep remembering one of my earliest camping experiences. My mother is standing in the rain holding an umbrella and boiling eggs. I'm huddled with my father and my two brothers and two sisters in the tent trailer doorway watching her.

My mother turns to my father and says with no heat at all in her voice but with that "I'll only say this once but you'd better believe I'm incredibly serious" voice, "Ross, there'd better be a cottage on this land by next summer." And there was.

Maybe that's what bugs me most about camping. What I most want to do when out camping is experience the satisfaction of turning to someone and saying, "You'd better get some land and get a cabin on it pronto buster because this is my last time out!"

Do as I say children. Not as I do

My husband and I had a minor squabble early one Saturday morning. The spat was not serious; just one of those stupid moments of irritation when you rub each other the wrong way and say so. As a long married couple we were wise enough to take a deep breath, apologize to each other and forgive our mutual lapse so that equanimity was quickly restored.

Nevertheless, as I walked to the kitchen, I was feeling a little bit shattered and sorry for myself to have started out my weekend this way.

It had been a fairly busy week. In addition to all the usual stuff that needed doing in an ordinary week, the addition of one sick kid, one ratty kid and a small crisis brewing at work had left me a bit stressed out.

After a few moments of self indulgence, I morally bucked myself up. I resolved not to let this inauspicious start to my day totally derail me or ruin everyone's day (for as we all know a mother in a bad mood infects the whole house).

After all it was Saturday morning and a whole weekend lay before me still untrammeled. I decided I would laze around and try to recoup my good mood. A leisurely second cup of coffee while reading the whole newspaper would go a long way to restoring my equanimity.

A half hour later everything was fine and harmony seemed restored to the house for about five minutes until the caffeine and sugar kicked in. In the process of enjoying my paper and a few too many cups of coffee I had fallen off the wagon and eaten an excessively large piece of birthday cake for breakfast.

Now I did rationalize that it was good, homemade from scratch cake, baked with eggs and all manner of real ingredients nevertheless it was an overly generous slice of chocolate cake with a thick lashing of chocolate frosting on top of three (two more than my usual) cups of coffee.

Before I could stop myself or even rein myself in a tad, I burdened my husband with the news that we needed to repaint the living room and to replace the missing mirror in my son's wardrobe, did up an exhaustive packing list for March break

[255]

vacation (still a month hence) then realized I had a terrible headache.

What is that well worn phrase of my husband's again? Oh yes, "I don't always do what I know."

I happen to know from bitter experience (because I am an adult who has had many years in which to test this theory) that a whack of coffee plus a dollop of sugary baking first thing in the morning is not of benefit to me nor to most people around me. I am encouraged to talk way, way too much and to plan too vociferously. The end is always the same; crash and burn.

By 10 am I had taken an Advil and gone back to bed to sleep off the excess.

See the happy bride smiling

It's wedding season. Cars festooned with decorations (see the happy bride smiling!) are abundant. Parks are littered with wedding parties posing for photographs.

Ah, it brings back such memories. Not of my own wedding mind you, but of my bridesmaiding days. In my late teens, in my prime for being a bridesmaid, my mother and I once attended two weddings on consecutive weekends. They were the last straw.

My older, city-bred cousin was the bride at a posh city wedding. I was honoured to be asked but I was completely out of my league with these older, sophisticated girls. For hours they discussed the wedding, the men in the wedding party, the wedding night, their dresses, hair and makeup. They were in a tizzy that I was too young to understand. I was not nervous before the wedding, just uncomfortable in the midst of so many city people in a much fancier dress than I had ever worn.

On the drive home I was never so thankful to be back in the bosom of my own sane family and away from all that city fanciness. Until the next weekend and the next wedding.

This was a very different wedding featuring a college friend and a small town. Decorating the church and setting tables for the reception we were plagued by an ongoing row between the bride and groom. The groom was spending the day out of the line of fire with various languishing male friends at the Legion imbibing because the bride was mad. The bride claimed to only be angry because the men folk were at the Legion.

The crisis atmosphere deepened when the power was discovered to be off at the Legion Hall. It was a sweltering day. We had to hope the salads would survive the wait.

I was dressed in a horrendous pastel gathered empire waistline puffed short-sleeved dress that unattractively accentuated my already overabundant bosom. A large wide brimmed matching hat surmounted this awful creation. We stood for hours in the heat at a high Anglican ceremony, which was not shortened one whit due to heat or mortification.

At the reception the bride and groom snapped at each other under their breath as we all ate possibly poisonous salads.

[257]

Annie MacInnis

That night I told my mother I believed these were cautionary experiences. I vowed not to participate in such an affair ever again, except as a blameless fringe participant arriving in time to enjoy oneself.

I kept my vow, getting married in a wonderful small Valentine's Day wedding at my parent's house with a wedding cake made by family, local moonshine, fireworks, and bagpipes,

I walked down the stairs from the bedroom I grew up in on my Dad's arm into my parent's living room as my Mom played "Here Comes the Bride".

Thank you Mom and Dad for the wedding of MY dreams.

Oatmeal Brown Bread

My hands sink into the soft, warm dough. I take a long slow breath and stare sightlessly out the kitchen window, looking inward rather than at the world outside. My thoughts slow to a faint, background murmur. My hands know what to do as I knead the last of the flour into the dough, turning, and then sinking my fists, gathering and turning the dough again.

This is memory bread, meant to comfort a friend whose mother has died. As I hold the warm dough in my hands, inert like a small sleepy baby exuding comfort from it's very warmth and heaviness my thoughts turn to mothers and daughters and cooking. I send good wishes to my friend's mother on her road to heaven.

I place the dough gently in my big old bread bowl greased with real butter. I put a clean tea towel over the top and set the bowl in the slightly warmed oven to proof.

In a while I turn out the risen bread to knead again, my hands remembering instinctively how to roll two balls of dough at once. I place the dough in my old greased bread pans and cover them again for the second rise.

When they finally come out of the oven, the loaves are crusty brown, the tops glisten as I brush butter on them. The smell of hot bread fills the kitchen.

I wrap the hot bread in a clean tea towel and add a bottle of my jam and a card to my offering.

A loaf of bread, jam and some words of comfort. Nothing fancy, but I know from my own experience the warm feeling I get when I know my friends are thinking of me during rough times.

Delivering comfort food and support to friends and neighbors during times of crisis, illness and bereavement is a time honored way to practice charity, to help those around you and to feel great yourself.

Annie's friend Lynn's Oatmeal Molasses Brown Bread

Pour 3 cups boiling water over 2 cups uncooked oatmeal and ¼ cup shortening. Let stand 20 minutes, stirring occasionally.

Meanwhile dissolve 2 teaspoons of white sugar in 1 cup of lukewarm water.

Sprinkle 2 tablespoons of yeast over water. Let stand 10 minutes then stir briskly with a fork.

Stir in 2/3 cup fancy molasses and 1 teaspoon salt.

Cool to lukewarm then add softened yeast to oatmeal mixture.

Beat in 2-½ cups white flour. Beat vigorously

Gradually add 5-6 more cups of flour working in the last by hand.

Turn dough onto floured surface and knead about 8-10 minutes.

Shape into ball, place in greased bowl, cover with a clean tea towel and let rise in a warm place until doubled (about 1 ½ hours).

Punch down. Shape into four loaves. Grease tops. Cover again.

Let rise until doubled (about 1 hour).

Bake at 400 for 30-35 minutes. Grease tops when you remove from the oven.

(This recipe makes three good sized loaves so there's enough for giving and some left for eating hot at home.)

The Boogie Man

Some years back I received a call from a lovely sounding woman. She indicated that we had met briefly at a mutual friend's party. She said that our mutual friend had spoken highly of my daughter. She said that she was looking for a babysitter for her six year old son for that Saturday.

Although I had been at my friend's house only the day before to pick up my son from a birthday party and although this woman had an unusual name, I didn't remember meeting her. However since I'm terrible at remembering names, I didn't concern myself.

I said I would leave my daughter a note to call her and that if my daughter was unable to baby-sit we could recommend one or two friends who might be able to instead.

I copied out a legible note for my daughter and threw away the scribbled scrap of paper I'd started with.

When my daughter got home I gave her the note. There was no phone number. I was sure I'd written down the number originally but rather than rummage through the garbage I called my friend.

After I made my request, there was a longish silence on the phone. Then my friend said, "I don't know anyone by that name and there was no six year old boy at the party!"

A thrill of horror swept through me. The boogie man (or woman)!

I had to sit down. My friend and I agreed my daughter should NOT baby-sit nor should we give the names of any friends should this PERSON call back again. We talked a while longer about how weird and scary this was. I told my daughter why I did not want her to call this person back.

The next day the person called again. She still sounded nice and normal but instead of challenging her, I was abrupt. No my daughter could not baby-sit. No, her friends were unavailable too. Goodbye.

When my husband got home that night, I told him the whole sinister scenario. I expected him to rear back at the mere thought of some nefarious plot directed at his precious daughter. Instead, he looked at me speculatively with a 'you can be a tad slow witted at times' look and said, "Do you suppose you met this

[261]

woman at our other (with the same name) friend's party just after Christmas?"

Ooops! Oh, yeah, that party, that friend. I called my other friend by that name and confirmed she had passed on our number.

Oh, @@$*@$(). I was flummoxed and embarrassed at the furor I'd created. Define sheepish, that's me. Who knew that beneath my usually reasonable, everyday surface there lurked a hysterical mother seeing the boogie man under every bush? Some days parenting seems to be just one long series of mortifying humiliations after another.

I asked my friend to make my apologies to her friend and indicate that although the mother was a nutcase, the daughter was still a good bet for a babysitter for another Saturday night.

A Blessed Event

A friend of mine recently announced she is expecting a baby in the very near future.

When referring to a woman who is expecting a baby, my mother always says they are "blessed-eventing." I have always loved that expression. Somehow it totally sums up the immeasurable, inexpressible feeling of joy, the sense of faith in the future, the helpless trust in the miracles your body is performing daily, the feeling of experiencing the world through new eyes, the new tenderness of your heart and in your feelings, as though you are now living your life closer to creation, at a deeper, more basic level than in the days before you became a cradle of life.

Watching my friend's tenderness as she lay one hand delicately on her swelling stomach, I recalled how I loved being pregnant. Oh, there were some nasty moments now and then and some scary and painful moments even prior to the birth itself but through it all I was always amazed at the sense of destiny I felt as my babies grew and moved ever closer to the moment when I would, God willing, hold them safe in my arms.

I was blessed to experience this joy twice in my life. Now, many years hence, with teenagers underfoot, I looked back across the years for a moment with a pang of remorse that this wonderful experience was forever behind me.

Then I smacked myself upside the head mentally. I went home gratefully to my two dear teenagers reminding myself that, for every time there is a season and…thankfully, as much as I adored the experience, my childbearing days are gratefully behind me.

I also reminded myself that the thrill and sense of wonder I felt when pregnant actually paled in comparison to how I felt the first time I held my babies in my arms. The first time you hold your child is the first time you hold your child regardless of whether you have borne your babies yourself, or adopted them newborn or later on. A friend of mine who has two adopted children says she finds it hard to remember that they have not always been hers because life without them is unimaginable.

The joy, pain, fear, and wonder that come with loving and raising a child can make you feel overwhelmed sometimes but also blessed. Watching your child grow and become a being apart from you is so momentous, so wondrous that you are forever changed.

No matter the age of your children these feelings persist below the surface of mundane, petty, day to day aggravations like homework, laziness, sauciness, etc.

Parenting is truly a "blessed event", Mom. It is a time of inexpressible joy, a leap of faith in the future, a trust in miracles, experiencing the world through someone else's eyes, a forever tenderness of your heart and in your feelings, for this new life growing and changing before your eyes.

Belly Buttons

Okay, I admit it. I'm over-the-hill fashion wise.

I can still spot some relatively cool clothes for my twelve-year-old daughter. I own a couple of pairs of bell type bottom pants and a pair of jeans with rickrack decorations on the bottom and have succumbed to a couple of polyester shirts but it's becoming increasingly obvious that I am no longer anywhere near the cutting edge of cool fashion anymore.

At least age and life experience have allowed me to realize I should not consider anything in the way of low-slung jeans. My first pair of purple velvet hip hugger bell-bottoms was a fashion error obvious to all except my pudgy thirteen-year-old self.

Nowadays I mostly wear what suits my body and my persona. I view most young people's fashion trends with an amused, indulgent eye and adopt the occasional mild trend. But there are some trends that really mystify me.

The current prevalence among girls is for short tops and low-slung bottoms worn with thong underwear showing and exposing the tummy, slash belly button area and for boys wearing bagging jeans with the waistband of their underwear deliberately on display.

I obviously date myself when I say that "my generation" was relatively careful NOT to expose those areas of our anatomy unnecessarily.

Any boy seen deliberately walking around with his underwear showing above the waist band of his jeans would have been shunned by his peers, jeered at by smaller children and no doubt older respectable women of the town would have felt compelled to take his mother to task for such slatternly disregard for her child's behavior.

A girl seen walking around with any aspect of her undergarments showing, let alone displaying the wearing of 'stripper' underwear would be taken aside personally by all manner of well-meaning friends, elders and teachers and would nevertheless have her reputation besmirched forever. Her mother would appear in public with trepidation and her father would rail against the fates in the privacy of his own home.

[265]

Annie MacInnis

Exposure of the tummy area was generally avoided unless one were washboard flat and flaunting their lucky genes in a bikini at the beach or pool.

But nowadays the sight of exposed saggy, bulgy basically unattractive adolescent and older stomachs everywhere confronts us.

Now I'm not advocating that all of us without the boon of perfect bodies cower in shame inside long-sleeved high-necked tent dresses. I dress in sleeveless shirts even though my arms are no longer as firm as they once were and occasionally wear slinky dresses even though my tummy is less than flat and like wearing shirts that are a little snug for some people's taste. But my tummy is always respectably clothed and hidden from the human eye except in the privacy of my own home.

I guess the generation gap these days is to be found within the distance between a bulgy tummy sporting today's choice of underwear and the owner's jeans and tops!

Wash your hands

It was exhilarating. My heart was instantly pounding.

It was startling. I staggered for a moment and braced my feet.

It was exfoliating. My skin was actually rippling a bit.

It was incredibly noisy but wow! Was it efficient!

After years of gritting my teeth each time I go into a public washroom, it was a joy to experience a washroom that was such a marvel of modern technology and design.

Usually I treat trips into public washrooms as though I am entering a typhoid ward in a pre-penicillin era. I handle my purse and coat with particularly careful regard to them not ending up inadvertently on the floor. I wince as I touch germ-laden taps or stand fruitlessly waving my hands under automatic taps that refuse to turn on. Often endeavoring to glean the last scraps of soap from at least one functioning dispenser is an added insult.

Washing vigorously for the requisite two rounds of Happy Birthday, usually results in me promising myself yet again to come up with some other song for a change. Getting a modicum of paper towel from the dispenser using my elbow, turning off the germ-laden tap, then struggling with the paper towel dispenser yet again for more to dry my hands is irritating and frustrating. The task is often complicated by being faced with the dilemma of only a hand dryer so how do I turn off the tap without re-infecting myself.

So, imagine my initial surprise and pleasure in this public washroom when it was clean and there was lots of nice soap and hot water. Rinsing my hands under the automatic tap (no quandary about getting it turned off) I was smiling until I turned and saw, with resignation, no paper towel dispenser. Only one innocuous hand dryer was mounted on the wall. Fat lot of help that will be if the washroom has more than one occupant I thought as I stepped unwittingly in front of the dryer. Planning on the usual lame attempt to get my hands dry and finishing the job on the sides of my pants, I waved my hands hopefully under the automatic dryer.

Instantly the noise was deafening and the blowing air a fierce gale. I felt like I was in a cartoon or a science fiction movie. If

[267]

anyone had looked at me, I am sure my hair was blowing backward and I was leaning as though into a strong wind. My hands were thoroughly dry, both sides (even between my fingers) in about 5 seconds!! I kid you not.

What with the noise and strong winds, I did feel a bit as though I was in a spaceship taking off for other worlds. This flight of fancy combined with the experience itself left me feeling faintly bemused as I exited this marvel of modern technology. I opened the door a bit cautiously just in case I was exiting into another dimension.

Thankfully, I was back where I started no worse for the wear, but totally impressed with that public washroom..

When I recounted my story the next day to my kids, I laughed and said I could write a story about that. My kids laughed and said you can't write a story about a hand dryer can you?

Watch me.

Bathing with Dinosaurs

When I became a parent I thought I was prepared for the emotional and physical changes parenthood would bring. I think that generally I have met the challenges of giving birth, nursing, sleeplessness, carrying a child most of the day, and performing all bathroom functions with a chattering/whining/fighting audience within inches of me.

But despite all the wondrous joys of parenting (especially the "I love you's", the tight hugs, and the times when they make you proud); the lack of breaks and other adults, the endless chatter (pretend that you're a baby mouse and I'm an alligator and then you say… and then I say…and then you say…) the never-ending accommodating (I didn't want my toast cut in triangles, I wanted squares, I don't want my red boots, I want my yellow boots, I wanted to be the leader), the constant physical and emotional contact can occasionally become too much. I've learned the hard way that as a stay-at-home parent you have to be vigilant at squeezing in minute moments that restore you and allow you to make it to the children's bedtime with some ragged remnants of your sanity still intact.

A case in point: I have been a calm, patient, organized model mother all day. We have made crafts, played outside, baked muffins, read books, and eaten healthy meals. We are happy, exercised and well-fed. We are proud of ourselves. I am feeling so content and indulgent I agree to bathe with my two pre-school children.

In the beginning all is well. We are crowded but happy. The children play separately on either side and I sit squished but lulled into false security by a few moments to read in relative, damp peace.

Suddenly one child leans over to hug me. With the competitiveness inbred in every sibling, the other instantly hugs me from her side. They smile possessively, challengingly across my chest at each other.

I shoo them away, gently admonishing them. Within moments they are back. Inevitably a small hand strays across to touch the other's side of me. The situation is fraught with the signs of imminent sibling warfare. Again, I gently, patiently, calmly try to direct their attention back to their respective bath toys but it is too late.

Annie MacInnis

The seeds of a good fight have been sown; their blood is up.
Within moments they are back, each with a hard snouted plastic
dinosaur. The dinosaurs eye each other impassively, then the
children slowly, deliberately hug me.

With the lightening speed so common to this stage of a sibling
fight (and so absent from mealtime and getting dressed) the
dinosaurs are pecking at each other. The protruding aspects of
my chest suffer the majority of the blows.

With the instant loss of rationality, calmness, and patience
known to all parents, this model of parenthood disintegrates. In
its place rears a wet harridan yelling about good touches/bad
touches and chanting Mr. Roger's refrain "your body is your body
and my body is mine". Then I slam the door really hard.

There is complete silence from the bathroom.

I stand in the hallway dripping water and guilt. Finally, I gather
my dignity and a towel about me and reenter the scene of my
most recent failure. I quietly apologize for losing my temper and
talk about what precipitated it. The children listen with wide,
innocent eyes. (Even the dinosaurs are set to face me and look
contrite.) The kids climb from the tub (hurrying surreptitiously to
be first).

I will probably feel guilty forever about the look on my children's
faces that night as I ranted but I've learned that children are very
forgiving about your frailties if you're honest with them when you
make a mistake. I've also learned not to share my bath with
children or dinosaurs.

All I want for Christmas…

Dear Santa,

It's been a long time since I've written to you. You've been doing such a great job over the years sending so many wonderful, cherished, longed-for, and absolutely perfect presents to our whole family, that I haven't really felt the need to request a special present for myself. But this year I do have a specific request…

As you are no doubt aware, Santa, Christmas is almost here. I'm pretty organized this year. I'm working hard at taming the children's gimmies and resisting the urge to buy more stuff. I'm focusing the family's attention on fun Christmas activities. We are immersed in crafts, baking, playing outside, and reading. As long as my husband's sanity holds up to the onslaught, we are evoking Christmas jollity by listening to Christmas music.

When the children's anticipation slash excitement level gets too intense even for me, I am coping by dint of frequent taste testing of our copious baking and resorting to my usual panacea for whatever ails me - baths.

Normally the combo of something sweet to eat and a hot bath is a no-fail recipe to cheer me. But today there is a fly in the ointment. I'm a bath aficionado. I consider baths to be one of the few achievable luxuries potentially available at a moment's notice to a parent in dire need of stress relief. The prospect of a nice hot quiet bath is, for me, almost always an alluring idea. Add a good book and subtract a solicitous child perched on the toilet seat "to keep you company" and you are halfway to a brief taste of heaven.

However Santa, while I hesitate to complain at this late date lest it be construed as 'naughty behavior,' today I am NOT enjoying my bath. Oh, there are many good features to today's 'mini spa.' I have an excellent book, hot scented water, the pleasing background sound of my children happily engaged elsewhere in the house, no dog scratching at the door, and no phone ringing. But all this is marred by one thing.

I am not quite alone in my bath.

The bathtub plug is missing in action AGAIN.

Annie MacInnis

It is possible the dog has chewed it into oblivion yet again for who knows what neurotic reason.

Alternatively, my son the inveterate construction engineer of esoteric dioramas may have once again appropriated a critical household item for his own nefarious building purposes in the heaving morass he calls 'his room.'

I am left with two choices: forgo my few moments of luxurious ablutions or locate the dreaded plug substitute. I opt for the latter and petulantly rummage under the sink for the bathtub plug substitute.

While I am all too aware of the perils of not-nice behavior at this time of year, I confess, Santa, that my mood is NOT NICE. I contemplate this latest inconvenience with a mood of irritation out of all proportion to one missing plug.

As is often the case is these sorts of situations, (does anyone ELSE have these sorts of situations?) the problem is not really a missing plug. The problem is the alternative 'plug' that is available. In our whole house crammed to the scuppers with who knows how many items which "we might need sometime," there is never an actual *made for this particular purpose* spare tub plug. Worse, there is only one item that will serve as a substitute.

I stare peevishly at the far end of the tub. In fact, as the tub slowly fills, my mood deepens to downright sullenness.

This is not my idea of a perfect Christmas! There, sinking inexorably beneath the bubbles, a brave, long-suffering smile pasted on its face, is one of those small, bald, cheery, armless and legless Fisher Price baby toys. The odious little figure smirks at me from between my ankles. I lean forward and turn it to face the wall.

It doesn't help. Even as the bubbles close over its little head, I take no pleasure from its disappearance. I remain irked.

Dear Santa, for Christmas I want one bathtub plug. Actually, could I please have two?

Yours truly (and always a believer),
Annie MacInnis

I had forgotten about this part of me

When my first child was born, I found the adjustment from working wife to stay at home mother abrupt. Motherhood overwhelmed me (in a good way). Parenting this newborn was so all consuming, there seemed no time or energy left for being a wife let alone a person who had a career, other interests and abilities.

My husband, while a wonderful father, seemed so adept at shedding fatherhood like a snake shedding its skin each time he walked out the door and back into his life while my former life seemed gone forever.

Yet, I loved being a mom, despite giving up a great career, in spite of the bad days and the hard days and the failures. Those wonderful heart swelling, emotion filled days were so satisfying, so all consuming that over the years I forgot about the me that existed BK (before kids). I loved volunteering at my children's school, cooking meals for my family, living my life at a slower pace than the majority.

Then one day my second kid finished elementary school and I realized the time had come to go back to work. The prospect of finding work again filled me with excitement and trepidation. What if prospective employers dismissed me as no longer relevant in the work world now that I had been "just a mom" for 14 years? What if my 2 degrees and 14 years working in my field were now passé?

Thankfully, my fears were unfounded. I found a great job that fits me to a tee. It's part time so home life still seems manageable although the house is a little grubbier and I confess I have succumbed (to my children's immense satisfaction) to stocking a couple of frozen store bought pizzas against the occasional day when life is a little too busy. Otherwise, my life seems wonderful in different ways these days.

Of course, the biggest, most obvious advantage to returning to work is the opportunity to wear clean, trendy clothes all day. It is thrilling to discover my brain still works as it used to, that I am still smart. The stigma (which largely was only in my own mind) of being "only" a stay at home mom even though I was doing a great job in a tough field, is gone.

[273]

Annie MacInnis

Now I return home to my family each day, proud of what I have accomplished 'out there' in that world. I remain grateful and humbled by what I know I bring to my family these days.

Most of the time the old stuff I gave freely of for all those years is still on offer – good meals, a welcoming home, a listening ear, a chauffeur, help with whatever. But now I also bring a renewed confidence in my ability to operate in both worlds, home and work.

These days life beckons me to stretch my wings with the clear and certain knowledge that home is here, safe and waiting for my return.

I love aprons

I mean really love them. I am a collector of aprons. I covet aprons I see on others. I look for aprons, new and even well used when I am shopping. I have aprons I haven't worn yet but just take out and look at sometimes when I am tidying, reorganizing or culling unnecessary clutter from the house. I have frivolous aprons and practical aprons. I have aprons I paid a pittance for, aprons my parents gave me for Christmas and aprons I inherited from my Nanna. I have new well-made aprons and frail old embroidered aprons. I have aprons that tie around the waist and bib ones that loop over the head. I have Christmas aprons - both full aprons for hard core Christmas baking and whimsical half aprons for serving Christmas dinner. I have beautiful white Belgian lace aprons and wild colourful cabbage roses aprons. I have meticulously embroidered aprons, frilly aprons and baker style aprons. I can supply an apron appropriate for almost any occasion.

I love to cook and bake and most days I put on an apron at some point so I am free to cook with gay abandon. I wipe my hands on my aprons and lean against the counter while I work and hold bowls against myself as I beat batter. I use my aprons and use them well.

Aprons are almost a lost art these days. Most people seem surprised that I actually use them and have lots.

Although I am pretty much a sucker for most any apron – if it's pretty I usually want to own it, nevertheless I do have some standards. I'm not just an addict who buys indiscriminately.

My favorite aprons (unless the occasion calls for dressy) are the over the head full length bib style aprons. I have a generous bosom that lends itself to scatterings of flour, dough and sauce so the full length apron is most practical. I like two good sized pockets, the better to stash baking implements, pot holders, and Kleenex. Knee length is good in case I'm beating dough and so there's lots of room to wipe my hands.

I NEVER buy cutesy aprons with slogans or people or creatures on them, rarely yellow unless it is butter yellow with embroidery, never orange, never utterly plain. But if an apron is vintage or has a beautiful flower pattern, I probably want to own it.

[275]

Annie MacInnis

Although a few of my aprons are for admiring only, most of my aprons are for using up and enjoying and tossing with love and without regret, for when they get too ratty I know they have seen me through many a delicious meal and dessert.

My aprons are well enjoyed, well loved and well used. My aprons support me in my passion for cooking and baking and remind me who I am at my core. Regardless of who I am out there in the world, I am descended from good cooks and take pride in that inheritance.

In memory of my friend and neighbour who also loved aprons and baking, Godspeed Eleanor.

Annie Pineo's curtains hang in my bedroom

I first saw the curtains more than 3000 miles from Calgary. They lay neatly pressed and folded on a picnic table on her front lawn.

Annie had recently died and her children and grandchildren were clearing out the house and selling the unwanted items at a yard sale. I was visiting my parents next door. As I poured myself a cup of my mother's wonderful coffee I spotted the unmistakable bustle of yard sale activity next door. Quite unable to resist yard sales at the best of times, I grabbed my wallet and sallied forth, coffee in hand.

I wandered Annie's front lawn looking closely at faces to see whom I knew. It's been 27 years since I've lived in this small town so there are still some familiar faces of school friends and their parents but many faces are unfamiliar to me nowadays.

There were lots of people I knew. As I visited with these old friends, the curtains caught my eye.

They lay lightly on the table, a creamy homemade vanilla pudding colour of rich pale yellow. They called to me from their place among the sheets and vases and Christmas ornaments. They nestled there as smooth and pristine as the day they had been purchased and put away in the linen cupboard *for good*.

I edged my way unobtrusively toward the table containing the curtains practicing the yard sale etiquette entailing not revealing how much an object appeals to you lest you alert other shoppers to your heart's desire before it is safely in your hands. An eternity later the curtains were safely cradled in my arms and a price had been agreed upon.

When I arrived home in Calgary, I placed the curtains reverently in *my* linen cupboard to keep *for good*. A few days later as I closed my linen cupboard door I looked at the curtains I had so coveted. Resolutely I picked them up and shook out their folds.

Now the curtains hang in my bedroom. They please me so much. They are exactly the colour I wanted in my bedroom. The sunlight shines *just so* through them, dappling my room with sun drops filled with memories.

[277]

Annie MacInnis

Like the vanity that I love because it was my grandmother's and the tea cozy I so cherish because my mother made it for me, these curtains please me on an intrinsic level but also because they remind me of my childhood.

When I was four my five-year old brother John judged an innocent but bare naked beauty contest held in a tent set up in Annie's back yard. The contestants were Annie's daughter Barb, her grandchildren Gwen and Cathy and me. Annie discovered us parading our wares and sent us out to play elsewhere with a flea firmly planted in everyone's ear.

When I was about eight, my older cousin Margot and I decided it would be great fun to stand together between the columns of Annie's high front step and to jump off the side onto her lawn below. I followed where I was led and went home crying with a cracked bone in my arm and Annie's fully justified chastisements ringing in my ears. My cousin was unscathed.

When I was a teenager I noticed Annie wandering in the early mornings in the fields behind our houses. After several days of watching her, curiosity finally overcame my adolescent feigned indifference. I walked out to meet her in the field and learned she was picking mushrooms. I wandered the fields with her many times after that, learning what she knew about mushrooms and bringing home my fresh gatherings. Before this experience I guess I hadn't thought of anything other than berries or flowers growing wild that would be worth picking. Now a whole new world of gleaning opened up to my wondering eyes.

Today when I walk in Alberta and spot wild sage or mushrooms or Saskatoon's I think of how Annie would love to have walked and filled her apron with these wild western things.

At that summer yard sale Barb, Annie's daughter gifted me with one of Annie's best bib aprons when I spoke of my memories of Annie. So now memories of Annie are in my bedroom and kitchen. Godspeed Annie, I love your curtains and apron. May flights of angels guide you to your rest.

Barbeque

It's a brand new year, the time of resolutions, of clearing clutter, out with the old and in with the new. All that Christmas loot has to go somewhere. As I cast a ruthless eye about the house and yard for dispensable things my gaze settles momentarily on the barbeque.

Even when it was brand spanking new it was unprepossessing, functional but not beautiful by any means. Although I chose it specifically from among many models and had to arrange with a friend who had a vehicle to help me get it home and hide it away until the birthday day it was nevertheless a rather practical, odd gift.

Nowadays twenty years later, it humbly continues to occupy a corner of the yard but looks fairly pitiful. Its legs are a little wonky. It lists quite noticeably to the left. The tray where you could lay your tools or a dish is no longer reliable but this is a barbeque with history.

It's not gas so it cannot be quickly turned on to cook a fast supper. It uses old-fashioned coals that take over an hour to be ready to cook on. Since it has never had a nice vinyl cover, it has been out in all weathers and looks it.

On several occasions friends have tried to unload older model gas barbeques on us presumably in an effort to force us to throw this one away and to upgrade a tad.

But this barbeque has been with us longer than our cars or our children or even our house.

I bought this barbeque for my husband's birthday in March the first year we lived in Calgary. That first winter here was a shock to two poor freezing Easterners. The year was 1982. We huddled in our balcony apartment in a funky old building dreaming of spring.

The barbeque cost me $60 and was an extravagant gift designed to cheer our poor homesick hearts with thoughts of spring, green space, barbeques with friends and an altogether brighter future.

Despite the freezing weather that March my husband decided we would begin barbequing right away.

Annie MacInnis

That year the sight of him standing at his ease barbequing on our balcony fueled my dreams of a future when we would have a fitting place of our own to put the barbeque. This was not some piddly little $8 tabletop hibachi that apartment dwellers would use. This was a big stand up barbeque for people who planned to have a house and a yard.

The barbeque came with us through a succession of apartments until we finally bought our home.

During our first days in our home a visiting friend 'with drink taken' tripped and fell over the barbeque giving it that distinctive leftward list.

Nowadays it sits to one side of the yard and, yes, it looks especially pitiful but this is a barbeque with history.

While we ate meals from this barbeque we made lots of friends and began to feel at home in this city. We got married, bought a house, had children, changed jobs, and grew up.

Even though the barbeque looks terrible it works fine. The food my husband cooks on this barbeque always tastes especially good because infused with the marinade and the meat and vegetables, soaked into each meal is the memory of those early days twenty years ago when my husband and I spent our first winter in a new city dreaming of home and spring and a brighter future here in the West.

This wreck of a barbeque will continue to reside in our yard for the foreseeable future and when I look out at it I never frown and think what a frightful looking thing that is. No, when I look at that old wreck I remember and smile a little smile and look elsewhere for something to jettison.

Ginger ale

In my twenties I was in the early days of learning to live with a chronic illness, Multiple Sclerosis. Balancing a newish relationship, my first big job and living in a new city far from friends and family meant I has an occasionally rocky day.

On one of those days when I had admitted I needed to stay home and rest, my husband checked with me before going to work if there was anything he could do before he left.

I asked him to bring up the bottle of ginger ale from the basement pantry and put it in the fridge.

After resting much of the day I decided to treat myself to a glass of that nice cold ginger ale. I got the two litre bottle out of the fridge and attempted to open it.

After numerous attempts with bare hands, a damp cloth and all the other aids I could think off I was stumped. I could NOT get the cover off.

Given that I was already feeling a little under the weather, I went straight to despair. If I no longer had enough strength in my hands to be able to open a bottle of pop, how long would I been able to continue to work, how could we even consider having children.

I spent the rest of the afternoon weeping and wallowing in self pity. By the time my husband came home from work, I was a complete wreck.

Close to incoherent, I related my sorry tale, my conclusions and my fears for my future. After hugging me and reassuring me, he offered to get me my ginger ale.

Tearfully I said, "yes please" and began to make some effort at pulling myself together.

I waited and waited.

Then my boyfriend came into the room without my drink. He gave me a huge smile and said, "There is something wrong with the bottle and the cover. Even with vice grips I cannot get the cover off!"

[281]

We both burst out laughing. How easily we catastrophize situations when we are tired or ill.

This early lesson in living with chronic illness taught me a valuable lesson. When things go wrong in my life, "It is not always about my Multiple Sclerosis. Sometimes it is about the ginger ale bottle."

Alice and Cecil

I don't know why we didn't stop while everyone was still enjoying the joke. We were just too full of our own cleverness I guess. Nevertheless, we made both children cry.

I was reading bedtime stories to our kids then ages 3 and 6. The dog, scrambling to be the first to greet my husband, overlaid the sound of the backdoor opening. Both kids instantly dived under the bedcovers for the next phase of the homecoming ritual.

My husband came to the bedroom.

"How was your day?" he asked.

"Good, how about yours?" I replied.

"Good," he said, "Where are the kids?"

The kids?" I usually mused absentmindedly. "Oh yeah, the kids, gosh, I can't think where they've gone…"

After a few moments along this vein, our usual routine was for my husband to feign tiredness and to lay down on the bed, but it would be lumpy and he'd gently chide me about trying to do a better job making the bed, then the kids would be unearthed giggling. Just one of those little family rituals except tonight we carried it a little too far.

When my husband asked where the kids were this night, in a fit of inspiration, I replied, chagrined, "I lost them. I was busy and I left them somewhere. I can't for the life of me think where. I'm really sorry. I know I said I'd be more careful after the last time. Oh well, let's just get new ones again."

My husband and I grinned at each other. Giggles erupted from the bedclothes but were quickly stifled.

Quick as always on the uptake, my husband tsked and said, "I can't believe you lost these kids too. When you lost the last ones you promised to be more careful. These kids weren't so bad. I was getting used to them even though I did really prefer Alice and Cecil."

"Oh Alice and Cecil," I remarked fondly, "weren't they lovely children! She was so pretty and nice and he was so sweet and well mannered. I do think I also might have preferred them a bit to these last two. Let's just hope the new ones will be more like dear Alice and Cecil."

There was an ominous silence from under the bedclothes as we twittered on about Alice and Cecil but we were too pleased with ourselves to stop.

Suddenly one child wailed, then both burst from the bedclothes. They were aghast, eyes brimming with tears. "You had other kids called Alice and Cecil and you LOST them???"

No, no, we tried to reassure them. It was just a joke. But they took a lot of convincing. They were still tearful and eying us doubtfully as we tucked them into bed. It was many nights before they ducked under the covers again and they stuck close to us whenever we went out for quite some time.

Nowadays mention of Alice and Cecil always elicits laughter. Funny how it's often the mistakes that make up family lore and the hardships that teach us lifelong lessons while the unremarkable nice days are long forgotten.

New Beginnings

I wish I could save this moment in time, to always live my life at this peak of pleasure! I feel such passion for life these days.

My life isn't perfect. Of course, there are occasional worms in my apple, a few bruised spots I just close my eyes to, but generally, life is so juicy and sweet that I find myself marveling at this process of growing older.

I'm at that time in my life when my hair is starting to show increasing strands of grey, my chin (and many other unmentionables) starting to sag a little (or a lot), and my face is long past the fresh flush of youth. My days have become filled with Ma'am's from young clerks and I have an increasing sense of being invisible to the younger generation.

What a pleasant surprise to discover that instead of feeling like an era is ending as that empty nest grows ever nearer, nevertheless this sense of new beginnings, this feeling that my future is still full of promise and that so much is possible is reminiscent of other times in my life.

When I first left home and went to university I rushed headlong into the world eager to dream great dreams and to gulp down knowledge and experience.

When my boyfriend and I decided to move to western Canada from small town Nova Scotia what an adventure life in a big city seemed.

When we decided to get married, how momentous that time seemed, how full of meaning and promise of a future together.

Each time I was pregnant I felt like a walking miracle, pregnant not just with new life but with incredible possibility.

But this latest passionate time crept up on me unawares. No dramatic event, no big change has accompanied this feeling. Rather, the realization has gradually grown on me that I am happy, content, fulfilled, in the truest, most fundamental sense of the words. I've discovered that day after day I am filled with gratitude for all the blessings I've been afforded in my life – health, marriage, children, parents, siblings, friends, my beloved ageing dog, job, home, enough to eat, a future for my children in a peaceful country. To be so blessed is a gift beyond measure. May you too, discover your own wealth of blessings this year.

The Flim flam man

Most Maritimers are fairly blasé about local politicians and bigwigs involved in shenanigans. We expect them to be a little bit crooked now and then. We are surprised when they don't line their pockets or favour their friends with grants, jobs, and/or money. Any attempts to reform such behaviour founder on everyone's hope to benefit from the system before it is changed.

Nevertheless, even we have our standards. I recently heard about a Funeral Parlour Director who tops my list of most scandalous shysters. Although they are sometimes regarded with inease, funeral directors nevertheless still hold a certain social standing within the community, especially in small towns.

Funeral directors are expected to be a cut above the rest, possessed of a finer moral fiber than the common riffraff. Regardless of how much a funeral director coveted the odd piece of jewelry worn by a client it is assumed that he would never succumb to such temptation. When circumstances warrant a hearty guffaw from everyone else, we expect the funeral director to resist indulging and to exude the proper level of obsequiousness.

The Funeral Parlour Director in THIS story was known not to be cut from the finest cloth, but the extent of his duplicitousness became apparent only recently.

This man was always accorded the respect due his profession even if his personal reputation was more of the nudge-nudge, wink-wink variety. Running the most popular funeral parlour in town is a big deal when one of the main topics of conversation is who died this week. Many people's social calendars revolve around whose wake you are attending, why you are attending (personal friendship, mere acquaintance, familial obligation, curiosity, an outing) and how the corpse looked.

Maybe that Celtic penchant for reveling in death and gloom and the tendency to relish angst under those so often lowering skies allowed his downward spiral to continue so long. Maybe, as is usual in most small towns, much was forgiven, because he was "a character." Certainly, for many years he was assumed to be guilty of no more than having drink taken. The resultant minor lurching and reeking while greeting mourners was easily forgiven.

[287]

Finally, though, the day of reckoning arrived.

The doors of the funeral home were padlocked pending investigation of the books. The town was abuzz with rumour, rife with speculation, and the funeral director was, wisely, nowhere to be found.

Gradually the truth emerged. One quarter of a million dollars worth of pre-paid funeral money was missing, squandered on booze, frittered away on gambling and the like.

One has to wonder at what point the slippery slope of 'borrowing just a little to tide me over until payday' turned into the runaway train of $250,000 in prepaid funerals missing from the coffers.

In the meantime, the town is still atwitter trying to determine who can afford to die and who will need to soldier on a while longer until they can be seen off in style.

A Christmas of yore

My Nanna's Christmas candelabra glows in the window as I walk toward my house.

To me it shines with memories of childhood and glows bright enough to seal the small ache of my heart as I spend another Christmas so far from my parents and siblings.

For a moment I am home again, a child again. I look way up at my father's face. We walk through the deep snow, my hand in my father's, to my grandparent's door.

I kick off my boots, throw down my coat and brush past my father and my Nanna to the living room. I fling past my grandfather in his favorite chair in the living room and skid to a halt in front of the tree.

It is an amazing tree, a tree for a house without a gaggle of little kids like my house. It shines gloriously, the lights reflected in the big living room windows behind it. I look especially for each of the wonderful blown glass ornaments full of coloured liquid that bubble as the heat from the Christmas lights warms them. I put my face really close to each of the ornaments. I can hear the liquid bubbling and feel the faint heat from the bulb underneath I peer around the room through the kaleidoscope of each one.

In the background the rise and fall of my father's voice in the kitchen is punctuated by my grandmother's murmurs as she works in the kitchen.

My grandfather sits near me in the living room, reading, maybe listening to the voices in the kitchen. We haven't spoken yet.

I kneel on the window seat cushion and press my face close to the glass. The snow falling outside the window gleams with rainbows from the candelabra on the sill. The glass is cold on my face. I hang my hands down between the couch and the sill where the register warms them. My breath fogs the window. Halos hover around the candelabra lights when I narrow my eyes.

I look back into the room past the tree at the back of my grandfather's head. His white hair curls softly along the back of his neck. The tweed of his suit coat looks scratchy against his neck. When I lunge across the room and fling myself onto his lap the tweed is scratchy. I rub my cheek against his shoulder as I hug him hello. "Hello Papoo," I carol. He gives me a gruff hello and a quick rub on the shoulder and goes back to his Financial Post newspaper.

I wander off to the kitchen. My Nanna is making small rectangle sandwiches on white bread with the crusts cut off, buttered, topped with cooked crumbled bacon and cheese then broiled until they are bubbly. She has made a nice pot of tea. I have milk in a teacup with only a splash of tea 'for colour'.

My father and Nanna talk quietly about their days. Her silver white hair sweeps up the back of her head anchored with beautiful combs. Her rings sparkle in the low light. I sit nicely and quietly in my chair. I sip my 'tea' and consider how many sandwiches I can get away with eating.

I look through the doorway to the tree and beyond to the candelabra. Their light glows to the back of my heart and lodges there forever as a symbol of what Christmas will always mean to me.

And in a blink I am back on the sidewalk of my grown up home thousands of miles from that childhood home and those long ago days breathless with the sudden loss of that Christmas and my return to the present.

My Nanna and Papoo live now only in my heart.

My favorite gift this year is the return of the Christmas memories of those bubbling glass lights, of how the cold glass felt on my cheeks, the tingle of my cold fingers as the warm air from the register swept over them and especially the sound of my Nanna's voice just there at the edge of time.

Let's Chat with our families about death

You know how it goes when you're visiting with family. One minute you're relaxed and idly following the conversation, trying to place in your mind Aunt Whosit's nephew's first wife's second cousin, you know, the one with the squint who moved away for a year in the 1970s, and when she came back she worked at the Hardware store for awhile, "You know! Brown hair, always wore bright shirts, big nose...W)W)($%*$)_%&_?????????.

You're nodding your head without commitment implying 'not entirely' but keep talking and maybe the memory will come to me...when, suddenly, while you weren't really paying close attention, inexplicably, the discussion has turned to death.

Worse, not just death in a pleasant sort of "you can have that tea cup when I'm gone, I'll put your name on it now with masking tape" way or even a directive such as whatever you do, make certain Aunt So-and-so does NOT sing at my funeral or as God is my witness type thing...

Oh no, the discussion has turned to the minefield of memorial wishes and there is rampant and passionate polarization of opinion. Never mind the whole burial versus cremation issue. Never mind the whole service/no service and church versus funeral home versus family home reception business. Been there, had those talks.

Oh no this was much worse. This day the conversation had taken a totally unexpected turn. Suddenly we were embroiled in a discussion about those who like to visit the graveyard regularly and pause to remember there and those who do not want to remember in a graveyard but instead want to picture the loved one as remembered in their day to day lives instead.

Strongly held opinions were being aired with gay abandon until suddenly everyone is treading warily realizing we were on delicate ground when one family member weighs in with a different opinion.

The family member was perfectly serious and spoke with conviction. He had recently seen a wonderful memorial tribute which he fully intended to order for himself. This company would create a 3D realistic head in living colour suspended in a large crystal cube and cunningly lit from below so that the cube could be placed on the fireplace mantel or other such prominent location. Perpetually plugged in, it would glow down on the remaining family members on a daily basis.

Normally I'm not so insensitive (I hope) but I was immediately transported imagining this glowing disembodied head eerily watching for you to enter the room with your morning coffee or benignly observing you as you watch TV of an evening. I guffawed and without thinking, I blurted out, "Oh my gosh! I couldn't stand that! I'd lie awake at the thought of you down there glowing the dark. I would have to unplug you and put you in the closet!"

The family member tried to persevere with his wishes but there was no going back. The room burst into unbelieving laughter and finally the family member gave up for the moment.

Later that evening I realized I would need to revise my mental list of best ever death discussions and choose new rankings for the friend known in university in the 1970s by the nickname "Mr. Compost". He wanted to be ground up and mixed in with the backyard compost along with yesterday's coffee grounds and potato peelings and used in the flower and vegetable gardens to create on-going beauty and sustenance for his family. Also assigned a new ranking would be the husband of a family friend who wanted his ashes scattered over the Bay of Fundy from an airplane. Due to an unfortunate gust of wind at the critical moment of release, the ashes ended up completely covering the group of mourners dressed in their Sunday best and huddled closely in the doorway of the small plane.

I drifted off to sleep smiling at the mental image of that disembodied eerily lit head with the words of that old song drifting though my mind, "I'll be seeing you in all the old familiar places..."

Made in the USA
Charleston, SC
27 April 2016